# Waiting for America

## A Civilian Prisoner of Japan In the Philippines

LARRY C. FLOYD

With

PATTY KELLY STEVENS

TC
TURNKEY
COMMUNICATIONS

ISBN 978-0-9893007-1-1 (soft cover)
ISBN 978-0-9893007-2-8 (ebook)

First edition, 2024

Published by TurnKey Communications
Oklahoma City, Oklahoma
www.turnkeycommo.com
info@turnkeycommo.com

Autographed editions of this book can be purchased at:

turnkeycommo.com

Bulk purchases at discounts are available in the U.S. for corporations, institutions, and other organizations. For more information, please contact the publisher at info@turnkeycommo.com

10 9 8 7 6 5 4 3 2 1

To the weary GIs
of the war in the Pacific
who returned for their
fellow Americans

———————————

# CONTENTS

CONTENTS

# MAPS

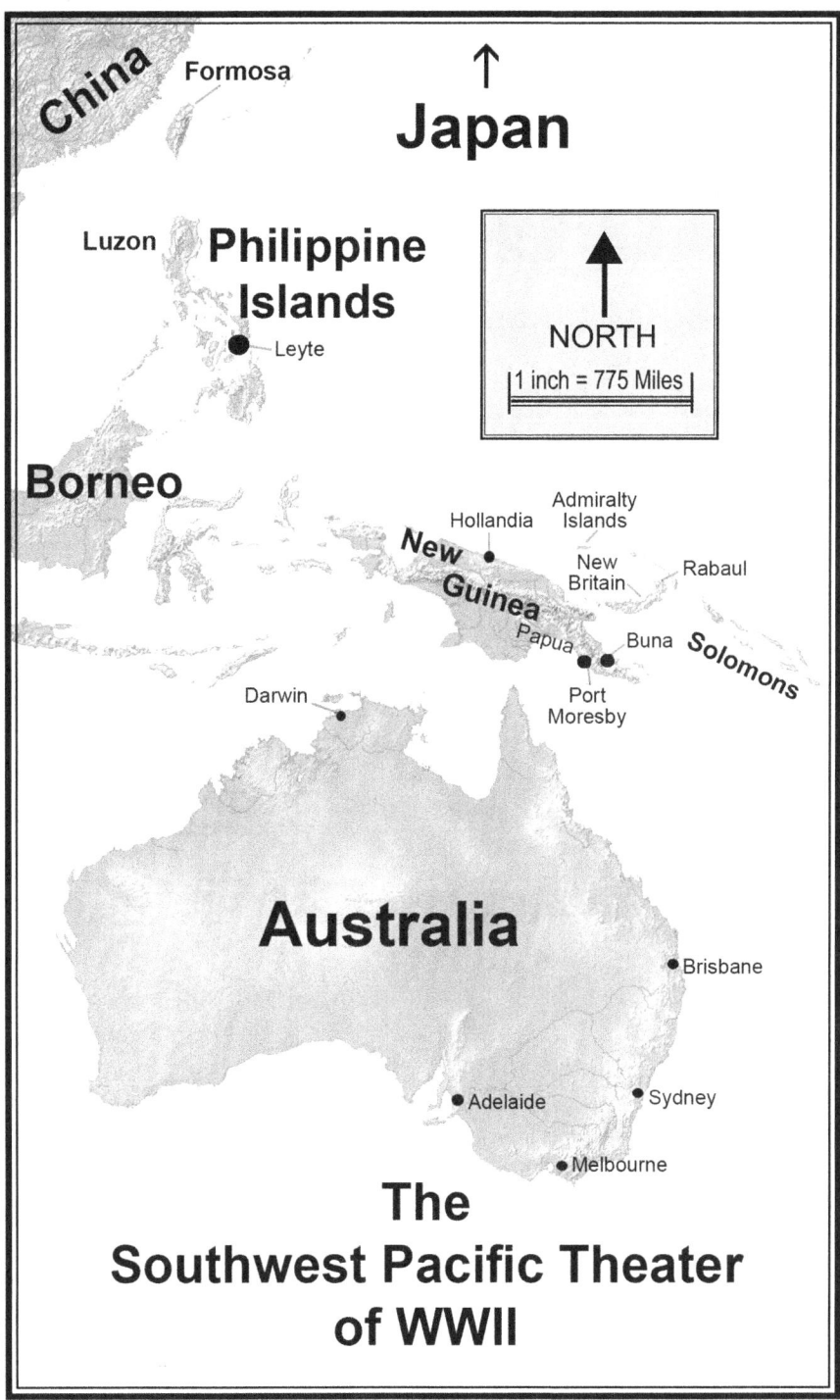

China

Formosa

↑ Japan

Luzon

Philippine Islands

● Leyte

NORTH

1 inch = 775 Miles

Borneo

Admiralty Islands

Hollandia ●

New Guinea

New Britain

Rabaul

Papua

Buna

Solomons

Darwin ●

● ● Port Moresby

Australia

● Brisbane

● Adelaide

● Sydney

● Melbourne

The
Southwest Pacific Theater
of WWII

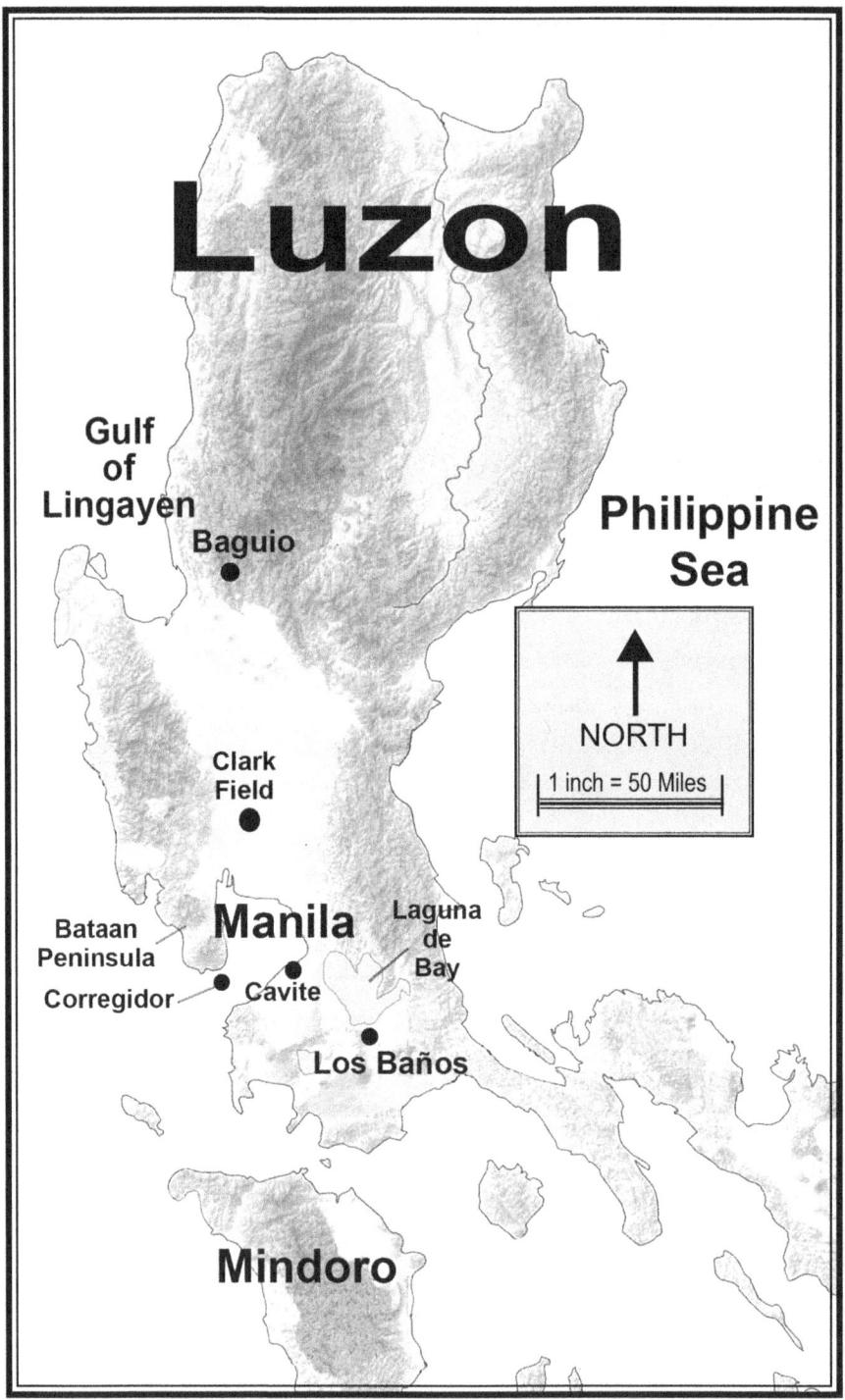

Luzon

Gulf of Lingayen

Baguio

Philippine Sea

NORTH

1 inch = 50 Miles

Clark Field

Bataan Peninsula

Manila

Corregidor

Cavite

Laguna de Bay

Los Baños

Mindoro

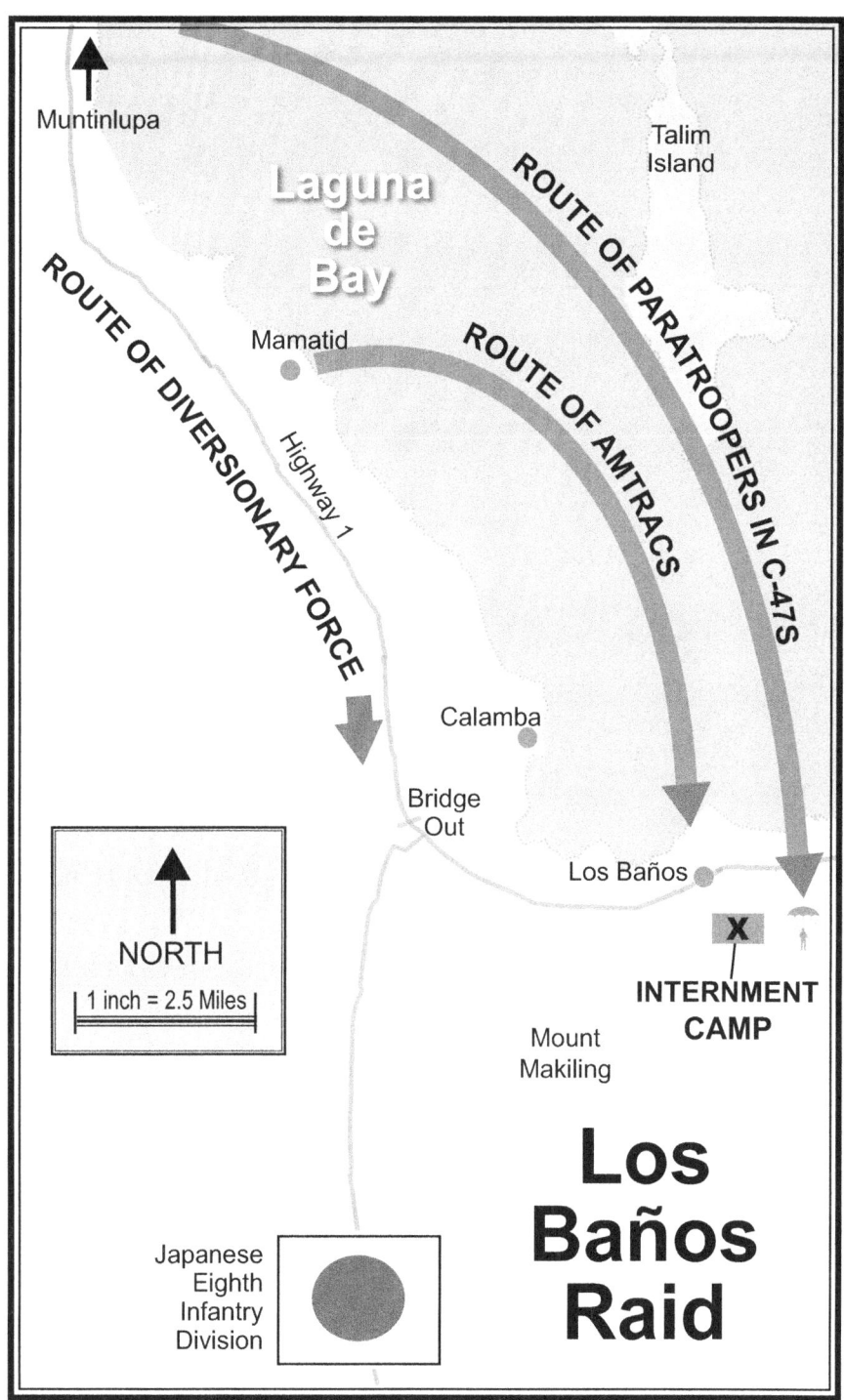

Muntinlupa

Laguna de Bay

Talim Island

ROUTE OF PARATROOPERS IN C-47S

Mamatid

ROUTE OF AMTRACS

ROUTE OF DIVERSIONARY FORCE

Highway 1

Calamba

Bridge Out

Los Baños

**X**

NORTH

1 inch = 2.5 Miles

**INTERNMENT CAMP**

Mount Makiling

Japanese Eighth Infantry Division

# Los Baños Raid

# PREFACE

MOST AMERICANS ARE UNAWARE of the more than 5,000 American civilians imprisoned for several years under ultimately horrendous conditions in the Philippine Islands during World War II. Captured by Japanese forces and crowded into what were essentially concentration camps, these wartime internees were part of the largest group of American civilians incarcerated by any enemy nation. More than 2,000 civilians from other Allied nations suffered in these same camps.

As the Japanese overran this U.S. territory, many of these American expatriates were working as doctors, teachers, engineers, religious workers, and businessmen preparing the Filipinos for their approaching independence. Some were America's "missionaries of democracy," sent by the U.S. government to instill American ideals and values. Thousands of these Americans had lived in the Philippines for decades, acquiring stylish residences and building flourishing businesses. Most who survived their wartime confinement returned to America possessing little more than the clothes they wore.

Although closely guarded by the Japanese, the captives were expected to administer and provide for themselves. That the majority of these civilians survived the disease, starvation and executions in these internment camps can be attributed to both the effective self-governments they formed and the self-reliant frontier spirit still resonant in these twentieth-century Americans. Separated from their homeland and increasingly desperate for food and basic necessities, the internees elected officials and formed operating committees to oversee the requirements of daily living in harsh, crowded conditions. Their internment communities functioned much like the towns and cities in America that molded many of these expatriates.

Although initially misled and seemingly abandoned by U.S. officials, the captives' faith that America would eventually come for them sustained them in their darkest hours. Their rescue came with General Douglas

MacArthur's celebrated return to the Philippines. Yet the arrival of U.S. forces and the internees' deliverance were far from inevitable. Many more, if not most, of the captives would have been starved or executed if not for MacArthur's insistence on a rapid liberation of the northern Philippines and his direct orders to liberate the two largest internment camps on Luzon. The miraculous rescue of the 2,146 captives at the second largest of the camps, Los Baños, is a military epic celebrated to this day.

To elucidate the human aspect of these historic events, *Waiting for America* includes the personal story of an American expatriate and her family inside the larger narrative of these thousands of beleaguered Americans and their eventual rescue. Patty Croft was about to complete her senior year at the American School in Manila when she, her mother, and younger brother were swept up in bewildering, life-threatening events beginning in December 1941. As a prisoner of Japan in both of the two largest internment camps, the personal account of Patty's trying ordeal provides a worm's-eye view of the hardships and hopes similarly experienced by thousands of her fellow captives.

The human aspect of this narrative reflects the patriotism commonly shared by these suffering U.S. civilian prisoners. Persecuted, starved, and occasionally executed, the internees knew their ultimate salvation lay with a distant America they connected with only from memory. Unabashedly sentimental and patriotic about their homeland during their three-year ordeal, they nurtured their American identity and traditions to keep hope alive. They had no future without the U.S. flag flying once more over the Philippines.

*Waiting for America* is a synthesis of first-hand accounts, original records, and respected historical narratives. Almost all previous writings on American internees in the Philippines are narrowly focused on one individual's experiences or a particular internment camp. Using a variety of sources, the authors hoped to provide a more complete understanding of the experiences of American civilians in Manila just before and during WWII, and of the ordeal they underwent as prisoners under Japanese forces and without aid from an America preoccupied by a global conflict.

This work's depiction of the military aspect of war in the southwest Pacific theater and the eventual liberation of the Philippines relies on numerous published accounts of these years. Douglas MacArthur's integral role in these events is explained in William Manchester's acclaimed biography, *American Caesar*, and Hiroshi Masuda's *MacArthur in Asia*. These accounts of MacArthur's actions and his ties with the American internees and the Filipino people provide much of the framework for the military aspect of *Waiting for America.*

Most have little knowledge that MacArthur was living in Manila as a U.S. Army retiree and commander of the Philippine military as the Japanese threat loomed in the late 1930s. Having lived in Manila among the American expatriates, MacArthur and his wife personally knew many of the U.S. captives and felt a deep obligation to save them. Recalled to active duty in the U.S. Army and subsequently ordered to flee the Philippines early in 1942, the general's efforts to defeat the Japanese aggressors and avenge America's greatest military defeat became inseparable from his personal desire to return to Luzon to free both the American captives and the subjugated Filipinos.

The personal aspect of *Waiting for America* draws from an American adolescent's recollections and her hidden diary while a prisoner. Like MacArthur's expatriate household, Patty Croft's family lived in Manila before the war. Her secretly recorded thoughts provide a window to the past and an insider's view of these historical events. Nearing a century of living, Patty embodies the best qualities of the rapidly vanishing generation of proudly patriotic Americans who emerged through the crucible of World War II. Shaped by the events of her late adolescence, her many years are a story of trial, survival, repatriation, and ultimately a life well lived.

Two other eyewitness accounts of life as a civilian prisoner of Japan in the Philippines were vital to the author's understanding of both the self-administering nature of the internment camps and the key policies and events affecting the lives of the captives. American internee Fred Stevens's limited-edition *Santo Tomás Internment Camp* provides important facts on key people and experiences in the largest of these camps. This obscure book's daily summary of important events in the camp over a three-year period was invaluable to the author.

Another account of the prisoners' experiences in a number of camps is A. V. H. Hartendorp's two-volume *The Japanese Occupation of the Philippines*. A British captive in Santo Tomás Internment Camp, Hartendorp's work includes numerous primary source documents related to the experiences of these wartime internees. This lengthy chronicle provides his and other eyewitness descriptions of the people and events in the camps. The detail and scope of these two volumes exceed all other accounts of civilian internment in the Philippines during World War II.

The plight of these civilian captives and the dramatic liberation of the Los Baños Internment Camp, where Patty and her family were interned, were the subject of a 2004 documentary, *Rescue at Dawn–The Los Baños Raid*. This account aired several times in summer 2023 on the American television network History (formerly The History Channel).

Although beyond the living memory of all but a few Americans, these captives' suffering, survival, patriotism and rescue are an obscure yet important and inspirational chapter in the American experience.

Larry C. Floyd and Patty Kelly Stevens
Oklahoma City, Oklahoma
January 19, 2024

# ACKNOWLEDGMENTS

WITHOUT THE CAREFULLY PRESERVED RECORDS and later publications of courageous Santo Tomás internees Frederic H. Stevens and A.V. H. Hartendorp, this book's account of daily life in the largest civilian internment camps in the war-torn Philippines would have been incomplete. Under threat of death by Japanese guards, these two heroic captives risked their lives to preserve a comprehensive account of the suffering and injustice endured by the thousands of Allied civilian captives in Luzon during World War II.

The comments, clarifications and suggestions of retired American University professor Martin Meadows—confined as a youth at Santo Tomás Internment Camp—added to the accuracy and integrity of this book. Another academician, University of Oklahoma history professor Jay Casey, provided useful improvements to this narrative. Gregg shorthand transcriber Dennis Hollier decoded Patty Kelly Stevens's nearly 80-year-old diary, and proofreader Kaylee Crampton did her usual thorough review saving the authors from potential embarrassment.

Finally, without the insight and persistence of Jim and Pat Wallis, former Oklahomans now living in Little Rock, Ark., and Paul J. Kelly Jr., sadly who died in the COVID-19 pandemic of 2020-2021, this book would never have been written. Paul had always been impressed with the life experiences of his mother, Patty Kelly Stevens, and worked to preserve her past. Following Paul's untimely death, his friends Jim and Pat persevered to convince Patty to share her inspirational story. Some of her experiences as an internee—like Stevens and Hartendorp's accounts—were preserved in her forbidden diary.

*May you live in interesting times.*

(Widely reported as an ancient Chinese curse)

# CHAPTER 1

✿ ✿ ✿

# Easy Living in Pre-War Manila

A TREASURED FLAG OF THE UNITED STATES was carefully stored among the household goods of Patty Croft's family during her years as an American expatriate in pre-World War II Manila, the principal city of the U.S.-held Philippine Islands. Almost ten feet wide, the immense banner with its forty-eight stars was rarely seen but always carefully safeguarded by the Croft family.

How the flag came to the Crofts was a source of pride to Patty's parents. Growing up, Patty often heard the story of how her father, Alfred J. Croft, had rescued this American flag from flames sweeping through the destructive Manila Carnival Fire of 1920. In recognition of this act of courage and patriotism, the flag had later been formally presented to Alfred by the distinguished U.S. governor-general of the Philippines, retired Maj. Gen. Leonard Wood.

Patty remembered nothing else being told to her about the flag's provenance other than these events had occurred in the early 1920s. That meant both the flag and Patty joined the Croft household at about the same time, with the flag preceding her birth in 1924 by only a few years.

No formal record appears to exist of Governor-General Wood's awarding the flag to Alfred Croft. But the size and quality of the flag—nine feet, six inches wide by five feet high and its manufacture by Wm. H. Horstmann Company, a prominent supplier of U.S. military banners, flags and sashes—would be commensurate with the kind of U.S. flag raised over an exhibit at the annual Manila Carnival.

Often called the Mardi Gras of the Orient, the carnival had been held annually since 1908 excepting a short hiatus at the end of World War I. The 1920 event marked a return of this popular event to the city and a celebration of the end of the Great War. Named the Victory Carnival, the nine-day exposition was brought to a sudden close by the disastrous fire, which consumed half the buildings and devastated several acres of exhibits.

One of the exhibits featured a number of De Haviland and Curtiss aircraft, some of which were saved from the inferno by soldiers. Alfred Croft was a prominent pilot and flight instructor in Manila at the time, and was likely present at this exhibit. A U.S. Army Air Service veteran of the First World War, he probably responded instinctively to save the threatened flag.[1]

Whatever the details of the flag's rescue, the awarding of the colors to Croft by the distinguished Governor-General Wood gave it historic significance. Wood's career and the Philippines had been intertwined for the previous two decades, culminating in his being named governor-general by President Warren G. Harding in 1921. A medical doctor by training, in the 1880s Woods had distinguished himself as a military leader and Medal of Honor recipient in the last of the Indian wars of the West. A full colonel in the Army as the United States entered the Spanish-American War in 1898, he was chosen to head the First Volunteer Cavalry Regiment, popularly known as the Rough Riders, with Lt. Col. Theodore Roosevelt as his second-in-command.

Celebrated for his role in the fighting in Cuba and later serving as the Caribbean island's governor-general, in 1903 Wood was sent to the Philippines as governor of Moro Province. The United States had annexed the Philippines as part of the spoils of war. Promoted to the rank of major general in 1903, Wood served in the Philippines until 1908 and on his return to the States was appointed Army chief of staff by President William H. Taft.

Personifying the assertive leadership and expansionist views of America in the first decades of the twentieth century, the popular Wood narrowly missed the Republican nomination for president in 1920. President Harding sent him on a special mission to the Philippines in early 1921 before naming him governor-general later that year.

Carefully preserving the flag presented by Wood, Patty's parents treasured this little piece of U.S. history that had become a part of their family lore. Growing up in Manila, Patty was somewhat indifferent to her father's awarding of the flag. "At that age, it just wasn't that important to me," she admitted.

She was, however, proud of her father's prominence as a pilot and flight instructor in the key seaport of Manila on Luzon, the largest and most populous island in the Philippine archipelago. Yet his career in aviation frightened her. She remembered him breaking his collarbone when his plane crash-landed in Manila Bay when she was five years old.

An incident on her eighth birthday added to her anxiety. She and some friends gathered outdoors to celebrate the occasion with her father providing entertainment for the girls with aerial stunts. As the party thrilled to the roaring two-seater swooping overhead, the girls suddenly screamed as they saw what they feared to be the pilot dropping from the sky. They were vastly relieved to learn that it was only one of the large seat cushions that had fallen out as the plane looped overhead.

That incident ended any thoughts Patty might have entertained about one day accompanying her pilot-father on one of his flights. "He would take my mother's friends up with him sometimes," Patty recalled, "but I was too scared after that birthday party."

Alfred Croft's flying career was certainly notable far beyond stunts at birthday parties. A self-trained pilot, the British-born aviator grew enamored with flying as a teenager in the early 1900s. Immigrating to the United States before the outbreak of World War I, Croft began his flying career in 1914 while working at the Curtiss Flying School on North Island in California's San Diego Bay. He was working as a civilian flight instructor in Mineola, New York, when the United States entered World War I in 1917.

As a member of the U.S. Army Air Service, his flight-training skills were put to use during the war at Brooks Field near San Antonio, Texas, a facility for the training of instructors and pilots. Some of the more illustrious aviation pioneers of the United States would be stationed at Brooks Field, including Charles Lindbergh, James Doolittle and Claire Chennault. Croft doubtless met some of these future leaders of the emerging U.S. Army Air Corps.[2]

Following the war, Croft moved to Manila to work for the Curtiss Aeroplane Company organizing and training the nascent Philippine Air Service. He soon fell for young nurse Selma M. Bergstrom, who had taken a position at Manila's Saint Luke's Hospital after wartime duty at a hospital in Oakland, California. In far northeast Manila, Saint Luke's had been founded by American missionaries in 1903, and Selma applied there at the urging of one of her nursing school classmates and to escape a faltering relationship with a doctor in Oakland.[3]

Married in 1920 at Manila's inter-denominational Union Church, the adventurous young couple were among a large community of U.S.-expatriate "missionaries of democracy," emigrants administering the government of the U.S. territory, instilling American values, and taking advantage of new economic opportunities. By 1921, Alfred had been named chief flight instructor for the Philippine Air Service with a salary of $6,000 per year, a sizable income at the time and enough for a comfortable lifestyle in the vibrant Manila of the 1920s.[4]

After appointment as governor-general of the Philippines, Wood abolished the Philippine Air Service, replacing it with the United States Air Service. Native-controlled air service in the territory would be put on hold for the next thirteen years, and Alfred Croft was suddenly looking for work. With aviation skills like his in high demand, he soon accepted a position in China with Dr. Sun Yat-sen's embattled Cantonese government. His duties included organizing and training the new South China air corps.[5]

Taking his new wife with him to a modernizing China in revolutionary disarray, Croft found himself in the midst of Chinese Nationalist Party leader Sun's attempt to unite the war-torn country through military conquest. With their first child soon on the way, Selma quite sensibly chose to leave Canton and return to the United States for the birth. Shortly afterward, Alfred narrowly escaped capture when Canton was overrun by forces from an opposing army. All of this may have been more adventure than the aviation instructor had bargained for. Arriving in Seattle on the Japanese liner *Kaga Maru* in September 1922, he joined his wife and new son, Alfred Croft Jr., in California.[6]

The Crofts soon moved from California to Honolulu, Hawaii, where daughter, Patty Gene, was born in November 1924. But the allure and economic opportunity of Manila called them back in 1926. With Alfred Jr. and 15-month-old Patty in tow, the young family departed on the *SS President Wilson* (forerunner to the later *SS President Wilson* passenger liner) for Manila in February 1926.[7]

Alfred Croft returned to his chief occupation as a flight instructor in Manila, but Patty remembered that he also worked for the General Motors Company during her childhood. In the early 1900s, the U.S. Army Signal

Corps brought to the Philippines a number of electric vehicles made by Woods Motor Vehicle Company, and from the 1920s until the early 1970s American-made cars dominated the automobile market in the Philippines.[8]

Popularly known as the Pearl of the Orient, Manila in the late 1920s was regarded as a peaceful cosmopolitan city of several hundred thousand celebrated for its scenery, leisure and luxury. This was certainly not the situation just a few decades earlier when much of the native population battled what they considered an army of occupation courtesy of the briefly imperialistic United States. In February 1899, the U.S. Congress had voted to annex the Philippines as part of its expansionist plans following the Spanish-American War and the Treaty of Paris that ended the fighting in 1898.

Led by Filipino nationalist Emilio Aguinaldo, the natives had initially allied with the American military to oust the longtime Spanish colonists from the islands during the brief fighting between the United States and Spain. After Aguinaldo and his nationalists declared the independence of the Philippine Republic in June 1898, they were dismayed to learn they had only traded one colonial master for another. American troops continued to occupy Manila, and the islands were claimed by the United States. The ugly guerilla war that ensued witnessed atrocities on both sides. Eventually Aguinaldo was captured and the so-called Philippine Insurrection ended in May 1902 with 4,200 Americans troops killed and more than 200,000 Filipino soldiers and civilians dead. Relations between the Filipinos and the much-hated *Yanquis* reached a nadir.[9]

The U.S. Organic Act of July 1902 recognized the Philippines as an unincorporated territory of the United States. The Filipinos would not be American citizens but would have the aid and protection of the United States. Moreover, a mutual understanding was reached whereby the islands could be granted independence at some point in the future. Relations between the Filipinos and their American occupiers began to improve.

The islands continued to be administered by a U.S.-appointed governor-general, but in 1916 the Filipinos were allowed to elect a bi-cameral legislature and organize their own government. Governor-General Wood reported in the early 1920s that the Filipinos were not yet ready for full independence, but by then the United States had divested of imperial ambitions and hoped to rid themselves of responsibility for the islands. American naval experts deemed the Philippine archipelago indefensible if attacked by a major power. The U.S. announced intentions to withdraw from the islands "as soon as a stable government [could] be established therein."[10]

By the time the Croft family settled into their new home in Manila in 1926, the Filipinos were largely accepting of the Americans, whom the natives began to value for economic development and political instruction as they moved closer to independence. Friendly locals aside, the exotic beauty and relaxed lifestyle of Manila attracted Americans and other nationalities from around the globe. Alfred and Selma Croft's desire to return to this pulsating western Pacific city would have been no surprise.

"There is no better proof of the worthwhileness of life in Manila than that those who have lived in the islands for two years always return," wrote a contributor to *Mid-Atlantic Pacific Magazine* in the 1920s. "They have eaten of the lotus." In his article entitled "Life Worth Living in Manila," the writer explained how "warm sunshine and summer haze convince that life is not all toil, nor the present merely a purgatory for future cleanliness of soul," and that "it is necessary to remember that there are two Manilas, the one in which man works, and the other in which man plays, the former yielding material success undreamed in poorer countries, and the latter, those emoluments of pleasure sought for in vain east of Honolulu and west of Suez."[11]

But the weather was not always "warm sunshine and summer haze," Patty recalled. "It was really hot, and the humidity made it worse. And we had occasional typhoons. Rains were sporadic but almost a constant during the monsoon season." She remembered the holiday season from Christmas through the first of the year as having the best weather with daytime temperatures around 80 degrees.

Inclement weather patterns were not the only negative aspect of life in the Philippines. The bothersome mosquitos were a part of everyday existence in the tropical islands. But Patty came to view the ever-present mosquito netting around her bed as a normal way of living. Even the finest hotels in Manila deployed this fine meshwork around guestroom beds.

Attractions of Manila included the cosmopolitan nature of the city and the sense of unfolding opportunity in a land awakening from colonial slumber. The coming of the Americans had meant the end of centuries of domination of Manila and the Philippine Islands by Spanish overlords. Once the Filipinos were convinced that American oversight was temporary, a true sense of partnership between the two peoples blossomed in the 1920s. The enterprising Americans with their money and technology could offer much to the future prosperity of the Filipinos, and the islands could in turn provide opportunity for U.S. emigrant families.

In her book *Captured: the Japanese Internment of American Civilians in the Philippines*, Frances B. Cogan describes the attitude of most American civilians at the time as a mix of "entrepreneurship and paternalism." The Philippines had untapped resources and business opportunities. Jobs were also plentiful in this environment, and the U.S. economic doldrums of the 1930s drove many Americans to the islands for work. The high standard of living and good economy would keep many of these U.S. emigrants in the islands even as war with Japan threatened in the late 1930s.[12]

The more paternalistic of the Americans included "dedicated teachers, eager missionaries, doctors in tropical medicine, American government bureaucrats, and civil engineers." The islands represented a worthy cause in which they could devote time and effort. Here was a backward land the Americans could help carry into the industrialized twentieth century. The drastically improved literacy rate of Filipinos, eradication of small pox and cholera, and network of modern bridges and roads testified to the Americans' success by the late 1930s.[13]

Attorney Alva Hill described the rich social life enjoyed in the 1930s by Americans in Manila like he and his wife, Martha. "Dinner parties are a favorite indoor sport, with cocktail parties a close second. The women invariably wear long dresses, and the men, white jackets. Bridge, poker, and mahjong parties are also popular. Ladies' afternoon bridge usually begins with an elaborate tea at 4:00 p.m., and continues until 7:00 p.m. Many of the men go to their clubs for tennis, or handball or swimming after office hours. In many homes dinner is not served before 8:00."[14]

If the Americans were living well off the Philippine economy, Filipinos also saw benefits from their U.S. occupiers. The tremendous gains in literacy experienced by the natives stood out as one of their chief profits. The Americans had rapidly built and continued to administer schools for the locals, from primary through university level. Despite the often-paternalistic attitude of the Americans, by the 1930s little racial tension existed between the natives and the newcomers. The separation between the two communities appeared more to be a class distinction than a racial one. And with the economic improvements fostered by the Americans, many Filipinos believed the income gap could narrow in the future.[15]

Most of the nearly 3,000 American *Manileños* (Manila residents) had taken homes in the Ermita and Malate districts of Manila, close to the

city's center and overlooking Manila Bay to the west. But the Crofts settled into the comfortable lifestyle of Santa Mesa, farther to the east and
surrounded by the Pasig River on the southwestern side and the San Juan
River on the southern and eastern side. The district's name reflected its
roots as a property of a Jesuit religious order during the Spanish colonial
era. The neighborhood had housed wealthy and aristocratic Filipino and
Spanish families, who built summer homes in the slightly cooler climate
of Santa Mesa. In 1899 the district's streets had seen fierce fighting between American troops and Filipino nationalists. But by the early 1930s,
the picturesque streets of Santa Mesa provided a playground for children
among the exotic *ylang-ylang* trees, with their yellow flowers used for
perfume.[16]

"It was an easy life for us," Patty recalled of her years growing up on
Manga Avenue. "Lots of parties and easy living in the 1930s, but it was a
bad place to raise children—I didn't even have to make my bed. We had
servants who worked cheap."

The Crofts employed five servants, including an *amah*, Tekay Marsigan,
who doubled as a housekeeper and nursemaid for the children. Younger
brother William had been born the year after the Croft's return to Manila,
so the three children kept their *amah* busy. Unmarried and middle-aged,
Tekay lived with the Crofts and eventually became part of the household.
"She didn't even speak English until my mother taught her," Patty remem-
bers. "She was with our family a long time."

In addition to their housekeeper, the Crofts had a houseboy, a chauffeur
for excursions around Manila, a *lavandara* (laundress), and a gardener.
While a household with five servants would be associated with wealth
on the U.S. mainland, Patty recalled this was common for middle-class
American families in 1930s Manila. "We weren't that well off," she said.
"The Filipino workers just really worked cheap."

With so many native servants around, Patty picked up some of the Tagalog language common to most of those indigenous to Luzon. She and
her younger brother occasionally dined with the household staff. "If Bill
and I didn't like what we were having for dinner, we would go into the
kitchen and have fish and rice with the servants."

Combining her Tagalog phrases with the four years of Spanish she
would take in school enabled her to converse with the Filipino store clerks
as a teenager. "I could dicker for a better price. You never paid the first
price for anything. For a long time afterward, I could talk just the like the

Filipinos with their accent."

In 1929 she began kindergarten at the private American School in Ermita. The area became urbanized during the American occupation, and the American School was founded in 1920 to offer U.S. expatriates an alternative to the Manila public schools. In the mid-1930s, the school was moved to Pasay, a district just south of the city's center. One of Patty's earliest memories of the school was of her father dropping her off in the morning and her asking for money to buy an Eskimo Pie, a chocolate-covered vanilla ice cream bar relatively new to the market at the time. "That must have sounded funny to my dad because my family kidded me a lot about it when I was growing up."

When Patty started third grade, her mother transferred her and her two brothers to Manila Central School, an English-language public school with a mix of native and foreign-born students. That lasted only a couple of years. "My mother took us out of there after a few years because she thought there were too many Filipino *mestizos* (Spanish and native mixed-bloods). We went back to the American School." Many of the American families at the time worried that their children would lose connection with their U.S. heritage if allowed too much exposure to the natives and their culture. Although this attitude might later be viewed as somewhat racist, it was common among American and European families at the time.

Although lily-white compared to the Filipinos, Patty admitted that as a child she felt more like a native of the Philippines than a U.S. citizen. Her family returned to the States only once every five years. "Walking around in the United States, it almost felt like I was in a foreign country," she reminisced. "And it seemed to me that I was treated differently when I would go into American stores and places. I just always felt like I didn't fit in on our visits to the States."

Trips back to the United States were both an adventure and an ordeal. With no passenger planes connecting the Philippines to the States, the Crofts boarded an ocean liner for the three-week excursion. "We usually went by way of Shanghai or Hong Kong or Yokohama," Patty said. "It was really educational for me."

The trip to the West Coast of the United States always included a visit with Patty's immigrant grandparents on Selma's side of the family, Charles and Matilda Bergstrom, who lived in Oakland, California. Though born in the States, Selma was a first-generation Swedish-American who didn't learn English until she started school. The conversations during Patty's visits were in Swedish, she recalled with amusement, but this may have added to her outsider feelings on her visits to America.

Back in Manila—and to Patty her familiar homeland—the American expatriate had no trouble fitting in and finding things to do. "Manila was a very social-type place to live. Almost all the Americans belonged to the Manila Polo Club."

The Polo Club was the center of life for the American community in Manila. In 1909 Governor-General Cameron Forbes had purchased forty acres of land in Pasay along Manila Bay and donated it to the founders of the Manila Polo Club. The club's Forbes Field would be rated one of the top polo venues in the world. The sport was popular among the American military on Luzon, and polo fields could also be found at nearby Ft. McKinley, Ft. Stotsenberg and Nichols Field.

The civilian American expatriates used the luxurious facilities at the Polo Club for parties, dances, and weddings. "Before the war started, they had lots of dances at the club, even for us teenagers," Patty said. "The Red, White and Blue Dance was a big party where we all had to dress in red, white and blue clothes. It was mostly ballroom dancing. What a great, easy way to live." The Red, White and Blue Dance was also a not-so-subtle reminder of where these Americans' loyalties were to remain.

The clubhouse design was Philippine with a high *nipa* (thatched) roof. The magnificent dining facility featured high ceilings and lighting suspended from wall-to-wall rafters. The heavy shade provided by the acacia trees surrounding Forbes Field provided an excellent setting for picnics or leisurely walks out of the blazing tropical sun. The club's large outdoor swimming pool included a diving platform and provided American-style luxury and respite from the island heat.[17]

Patty remembered hours of childhood pleasure in what she called "that wonderful swimming pool," although she recalled once being pushed off the high dive and landing awkwardly in the waters below. Her memories of the Polo Club included numerous social events and activities. "Every Sunday afternoon they would have polo matches. It was a wonderful afternoon. The club was right on the beach. They always served dinner in the evening. It was quite a social affair. They had indoor badminton courts, which is what I really liked. It was too hot outdoors to play tennis."

Membership in the club was overwhelmingly Caucasian. The Americans in Manila, as well as British, Dutch and other European nationals, were living in what was for the most part a segregated society. The

Filipino natives lived in neighborhoods apart from the lighter-skinned American and European immigrants, mingling with them chiefly as servants or laborers. Although Patty would grow to adulthood in the islands, she claimed few native friends.

"I remember my older brother was swimming in the Polo Club pool once," Patty recalled, "and a friend said to me, 'I didn't know they allowed Filipinos in this club.' My brother was so suntanned from sailing on Manila Bay with his friends that he could pass for a native."

Another social center for Americans was the Elks Club. Patty's father was an Elk, and the family occasionally attended the group's events. The club was near the distinctive statue of Filipino national hero José Rizal, whose name Patty and her friends Americanized as "Josey Rizzle."

She remembered the Christmas party at the Elks Club when she realized that the Santa was just an imposter. Her father had flown in old Saint Nick and landed the plane just outside the Elks Club. When Patty requested her gift from Santa, she recognized him as a friend of the family. "When I told him what I wanted, I called him by his name—Uncle Derry," she said. "For some reason we called our parents' good friends *uncle* and *aunt*."

Some of her early memories included fun-filled trips to the stores and food vendors along Escolta Street in downtown Manila. The Escolta section was the center of European and American commerce. The intersecting streets and plazas along Escolta lay just across the Pasig River from the Intramuros, the ancient Walled City of Manila that had served as the official and residential habitat of Spanish colonial aristocracy. The Walled City was—and still is—one of Manila's key tourist attractions.

"Talkie" theaters were commonplace along Escolta Street by the 1930s, but Patty remembered more the drug store in the Botica Boie Building. "We kids always wanted to stop at that drug store because they had the best strawberry shakes in the world." Visits to the drug store were often followed by shopping trips to nearby Heacock's Department Store, which was much like many of the department stores in the States.

With the U.S. Congress's passage of the Tydings-McDuffie Act in 1934, the Philippine Islands transitioned from mere territorial status to that of the Commonwealth of the Philippines with their own democratically elected leader in lieu of a U.S.-appointed governor-general. Manuel L. Quezon was elected president in 1935, and Manila was officially proclaimed the capital of the new commonwealth. Most important to the Filipinos, the act mandated U.S. recognition of the islands as a free and independent nation by July 4, 1946.

Another milestone in the modernization of the islands occurred around this same time with the landing of a Pan American Airways seaplane in Manila Bay in November 1935. The *China Clipper* was the first of three Martin M-130 four-engine "flying boats" built for Pan American to provide commercial air service from San Francisco to Manila. The sixty-hour inaugural flight delivered 110,000 pieces of mail via Hawaii, Midway Island, Wake Island and Guam. Navigator for the flight was Fred Noonan, who would also navigate for pioneer aviatrix Amelia Earhart on their ill-fated attempt to circumnavigate the globe in 1937.

Hailed as the beginning of a new age, the *China Clipper*'s arrival marked the first regularly scheduled flight across the Pacific Ocean. Mail would be the priority for the initial Pan Am flights, followed by cargo, then passengers in 1936. The American expatriates in Manila now had an air link to the States.[18]

Eleven-year-old Patty remembered the great excitement in the Manila community on the day of the first flight's arrival. She accompanied a friend, Lolita Rifkin, to Manila Bay to mix with the excited throng as the *China Clipper* splashed down to great fanfare. "That was a real thrill. It was a big deal for everyone in Manila."

With the Philippines now a self-governing commonwealth, the Filipinos shared in the celebration alongside the Americans. By the time of this new air link to the U.S. mainland, the Filipinos' national flag was flying side by side with the Stars and Stripes. The new Philippine banner was a horizontal bicolor flag with equal bands of crimson red and royal blue. Patty remembered that the U.S. flag had always been prominently displayed alone in many Manila locations during her early childhood, and the Philippine banner now flying beside it seemed a harbinger of changes ahead.

Socializing in the Santa Mesa neighborhood, Patty occasionally visited a spacious resident at the top of a hill on Manga Avenue. It was a beautiful home named Casa Blanca built by a wealthy Jewish couple whose last name was Bachrach. Emil Bachrach was Manila's richest car dealer. "They had a swimming pool and even a bowling alley. It was a gorgeous place. I went there a few times as a girl to swim, but they kind of kept to themselves. They moved away before the Japanese came." She later remembered General Douglas MacArthur making the Bachrach house his temporary residence in 1945 after his return to the Philippines.

But the Japanese invasion and MacArthur's historic return was a world away from her carefree years in the mid-1930s. The lighthearted girl was looking forward to new friends and new adventures during her upcoming high school years at the American School. She was blissfully unaware of the great world affairs unfolding around her in the Philippines, and just how much her life—and the lives of all the Americans in the islands— would be entwined in these historical events. "Sometimes I wish my life had not been," she mused much later.

THE INTERNATIONAL EVENTS that would soon shatter the comfortable lives of Patty Croft and the American expatriates were instigated by the newly industrialized and imperialistic nation of Japan, whose militaristic leaders determined to forge a new political order in the western Pacific. The Japanese navy had shown its new might with victories over the Chinese fleet in the 1894-1895 war and again with the smashing victory over the Russian navy at Tsushima in the Russo-Japanese War of 1904-1905. Japanese naval officers studied the writings of U.S. naval strategist Alfred Thayer Mahan and his 1890 publication *The Influence of Sea Power Upon History* with its emphasis on a strong navy supported by overseas bases as a key to a nation's economic and political power. The book's persuasive ideas were translated into Japanese before any other foreign language, and by the 1920s the Japanese navy looked much like that of the United States. With so much of the Japanese imperialistic aspiration surrounded by the waters of the Pacific Ocean, the island nation's naval leaders naturally advocated for a powerful fleet.

Mahan's writings had also influenced American leaders to annex the Philippine Islands in 1899. The archipelago and other Pacific islands could provide resupply stations for America's coal-fired navy, and these possessions gave the U.S. a base of operations to protect its trade with the emerging Chinese market. But early on American military planners foresaw problems defending America's new possession in the Pacific. An attack on these islands by a Japanese fleet would require a lengthy sortie by the U.S. Navy to rescue these holdings.[19]

In the years after World War I, U.S. geopolitical strategy took a twofold approach to check the growing threat from Japanese naval power in the Pacific: diplomacy and war planning. On the diplomatic side, the Washington Naval Treaty of 1922 was the culmination of U.S.-led efforts to limit the number and size of major powers' naval forces. Japan signed this accord, along with Great Britain, the United States, France and Italy, all agreeing to forego a naval arms race by limiting construction of large warships.

The war planning aspect of the U.S. strategy included the development of a military response in the event of war with Japan. Planners assumed a Japanese naval force could land troops and effectively blockade the Philippines and other U.S. holdings in the western Pacific. The response to this attack envisioned U.S. forces in the Philippines holding out against the Japanese invasion long enough for a mobilized American naval force to arrive and defeat the enemy fleet.[20]

Yet serious concerns were raised in the early 1920s when the plans were tested by U.S. War College analysts using various invasion scenarios. The first War Plan Orange defensive strategy resulted in a failure of U.S. forces to hold out more than a few months against a hypothetical Japanese attack on the Philippines. This probably would not allow enough time for the U.S. Navy's arrival. War planners were ready to write the islands off as indefensible, but in 1923 Governor-General Leonard Wood argued for revisions in Plan Orange, which he hoped would ensure a more successful defense.[21]

The rapidly developing Japanese air capabilities in the 1920s added further doubts to the adequacy of Plan Orange. The use of American naval power was key to the Orange strategy, but analysts pointed out the growing vulnerability of U.S. ships to Japanese air attacks. Japan's acquisition of numerous western Pacific islands in the 1920s and 1930s enhanced its ability to project air power in the region.[22]

While the U.S. military wrestled with the problem of defending the Philippines against a Japanese attack, 42-year-old Brig. Gen. Douglas MacArthur was assigned to a three-year tour in the islands beginning in 1922. MacArthur took command of the Manila military district and proudly directed the Philippine Scouts, a U.S. military unit of Filipino soldiers. He was welcomed to the islands as "Young General MacArthur" by Filipinos who had developed a high regard for his father, Lt. Gen. Arthur MacArthur Jr., who had been the military governor of the islands from 1900 to 1901. Like his father, Douglas MacArthur showed no racial prejudice toward the Filipinos and developed a friendly relationship with rising Filipino politician Manuel Quezon.

Reassigned to the Philippines in 1928 as army commander, MacArthur struggled with the potential Japanese threat. Several iterations of Plan Orange had evolved by the end of the 1920s, and MacArthur had doubts about each. With only 17,000 American and Filipino troops at his disposal, he saw no way to hold off a Japanese attack long enough for the U.S. Navy to arrive. He also worried about the increasing number of Japanese workers and businessmen in the islands.

After returning to the States in 1930 to serve as U.S. Army chief of staff with the rank of full general, by 1935 MacArthur was preparing for a second career in the Philippines. His old friend Manuel Quezon, by then president of the new Commonwealth of the Philippines, had recruited him to take charge of the Philippine military. With independence planned for the islands by the mid-1940s, the Filipinos would soon be responsible for their own defense. By a combination of U.S. legislation and a personal agreement with Quezon, MacArthur accepted a reduction in rank from general to major general in the U.S. Army while receiving a generous allowance from the new commonwealth and the courtesy title of General of the Army.

The divorced MacArthur and his 84-year-old mother, Pinky, boarded the steamship *President Harding* in San Francisco for the voyage to the Philippines in fall 1935. Attending a party while aboard, MacArthur met his future second wife, Jean Faircloth, a world traveler from a wealthy Tennessee family. They would marry two years later. A trooper to the end, Pinky MacArthur would die of a stroke not long after arriving in Manila with her son in October. Along with his mother and new girlfriend, MacArthur brought a number of staff officers from Washington, including 45-year-old Maj. Dwight D. Eisenhower. MacArthur and his staff would be tasked with planning a more viable defense of the Philippines.[23]

As he did for most of the American expatriates in Manila, MacArthur made quite an impression on young Patty Croft the first time she saw him. "My mother and I went to the Manila Hotel to pick up one of her friends," she vividly remembered. "While I was waiting in the lobby, I saw this good-looking guy coming down the stairs in a beautiful white suit." She was awestruck by the regal general, then nearly sixty. Selma Croft soon began playing bridge with Jean MacArthur, who socialized with other wives in the American community.

As part of his compensation for overseeing the Philippine military, MacArthur had required accommodations equal to that of Quezon's residence at Malacañan Palace, which included seven bedrooms and an immense dining room. A local architect suggested a penthouse be constructed atop the elegant Manila Hotel to meet the new commander's specifications. MacArthur's entire sixth-floor residence would be fully air-conditioned and carpeted.[24]

While the teenage Patty may have been awestruck by the revered American general, older Americans in the Manila community were calmed by his presence. As the world grew increasingly dangerous in the Philippines of the late 1930s, a seasoned military leader like MacArthur could be reassuring. Wrestling with the vexing problem of devising a credible defense of the islands, MacArthur's military staff were less assured. Their assessments left them with few illusions about the fate of the thousands of Americans on Luzon in the event of war with Japan.

In the closing years of the 1930s, the Croft family and other American civilians in Manila were barely aware of their increasingly perilous position so close to imperialistic Japan. American officials did little to nothing to alert them to the growing danger. The cocktail parties continued with regularity at the Polo Club, the Army-Navy Club, and the Elks Club. One could always spend an afternoon playing bridge at the Manila Hotel. It was an easy life for expatriate Americans in the Pearl of the Orient.

# CHAPTER 2

✼ ✼ ✼

# War Clouds Over the Philippines

LATE IN 1935, ELEVEN-YEAR-OLD Patty Croft and her family boarded a steamship for a visit to the United States. Five years had passed since the Crofts' previous journey to the West Coast. As with previous visits, much of the time would be spent with Selma Croft's parents in Oakland. This trip would overlap Christmas and the first of the new year, so they would not return to Manila until early 1936.

The America they visited still struggled to recover from the Great Depression, an economic downturn unseen in the vibrant, growing Manila economy. The depressed local economies in California went largely unnoticed by the carefree Patty as the family drove up the Pacific coast in their late model Chevrolet. The Crofts had shipped their car over with them as they intended to make a number of road trips, including a visit to Texas where Alfred Croft had trained pilots in World War I.

"I remember we stopped for gas along the Coast Highway, and the station attendant noticed our Manila car tag," Patty said. "He joked to my dad, 'My gosh, man, did you drive that car all the way across the ocean.' I think we shipped our car over because rental cars were not as available back in those days."

They later visited some friends of the family who had lived in Manila before retiring and moving to Pasadena, California. Patty remembered a lot of Americans from Manila moving to California upon retirement.

Patty and her younger brother, Bill, stayed with their grandparents in Oakland while her older brother, Al, and their parents made several other trips around California. Al was planning to move to Oakland in 1939 to live with his aunt and uncle during his senior year of high school. After graduation he planned to attend college in California.

That Christmas, Patty had told her mother and grandmother that she wanted money instead of presents. She determined to buy a puppy of her own that year. Before boarding in Los Angeles for the return trip, the family drove to a pet store so Patty could look at puppies. She found what she wanted, a cute wire-haired fox terrier. The breed was rare in Manila pet stores.

"The store clerk asked whose name it should be registered in," Patty remembered, "and of course I said, 'My name!' My brother Al got mad because he wanted it registered in his name for some reason or another. He got so angry he stormed out of the pet store and stomped down Long Beach Boulevard. It was just kid stuff."

At the time, Patty was sandwiched between thirteen-year-old Al and nine-year-old Bill and often suffered for it. "It's terrible when you're the girl between two boys. They were beating on me all the time, smothering me with pillows and drowning me in the pool. They could be mean."

On the return trip, Patty kept her new puppy on the top deck tending to her pet's needs each day. She wasn't sure what to name her terrier until an American friend of the family—who was the editor of the *Manila Daily Bulletin* newspaper and on the ship back to Manila—suggested the name *Chiquita*. It sounded perfect.

Each morning for more than two weeks, Patty diligently fed and cared for little Chiquita in her pen on the top deck. The voyage home took only a little more than two weeks. Instead of the longer northerly route from Hawaii to Japan and down the Asian coastline, the liner took a more direct route through the Solomon Islands and on to the Philippines.

As the American girl stood on the upper deck gazing at the tropical beauty of the tranquil Solomon Islands, she thought how she would be nearing the end of her high school years before her next visit to the States. But more than nine years would pass before her next return trip and much would be changed by then. Before her return to America, the once-obscure Solomon Islands would be a familiar name to many Americans following news accounts of savage fighting and death in the green hell of Solomon outposts like Guadalcanal, Tulagi and Bougainville. Before her return to

America, both she and the entire world would be vastly changed by unforeseen events.

DESPITE THE INCREASING BELLICOSITY of fascist nations in Europe and Asia, the United States left behind by the Crofts on their return to Manila in 1936 was more concerned with avoiding foreign conflict than preparing for it. In February, Congress strengthened its recently enacted embargo on U.S. arms shipments to belligerent countries by adding a prohibition on loans or credit to these warring nations. With the general election looming in November, President D. Franklin Roosevelt faced a more immediate threat from isolationists at home than potential hostility abroad. Focused on avoiding international conflicts through strict neutrality laws, Congress was in no mood for increases in military appropriations.

While the United States was choosing to avoid or ignore foreign threats, Japanese militarists were expanding their armed forces. Early in 1936 Japanese negotiators walked out of the second London Naval Conference, a meeting of great naval powers with the intent to limit key nations' naval forces. Japan's expansion of sea power at the time was crucial to its designs on the lands and waters of the western Pacific.

Japan intensified its imperial quest in July 1937 when a minor incident between Japanese and Chinese troops at the Marco Polo Bridge in Peking (Beijing) led to a full-scale attack by Japan on the Nationalist Chinese government led by Chiang Kai-shek. The Nationalist Chinese Party had been controlled by Sun Yat-sen and based in Canton when Alfred Croft helped train its air corps before fleeing the fighting and returning to the United States in 1922. Following Sun's death in 1925, Chiang had largely succeeded in unifying China under his rule, but in 1937 and for years afterward he would be fighting to prevent Japan from overrunning China.

Directly threatening to the United States, an attack by Japanese warplanes on the United States gunboat *Panay* as it lay at anchor in the Yangtze River set alarm bells ringing in Washington, D. C. In December 1937 the *Panay* had been rescuing American and Chinese civilians from murderous Japanese troops as they rampaged through Nanking, China's Nationalist Party capital. Japanese warplanes sank the *Panay* as the city fell, setting off several weeks of slaughter and rape by Japanese troops in what was later called the Rape of Nanking. More than 200,000 Chinese died at the hands of the Japanese military after the capital city succumbed. Japan later apologized and paid reparations to the United States for the *Panay* incident, but the Japanese invasion of China would set in motion events ultimately leading to an attack on the United States—and devastating to the Commonwealth of the Philippines.[1]

The Japanese aggression in China intensified efforts by Maj. Gen. Douglas MacArthur and his military mission in Manila as they planned for the defense of the Philippines. Although MacArthur privately shared doubts with war analysts about the defensibility of the islands, he evinced only confidence. When Manuel Quezon approached the general in 1934 to recruit him for the military mission in the Philippines, he asked MacArthur if he truly thought the islands could be defended. "I don't *think* that the Philippines can defend themselves," the then-army chief of staff confidently replied. "I *know* they can."[2]

To make good on this boast, late in 1935 MacArthur tasked his two chief military planners, Majors Dwight Eisenhower and James Ord, to begin formulating long-term strategy to defend the archipelago. By 1936 they had fleshed out a ten-year plan, although Eisenhower had little confidence in getting the necessary funding. The final implementation of the strategy was to coincide with Philippine independence in 1946.

The plans included training 40,000 Filipino troops each year from one of the ten military jurisdictions, so that by 1946 some 400,000 citizen-soldiers in forty divisions would be ready to defend their new country. To support this effort, 128 new army bases were to be established across the islands with training support by both American and Filipino military personnel. Additionally, a new Philippine navy would include fifty patrol-torpedo (PT) boats, and the country's new air force would boast 250 warplanes.[3]

Essential to these plans, of course, would be adequate funding from both the United States and the new commonwealth. This proved to be the biggest stumbling block as the Japanese threat loomed in the late 1930s. Even the awe-inspiring MacArthur would lack the clout to overcome this funding obstacle—especially in the critical early years of this planned buildup.

Playing a central role in these plans, Eisenhower grew increasingly frustrated in his efforts to implement a defensive strategy and increasingly exasperated working under *Generalissimo* Douglas MacArthur. Eisenhower had not wanted this staff assignment in the first place, but "General MacArthur lowered the boom on me, so to speak...I was in no position to argue with the Chief of Staff," he later said. He had temporarily left his wife, Mamie, behind with their son, John, while the boy finished the eighth grade in the States.[4]

Eisenhower and the others in MacArthur's military entourage dressed in civilian clothing and reported for duty in a modest building in a section of the old Walled City called the Cuartel de España. Staff usually ended their workday by 1 p.m., and Eisenhower routinely joined a group of Manila businessmen for an afternoon of bridge at the Manila Hotel. He had initially been provided a stuffy, two-room suite on the third floor of the hotel, three levels below MacArthur's air-conditioned penthouse. When Mamie and John joined him in October 1936, she was dismayed by the heat, mosquito netting around their beds, and the small lizards scurrying across the ceilings. The Eisenhowers soon located to an air-conditioned suite on a lower floor, upsetting the imperious MacArthur, who thought this an extravagant accommodation for the newly promoted Lieutenant Colonel Eisenhower.[5]

Early in 1937 President Quezon and his recently christened Field Marshal Douglas MacArthur, a rank no other American officer has ever held, were invited to Washington, D.C., for the swearing-in of Paul McNutt as U.S. high commissioner for the Philippines, succeeding Frank Murphy. While in the U.S. capital MacArthur hoped to gain funding for more military weapons and supplies for his nascent force of Filipinos. Meanwhile, Quezon tried to drum up support in Congress for an earlier independence date for the Philippines. Neither was successful. Disappointed, Quezon sailed for home leaving his field marshal in New York City. While there, MacArthur took the opportunity for a trip to the Municipal Building to marry Jean Faircloth, who had come over alone from Manila. Ten months later Jean would provide MacArthur the son he had long wanted, giving birth to Arthur MacArthur IV at Manila's Sternberg Hospital.[6]

Adding to MacArthur's difficulties getting his requested funding, in 1937 several influential officials and politicians in the States tried to end his military mission to the Philippines. Senator Millard Tydings, an isolationist from Maryland, wanted the United States to withdraw from the western Pacific entirely. Former high commissioner and later governor of Michigan, Frank Murphy, feared the militarization of the Philippines under MacArthur. The two pressured U.S. Army Chief of Staff Malin Craig, who had replaced MacArthur in 1935, to reassign the Philippine field marshal to stateside duty. To avoid this maneuver, MacArthur promptly resigned from active duty in the U.S. Army, effective December 31, 1937.

He would then command the military of the Commonwealth of the Philippines as a U.S.-expatriate *Manileño*.

Disheartened by lack of U.S. funding and MacArthur's new estrangement from Washington, Quezon contemplated Philippine neutrality, seeing this as a means to ward off a potential Japanese invasion. To MacArthur's dismay, Quezon sailed to Tokyo for discussions with Japanese officials in July 1938. Returning, Quezon tried once again to accelerate Philippine independence. Failing to gain support in Washington, he retaliated by cutting Philippine funds for defense of the islands and threatening to terminate MacArthur's ten-year plan.

Stating aloud what new High Commissioner Francis Sayre and Lieutenant Colonel Eisenhower privately thought, the mercurial Quezon told an audience in Manila's Rizal Stadium that despite what MacArthur and a few optimists were saying about successfully defending the islands, the Philippines "could not be defended even if every last Filipino were armed with modern weapons." Quezon's speech naturally had a demoralizing effect on the commonwealth's morale, and by late 1939 many Filipinos were refusing to register for the draft. MacArthur's standing army of Filipinos dwindled to 468 officers and 3,697 enlisted men.[7]

Hoping to change Quezon's pessimistic position on defensive of the islands, MacArthur called the president's secretary, Jorge Vargas, for an appointment. He was told that Quezon was too busy to see him. "Jorge," MacArthur presciently warned the secretary, "some day your boss will want to see me more than I want to see him."[8]

MacArthur made a desperate attempt to borrow weapons from the U.S. Army in 1939, but was told that even if the Philippines were loaned these weapons, the U.S. military could not spare ammunition. Isolationist congressmen and the diminished U.S. economy of the 1930s had drained even its own military of needed appropriations. Any transfer of arms and ammunitions to the Philippines would further undercut U.S. preparedness.

In despair as time ticked away and the Japanese threat loomed, MacArthur wrote to an American journalist blaming both Manila and Washington for the failure of his military mission to implement a sound defense "The history of failure in war can be summed up in two words: Too Late," he pronounced. "Too late in comprehending the deadly purpose of a potential enemy; too late in realizing the mortal danger; too late in preparedness; too late in uniting all possible forces for resistance; too late for standing with one's friends." That in a nutshell described the half-baked Philippine defense initiative as the 1930s drew to a close.[9]

This depressing situation was known all too well by Lieutenant Colonel Eisenhower as he hunched over a radio in the Manila Hotel in early September 1939 listening to a broadcast of the German invasion of Poland. This meant war in Europe, and MacArthur's chief staff officer in Manila balked at being mired in the intractable problems of defending the Philippines when he could be more useful in Washington.

Eisenhower had been unhappy for some time serving under his often overbearing and overly dramatic boss. The death of his friend and fellow planner Maj. James Ord in an airplane accident in 1938 had added to his melancholy. Eisenhower wanted a transfer. He wasted no time in telling MacArthur just that. Being Douglas MacArthur, Eisenhower's senior felt slighted by his underling's request to transfer from his command. "MacArthur said I was making a big mistake," Eisenhower later said, "[that] the work I was doing in the Philippines was far more important than any I could do as a mere lieutenant colonel in the American Army."[10]

But MacArthur would not stand in his way. In a rare show of magnanimity toward his subordinate, MacArthur and his wife saw the Eisenhowers off as they sailed for the States in December 1939. Eisenhower's son, John, later recalled the MacArthurs waving cordially as the *SS President Coolidge* pulled away from the Manila dock.[11]

The two army officers would not see each other again until after the cataclysm of World War II. Long after Eisenhower's ascension to five-star rank equivalent to his former boss, MacArthur dismissively called him the "[b]est clerk I ever had." When Eisenhower was later asked if he had ever met MacArthur, he replied, "Not only have I met him, ma'am, I studied dramatics under him for five years in Washington and four years in the Philippines." Despite his discontent working for MacArthur, in future years Eisenhower praised his former commanding officer's qualities as a soldier.[12]

PATTY CROFT FIRST MET John Eisenhower in fall 1938 when her American School basketball teams squared off against his Brent School squads in Baguio, 130 miles north of Manila and just east of Lingayen Gulf. By her freshman year of high school, Patty stood five feet six inches high, not particularly tall for the girls basketball team but rangy enough to play as a guard. With light brown hair and brown eyes, the fourteen-year-old was also blossoming into an attractive young lady.

"I met John my first year in high school when we took that winding road up the mountains to play basketball with Brent," she recalled. "We all called him 'Eyezy.' He was a couple of years older than me. John was just another guy. His dad was not well known at the time."

Patty had become familiar with the mountainous terrain around Baguio from around the age of ten when she began spending a month each year at Yosemite Summer Camp. The area's altitude provided relief from Manila's tropical climate. Camp attendees took day trips and hiked in the mountains. "I remember going on an orchid hunt and getting leeches up my legs," Patty remembered. "But I did bring orchids back—wild orchids."

John Eisenhower stayed at the Christian boarding school with other children of mostly American missionaries and military families, some from nearby Camp John Hay, a small U.S. Army installation. Girls also boarded at Brent School, which developed a strong sports rivalry with the American School in Manila. The school and its proximity to Lingayen Gulf and Camp John Hay would place it in the midst of bloody fighting in World War II. The military post would ultimately be the site for the final surrender of holdout Japanese forces in the Philippines in September 1945.

Patty's home life saw disruption by her freshman year in high school. Her parents had quarreled over Alfred's drinking habits throughout her childhood, and these arguments reached a climax in 1938 when they agreed to separate. Alfred moved to Hawaii to work at Hickam Field, using his aviation experience in an administrative role at the rapidly developing military airfield at Pearl Harbor. Just northwest of Honolulu, the air facility was officially completed that year in September.

Although Alfred Croft continued to send support to his family, Patty and her mother and brothers moved from their house in Santa Mesa to a large apartment in Pasay, just south of the center of Manila and along the harbor. "We lived in a four-story building with an elevator," she recalled. "Each floor housed a family. We had the second floor. I remember one of the families was from Vienna, Austria. It was close to the American School, so we could easily walk to classes."

With finances more of a concern, the family would have to manage without full-time servants from their household in Santa Mesa. The exception was their *amah*, Tekay, who played an important role in the family household and continued to live with the Crofts. The other servants would be employed only when necessary.

Patty now lived closer to her friends from school, so her social life improved. Her closest friend was basketball teammate Eileen Aaron, introduced to Patty by her older brother, Al. "She was a year ahead of me in school," Patty said, "but we played both basketball and softball together. Her dad was from Britain, so she had British citizenship."[13]

The teammates would meet for ice cream and gossip about school friends. "Eileen lived pretty close to me, and we'd go over to the school, or our little store and hang out," Patty said. The two would grow much closer in their years after high school with shared life experiences much different from what they had planned.

Although outgoing and attractive, Patty had no serious boyfriends during her high school years. "We only had four boys in my senior class, the other thirteen were all girls," she remembered. "The boys had their pick of us girls."

Now separated from her husband, Selma Croft began working as a private-duty nurse for hospitalized patients. Most of her work was at St. Luke's and St. Paul's Hospital. She had worked as a nurse at St. Luke's before meeting her husband in 1920. "If anyone in the American community was having some kind of serious surgery, they wanted my mom to be their nurse," Patty said of her mother's return to nursing. "She was in demand and made good money private-duty nursing."

About forty-four at the time of her separation, Selma's blue eyes, light-brown hair, and facial features reflected her Swedish heritage. She was intelligent and assertive, and fully in her element in a medical setting. Patty had a warm relationship with her mother, even during her sometimes-difficult teen years. "My mother rarely got cross with me. About the only time I remember her really getting after me was when I didn't get home from a date when I was supposed to."

By summer 1939, Patty's brother Al had left for his senior year of high school in Oakland, California. He would be staying with Selma's married younger sister, Florence, who had no children of her own and always wanted to adopt one of her sister's. Patty remembered Al leaving for the States with a classmate from the American School. They boarded a military ship for the voyage to California, so Al's classmate may have been from a military family. Military dependents began leaving Manila more frequently after 1938, Patty noticed.

Al's departure left Patty and Selma with twelve-year old Bill as the only male in the household. Patty grew close to her younger brother, who looked more like his mother with his blonde hair. Bill's chosen sport growing up was baseball, so he and his older sister spent little time together playing basketball.

After the family's move to Pasay, Patty's terrier Chiquita was bred with their Austrian neighbor's wire-haired terrier. All but one of Chiquita's puppies were sold by Patty, who used the money to purchase an accordion. Patty named the remaining puppy Suzy. Living on the second floor of their apartment building, Patty took her dogs downstairs for walks several times each day. Although Selma and Bill thought of the little terriers as "the family pets," Patty always considered Chiquita and Suzy her own.

Naming her dog Chiquita had reflected her fondness for the Spanish language, in which she was immersed in her everyday life. She also took a Spanish language class in each of her high school years. That she favored her Spanish classes best of all her studies must have been obvious to her teacher. "My Spanish teacher was a man from Spain," Patty said, "and he nicknamed me *Elliandra*." She thought the name translated roughly as "butterfly," but she wasn't certain what it meant.

About the time she started high school, Patty began accordion lessons with a German instructor she addressed as "Mister Beutel." He taught at his house where he lived with his Polish wife. The lesson room was decorated with a large Nazi flag on one wall making Patty uncomfortable during her sessions. By the late 1930s most Americans, even those in Manila, had heard enough negative stories about Adolph Hitler and his Nazis to be suspicious of their supporters.

Nevertheless, she continued to develop her accordion skills under the somewhat mysterious *Herr* Beutel. Before long, her musical talent had outgrown her small instrument, and her instructor found her a larger, more sophisticated one. The new accordion was purchased from a Jewish-German who had emigrated from Germany across the Soviet Union, arriving in Manila from Vladivostok, the eastern Soviet port city across from Japan.

"He brought three accordions with him when he left Germany," Patty said. "I've thought about that many times. I think he had money or jewelry hidden inside those accordions. Why else would he bring three accordions with him all the way from Germany?"

As her accordion skills improved, Beutel asked her to accompany him at performances on military bases around Luzon. Patty also began playing with the Manila Junior Symphony under the direction of American violinist Grace C. Nash, who had come to Manila in fall 1936 to marry an

American engineer named Ralph Nash. Grace became a featured violinist with the Manila Symphony and taught music at the American School. Patty's affiliation with Grace Nash would continue much longer than the high schooler anticipated at the time.[14]

In fall 1940, Patty began her junior year at the American School. Busy with classes, basketball and music, she still found time to meet some of the many young American military officers stationed at various locations around Manila. American girls were much in demand for socializing and dancing at local soirées. Life seemed idyllic for the flowering sixteen-year-old, who paid scant attention to the gathering geopolitical storm around her.

IN NOVEMBER 1940, JAPAN JOINED fascist Germany and Italy in the Tripartite Pact, a defensive military alliance that would form the backbone of the Axis powers. The Axis nations would eventually align against the Allies—primarily Britain, the British Commonwealth, France, the Soviet Union, China and the United States. Japan also signed a non-aggression agreement with the Soviet Union essentially securing the Japanese northern flank from a Soviet threat. Although the Japanese empire would continue its war of aggression in China, the island nation's militarists could now more freely expand southward in the western Pacific.

The Japanese move into Southeast Asia and the South Seas was initially opposed by Japanese naval leaders. Vice Navy Minister Isoroku Yamamoto and naval theorist Admiral Shigeyoshi Inoue were wary of a southward thrust that could result in conflict with Britain and the United States, countries with the world's two largest navies. But when their German ally shared secret documents indicating Britain would not go to war to defend French Indochina, Yamamoto and Inoue acquiesced to the southward expansion. Directly south of Japan and potentially blocking this thrust was the American-held Commonwealth of the Philippines.[15]

Another impediment to Japanese designs in the Pacific was the move in May 1940 of the U.S. Pacific Fleet from San Diego to Pearl Harbor on the island of Oahu in Hawaii. Roosevelt's orders to position the U.S. Navy closer to Japan was hoped to have a deterrent effect. Yet it also better allowed the Japanese to eavesdrop on U.S. radio telephone transmissions to the fleet. When U.S. military leaders learned the Japanese were able to monitor this communication, they began to use only telegraph transmissions for top-secret messages between the mainland and U.S. military in the Pacific, more secure but not as expedient. This would have severe consequences in early December 1941.

Viewing the Japanese threat with increasing alarm throughout 1940, MacArthur and his staff's planning for the defense of the Philippines moved into higher gear. The defense effort would eventually receive greater financial and material support from the United States military—but not until late in 1941. Eisenhower's vacancy was filled with the promotion of Lt. Col. Richard K. Sutherland as chief of staff. Most considered Sutherland efficient but ruthless. Some thought him arrogant and egotistical. Even the domineering MacArthur once told his new chief of staff, "The trouble with you, Dick, I am afraid, is that you are a natural-born autocrat." Telling words indeed coming from Field Marshal MacArthur.[16]

Another key addition to MacArthur's staff was his intelligence chief, Col. Charles Willoughby, who joined the team in 1939. A native of Germany, his original name had been Karl Weidenbach. Willoughby spoke with a heavy German accent and openly admitted his admiration for fascist Spanish leader Francisco Franco.

Even as the outlook for a successful defense of the Philippines worsened, MacArthur maintained a confident pose. He rather naively stated that Japan had no good reason to attack the Philippines and that such an amphibious operation exceeded Japanese abilities. But most of all, he based his confidence on renewed expectations of support from the United States, help that had failed to materialize in the last years of the 1930s. By 1940 MacArthur was calling the islands' defense the "ultimate responsibility" of the United States, a different approach than when he had confidently told Quezon in 1934 that the Filipinos could defend themselves.

Unknown to MacArthur at the time, Washington elites had already begun to acknowledge U.S. responsibility and pondered the advisability of a military buildup in the Philippines. MacArthur was often in the dark on Washington's war plans after his resignation from the army had left him outside the loop of the U.S. military establishment. MacArthur biographer William Manchester calls this situation "absurd" in his highly acclaimed biography *American Caesar*. As head of the military mission, MacArthur was overseeing the recruitment and training of the native citizen-soldiers on one hand; the commander of the U.S. Army's Philippine Department, Maj. Gen. Walter Grant, was directing U.S. military personnel and Philippine Scouts on the other. "Indeed, of all the blunders perpetrated by the United States as the Filipinos awaited the onslaught of the Japanese, one of the worst, in retrospect, was the division of army command until it was too late," Manchester argues. *Too late*: an echo of MacArthur's earlier summary of the history of failure in warfare.[17]

But in spring 1940, MacArthur caught a break when his old friend Maj. Gen. George Grunert was assigned to replace Grant as commander of the Philippine Department. By summer Grunert was urging Army Chief of Staff George C. Marshall to be more resolute in defense of the islands and send more U.S. troops, warplanes and submarines. Bucked up by MacArthur and Grunert, President Quezon reversed his defeatism and wrote Marshall pressing for a stronger U.S. military presence. Grunert also informed Marshall that current news accounts about the stout Philippine army were greatly exaggerated, but he absolved MacArthur for this shortcoming.

In a blow to MacArthur's efforts, in October 1940 the U.S. War Plans Division recommended the withdrawal of all U.S. forces west of the 180-degree meridian, which meant an abandonment of the Philippines, Guam and Wake. The now obsolete War Plan Orange had theorized the United States in a one-front Pacific war; recent events in Europe pointed to a two-front war. The new Rainbow Five war strategy was premised on a "Hitler first" effort, with the U.S. working with its allies to defeat Nazi Germany before turning full attention to the Pacific theater. As stated in the Rainbow Five plans, "strategy in the Far East will be defensive" as "the United States does not intend to add to its present strength" in the region. Although not specifically stated, Rainbow Five largely left the Filipinos to fend for themselves without U.S. assistance. Ominously for the thousands of U.S. civilians in the islands, the plans made no mention of their evacuation.

Still outside the loop since his retirement, MacArthur knew nothing of Rainbow Five. In February 1941 he wrote George Marshall exaggerating the readiness of his Philippine defense forces and asserting that a Japanese invasion could be repelled—if only he could get more guns and munitions from Washington. He heard nothing back from Marshall. MacArthur next sent a message to Roosevelt's press secretary, an old acquaintance of the general, nominating himself to command all Philippine and U.S. military in the islands. Hearing discouraging news from informal sources, MacArthur assumed he could do no more to help the situation. In a carefully written letter to Marshall on May 29, he told the chief of staff he was quitting his military mission in the Philippines and leaving Manila.

Finally, Roosevelt intervened. On June 20 Marshall wrote MacArthur that Secretary of War Henry Stimson planned to make him overall commander of U.S. military in the Far East if a crisis developed. With U.S. scout planes spotting Japanese troop ships moving southward in the South China Sea in early July, MacArthur believed the crisis was at hand. He wrote Washington urging a unified command in the Far East. By July 27, MacArthur was reappointed to the U.S. Army as a lieutenant general and made overall commander of the U.S. Army Forces in the Far East (USAFFE), which now included the Philippine Scouts as part of regular U.S. Army forces.

After a Japanese fleet sailed into Vietnam's Cam Ranh Bay and 30,000 Japanese troops entered Saigon in late July, the U.S. president prodded events closer to war between the United States and Japan with the embargo of U.S. sales of oil, iron and rubber and the freezing of Japanese and Chinese assets. Dependent on these resources to maintain their war machine, the Japanese had only two realistic choices: end their war in China or seize these raw materials from Malaya and the Dutch East Indies. That same day an intercepted cable from the Japanese foreign office to its ambassador in Berlin stated that the situation was "so horribly strained that we cannot endure it much longer..."[18]

A Japanese attack on U.S. allies in Malaya and the Dutch East Indies would likely trigger a response from the U.S. Pacific Fleet at Pearl Harbor. To remove the U.S. threat, Japanese Fleet Commander Yamamoto was ordered to plan a knock-out blow of U.S. naval forces at Pearl Harbor. With the monsoon season constraining the timing of this attack, the months of December and January were deemed most suitable. If negotiations between Japan and the United States failed to end the U.S. embargo by December 1, Yamamoto was ordered to put his plan in effect.[19]

Yamamoto had attended Harvard University and completed two tours as a naval attaché in the United States, developing a taste for poker and American whiskey. He had also been greatly impressed by U.S. industrial capacity. Before he unleashed his attack on the U.S. fleet, he must have felt a certain trepidation about the long-term result. "I will run wild for six months," he informed his superiors. "After that, I can promise nothing."[20]

Now with the command that MacArthur believed had been his "destiny," the head of the USAFFE was authorized by Washington to spend $10 million to defend the Philippines. President Quezon had been unreceptive to MacArthur the past several years, but upon hearing of the general's resurrection and the new money from Washington, he was eager to see his old friend—as MacArthur had predicted. Visiting his field marshal, he pledged Philippine loyalty to the United States.

Yet the military buildup from a suddenly supportive Washington would be slow, and MacArthur was unaware of how little time he actually had. Although he was promised 50,000 more U.S. troops by February 1942, by early December only 6,000 American regulars had arrived, bringing his command of U.S. and Philippine Scouts to only 22,000 troops. Additionally, he had 80,000 ill-trained Filipino militia, many of whom had never fired a rifle.

By late October, MacArthur had finally been shown the strategy spelled out in Rainbow Five, although it had been revised with a limited defense of the Philippines including Manila Bay. The commander considered it too "negativistic," and urged a defense of the entire archipelago. Predicting no Japanese advance on the Philippines until April 1942, the forceful MacArthur convinced Marshall and the Joint Army-Navy Board to approve his plans to defend all the islands.

The acquiescence of the highest echelon of the U.S. military to MacArthur's overly optimistic plans to repel Japanese landings on the Philippine beaches could be attributed to the strength of the general's personality and his earned reputation. But MacArthur's eleventh-hour planning would prove disastrous, especially for the defense of the Bataan peninsula. The stored munitions and supplies that were to be stockpiled on Bataan under the old Rainbow Five plan were instead dispersed by the general at four depots across the Luzon central plain.[21]

The flurry of hurried initiatives by MacArthur and Washington military staff in fall 1941 might have made a real difference in the defense of the Philippines if the Japanese had delayed their plans by six months. But Tokyo's timetable for war had been set for late 1941. So the last-minute efforts to cobble together an adequate defense for the islands would again be a classic illustration of MacArthur's own two-word summary of failure in warfare—*too late*.

ABOUT TO START HER SENIOR YEAR in fall 1941, Patty Croft paid little attention to the gathering storm. She was aware of a few Japanese store owners and residents around Manila but felt no threat from them. Much later, she had no recollection of any Americans in Manila at that time expressing concern about the local Japanese population.

Almost 5,000 *hojin* (Japanese expatriates) worked in Manila as retailers, gardeners, elevator operators, and other jobs. They were a part of daily life in the tropical city. Doubtless, more than a few were spying for the Japanese government. Some of these *hojin* would later be seen wearing the uniforms of Japanese officers during the occupation.[22]

Patty's junior year in high school had been an adventure of basketball games, accordion performances, and dancing with handsome young officers at the Polo Club and the Army-Navy Club. She continued to share many of these activities with her best friend, Eileen Aaron, but Aaron would graduate from the American School one year ahead of Patty and enroll at Manila's Santo Tomás University in fall 1941.

Dividing her spare time between basketball practice and accordion lessons, Patty began performing with her pro-Nazi accordion teacher, Mr. Beutel. One of her first shows was in front of two hundred American sailors quarantined aboard ship because of a measles outbreak. "I was a nervous sixteen-year-old and shaking so on the stage that I dropped my music," she said. "One of the sailors in the back yelled out, 'She did that on purpose.' I blushed bright red. It was funny."

One of her accordion shows was an ad hoc performance on board the *USS Houston*, the heavy cruiser and flagship of Adm. Thomas Hart's warships assigned to the Philippines and anchored at Cavite Naval Yard. She and several girlfriends had been invited to dinner aboard the vessel by a "cute ensign," Patty recalled. "We got all dolled up, went down to the dock, and rode in the little dinghy to the ship. After we climbed up the little stairs to get onboard, we heard over the loudspeaker, 'Now hear this. Girls on board.'" While being escorted to the dining area, Patty came upon a sailor struggling to play a popular accordion tune. She offered her help and ended up playing the tune as sailors gathered around her.

The evening on the *USS Houston* would be a pleasant memory for the high school girl until the following year when she heard of the ship's sinking by Japanese forces in Sunda Strait in the Dutch East Indies. Most of the crew were killed in the late February 1942 attack, many machine-gunned in the water after abandoning their ship. When Patty heard the news, she wondered how many of the cheerful American sailors she had met earlier were now dead.

Yet that was still in the future for the lighthearted high school senior in fall 1941. On weekends, she was frequently being asked by her German accordion teacher to perform with him at nearby Fort McKinley and other U.S. military bases around Manila. But one day that fall, the Nazi-friendly

Beutel and his wife vanished without notice. "I went for my lesson one day," she said, "and they were gone. They just disappeared. He was a nice man, but looking back, I'm suspicious now. He left just a few months before the Japanese attacked, and he was always wanting us to play at the military camps. I suspect he was spying."

Some of Patty's high school friends from military families began leaving the Philippines in 1941. One of those was her close friend, Nancy Taylor, the daughter of an army major who may have been working with MacArthur's military mission in the Cuartel de España. Military families arrived and left with regularity, Patty remembered, so it was difficult to know if they were being evacuated or merely reassigned.

Patty overheard her mother speaking with friends about American civilians having a difficult time trying to leave. "I heard about several men who went in a group to talk to the high commissioner about getting us civilians out," she recalled. "This was several months before the war started. They said the Filipinos couldn't handle it if Americans started leaving."

In her book *Captured*, Frances Cogan provides well-sourced information about Japanese internment of American civilians in the Philippines and reports several reasons why so many civilians stayed in the islands until it was too late to escape. Corroborating Patty Croft's remembrance, Cogan explains that "the Far East Division of the State Department was opposed to the early warning and removal of American civilians" as their continued presence was believed to have had a calming effect on the Filipino population as the Japanese threat grew.[23]

Government silence regarding the potential peril of the civilians apparently extended to the highest levels of the U.S. State Department. By fall 1941, Philippine High Commissioner Francis P. Sayre had received no notice from Washington encouraging U.S. civilians to evacuate the Philippines or even warning of their jeopardy. "I had decided in my own mind the issuing of such a notice," Sayre later wrote in a letter to Congress after the war, "but my advice from Washington was not to do so."[24]

Outside this reticence by U.S. officials, civilians had other reasons for not leaving, Cogan further explains in her book. Underestimating the Japanese threat factored in this decision for many, understandable in light of the U.S. military's outward confidence in repelling an attack. Also, many frightened civilians chose to stay rather than desert a family member reluctant to leave. Such was the situation with Patty Croft's Junior Orchestra conductor, Grace Nash. Her husband had an important job with an engineering company and refused to leave his work.

"I was in the minority; almost an outcast in the conversations," Nash would later say about her fears of getting trapped in a war zone. "I had a gut feeling, without any facts, figures, or geographical knowledge to back it up. I just felt that war was coming; that the islands were defenseless." The former farm girl from Ohio and mother of two young boys had good intuition. She would be proved right in every respect as 1941 drew to a dramatic close in the Pearl of the Orient.[25]

Saturday morning, December 6, Patty Croft and her American School girls and boys basketball teams boarded a train in Manila for the first leg of their trip to Baguio, where the teams would square off against archrival Brent School that afternoon. The train took the teams and supporters to Damortis Station just off the Gulf of Lingayen. From there, they took buses along the steep switch-back road as it zigged and zagged up the hills to the cool altitude of Baguio.

The games played out with the usual intensity, and that night a dance was held at Baguio's Tuesday Club for the two schools. A few enlisted men from nearby Clark Field dropped by to ogle the girls in their colorful dresses. The American School teams spent the night in Baguio, and the next morning, December 7, learned that an air-raid drill was planned for the town and nearby Camp John Hay. Fear of a Japanese attack had been building in early December, but most took those warnings in stride. The American School students received permission from principal Lois Croft (no relation to Patty Croft) to skip the drills and catch a movie at a local theater.[26]

After the movie, everyone boarded the busses for the zig-zag ride downhill and back to Damortis Station to catch the train. Before boarding the train, Patty looked westward over the gently rolling, blue expanse of the Lingayen Gulf. "I just couldn't believe it," she said of the normally busy waters. "There wasn't a single ship in sight."

Back home that evening in Pasay, the tired teenager readied for school the next morning. She crawled through the mosquito netting around her bed and was asleep shortly after 9 p.m. With the Philippines just west of the international date line marking the beginning of each new day, the clocks in Manila were many hours ahead of most the world. As sleep overtook Patty that tranquil evening just off Manila Bay, Sunday, December 7, had barely begun in Honolulu, Hawaii.

WHILE HONOLULU SLUMBERED PEACEFULLY, a number of military officials in Washington, D.C., were growing frantic the morning of December 7. A fourteen-part decrypted message from Tokyo to its Washington embassy had been received by U.S. military intelligence staff late the evening before. The Japanese Purple code for top-secret communication had been broken several years earlier, and U.S. officials referred to these intercepted messages as Magic, an appropriate name for this astounding intelligence coup. With the United States and Japan in tense negotiations over the U.S. embargo, advisories from Tokyo to its negotiators in Washington were being closely monitored by U.S. intelligence officers.[27]

Significantly, the Magic interceptions forwarded to key army and navy staff on December 6 had contained instructions for Japanese embassy staff to dispose of their Purple code machines used to decipher messages from Tokyo. The fourteenth and final part of the decrypted message was not received by Col. Carlisle C. Dusenbury, an officer assigned to the Far Eastern unit of military intelligence, until near midnight. The message instructed Japanese negotiators to discontinue talks with their U.S. counterparts and make this break official at precisely 1 p.m. in Washington on December 7. Owing to the lateness of the hour when the fourteenth part was received, Dusenbury did not distribute all of the fourteen parts of this message until Sunday morning, December 7.

When the unsuspecting Dusenbury handed the decrypted message to Col. Thomas T. Handy in the Operations Department at 9 a.m., Handy was aghast. The instructions to the Japanese embassy to destroy their Purple coding machines and end negotiations was shattering news. "This means war," the stunned Handy said.[28]

Chief of Staff George Marshall was promptly informed. He immediately ordered an encrypted warning be sent by radio to the military at Pearl Harbor in Hawaii, in Manila, and in the Panama Canal Zone. Fatefully, Marshall chose not to use the telephone lines because of the earlier concerns about the Japanese monitoring of telephone communications between Washington and military installations in the Pacific.

With War Department staff failing to reach Pearl Harbor by radio around 11:30 a.m. Washington time, 6:30 a.m. in Honolulu, a staff officer decided to send the message by commercial cable. The message was received by Western Union in San Francisco and from there forwarded by Radio Corporation of America (RCA) commercial radio to Honolulu, where it was received at 7:33 a.m. As the message arrived, dawn was breaking over

Pearl Harbor and Japanese warplanes were less than 100 miles away.

But any hope of a last-minute warning to U.S. forces died with the failure of the teletype hookup between the RCA office and Fort Shafter, the center for senior U.S. Army headquarters in Hawaii. A boy on a bicycle was sent to Ft. Shafter to deliver the critical dispatch.[29]

At 7:53 a.m. and well before the warning reached headquarters at Shafter, the commander of the Japanese strike force looked down from the lead bomber and saw the American Pacific Fleet docked serenely and unprotected alongside Ford Island at Pearl Harbor. He broke radio silence with the code words *"Tora! Tora! Tora!"* signaling complete surprise had been achieved. Two hours later, eight U.S. battleships had either been sunk or heavily damaged.[30]

While en route to Fort Shafter, the bicycle messenger was forced to take shelter from the Japanese air attack. But steadfast to his mission, he presented the warning to headquarters at 11:45 a.m., almost four hours after the first bombs and torpedoes struck U.S. warships at Pearl Harbor. MacArthur's admonition once again comes to mind—*too late.*[31]

When the first bombs fell at Pearl Harbor, Manila was in deep slumber several hours before daylight on Monday, December 8. At around 3:30 a.m., the phone rang in MacArthur's bedroom at the Manila Hotel. His chief of staff, Lieutenant Colonel Sutherland, broke the news of the attack. "Pearl Harbor!" MacArthur cried in astonishment. "It should be our strongest point!" Greatly underestimating the ability of the Japanese to accomplish such a feat so far from Japanese waters, MacArthur and senior U.S. military officials had not considered Pearl Harbor a likely target in the event of hostilities.[32]

Just a few miles southwest of the Manila Hotel in an apartment building in Pasay, a ringing telephone woke Patty Croft around 5:30 a.m. The seventeen-year-old heard her mother's voice talking excitedly with the caller, a friend who worked at the *Manila Daily Bulletin* newspaper. A few minutes later, Patty's bedroom light came on. Through the mosquito netting around her bed, Patty saw her mother standing over her. Selma Croft was sobbing.

# CHAPTER 3
❧ ❧ ❧

# Black Christmas

PATTY CROFT AND HER younger brother, Bill, did not go back to sleep after their distraught mother woke them in the early morning hours of that Monday, December 8, 1941. They knew the Japanese attack on Pearl Harbor likely meant war was coming to the Philippines—frightening for sure, but difficult to foresee its effect on their lives.

Pulling herself together, Selma told her two children to get ready for school. They would go on as normally as possible as long as they could. Walking to school with Bill, Patty wondered about the coming months. With the school year in Manila ending in March, she was only three months from her high school graduation. She planned to be in California by late summer and ready to start college in Pomona. Suddenly, she had serious doubts whether this would happen. "It was all like a bad dream was starting," she recalled.

About an hour after classes began at 7:30 that morning at the American School, the first bombs fell on Camp John Hay at Baguio. Indicative of the surprise and confusion from this attack, the air-raid siren in Baguio didn't sound until an hour after a formation of seventeen Japanese bombers attacked the army base. Just twenty hours earlier Patty and many of her schoolmates had been boarding the buses in Baguio for the return trip to Manila after their basketball games with Brent School.[1]

Just before the American School classes ended near midday, word reached the principal's office of the air raid on Camp John Hay and the beginning of a massive attack on the air force base at Clark Field, forty miles north of Manila. Clark was being hit by a fleet of Japanese warplanes—fifty-four Mitsubishi bombers and a swarm of Zero fighters. The students were told to go straight home. As the departing students walked through their neighborhoods, a great pillar of black, oily smoke climbed on the far northern horizon. By 1:30 p.m. the hangars at Clark Field and dozens of planes alongside the runways were demolished.[2]

Arriving home, Patty and Bill found their mother listening to the radio and crying. Selma Croft's estranged husband was in Hawaii and her oldest son was in his first year of college in California. She alone would be looking after her teenage daughter and son as their world in Manila exploded. "We certainly stayed in the house that night," Patty said. "We just didn't know what to expect."

There would be no classes at the American School the next day—nor for a number of years to come.

AT MACARTHUR'S HEADQUARTERS in the Walled City, all was chaos as the general arrived before 5 a.m. that Monday. His chief of staff, Lt. Col. Sutherland, was already there. Alert to the growing tensions of early December, Sutherland had been sleeping on a cot in the office when he received news of the attack at Pearl Harbor. He immediately called MacArthur. Admiral Thomas Hart, Asiatic Fleet commander, was also there as MacArthur arrived. Maj. Gen. Lewis H. Brereton, U.S. Army Air Force commander in the Philippines, was on his way.

Brereton had been in the Philippines only since early November but by then had more than two hundred warplanes at his command, including seventy-four bombers. Many of these planes had just arrived as part of Washington's eleventh-hour reinforcement of the Philippines. More had been scheduled to arrive in coming days and weeks. Owing to hesitation, miscalculation, and plain bad luck, many of Brereton's planes would be destroyed on the ground by Japanese bombers and fighters within nine hours of MacArthur's learning of the attack at Pearl Harbor. The loss of these planes and the destruction of Clark Field virtually crippled the general's plans to defend the Philippines.[3]

Shortly after his arrival at MacArthur's office, Brereton urged Sutherland to get authorization for an air raid on Formosa where Japanese troops would be staging air attacks and landings on Luzon. This action could strike a preemptive blow and, importantly, get U.S. warplanes off the ground where they were most vulnerable. Accounts differ on what transpired that chaotic morning in MacArthur's office, but Brereton failed to get timely authorization from MacArthur to strike with his considerable force of B-17 bombers and P-40 fighters.

It is apparent that Douglas MacArthur was far from his best that frenzied morning of December 8. Perhaps he hesitated under the influence of Manuel Quezon, who held last-minute hopes of Philippine neutrality in the coming cataclysm. Perhaps the 62-year-old commander suffered from input overload with rapid-fire questions and requests from Washington, his immediate staff, and his air and naval commanders. Whatever the cause, MacArthur seemed strangely and uncharacteristically indecisive in the midst of this crisis. His hesitation cost him much of his air force, and with that loss any realistic chance to repel the impending Japanese invasion.

While MacArthur pondered his moves that morning, Brereton received a phone call from Washington. Lt. Gen. Henry "Hap" Arnold, chief of the U.S. Army Air Forces, ordered him to disperse his seventeen B-17 Flying Fortresses and thirty-six P-40 fighters at Clark Field to avoid their getting caught on the ground. The planes went up, circling not far from their base. Around 11 a.m. Brereton ordered his B-17s back to Clark to arm and refuel for a belatedly approved bombing mission later in the day.

As the U.S. warplanes were being readied at Clark, a V of Japanese Mitsubishi bombers appeared high in the western sky around 12:30 p.m. The Japanese airmen could hardly believe their eyes when they peered down on the rows of B-17s and P-40s at Clark Field compliantly awaiting their impending destruction. The Japanese air armada from Formosa had been fogged in earlier that morning, so the attackers had assumed the worst as they left their base later in the day. After the war, a senior Japanese officer who had been stationed on Formosa told the enemy's side of the story: "We were very worried because we were sure after learning of Pearl Harbor you would disperse your planes or make an attack on our base at Formosa. We put on our gas masks and prepared for an attack by American aircraft." It was an attack that never came.[4]

Incredibly, it would be a repeat of Pearl Harbor for the confused, unprepared U.S. military on Luzon that day. As the last Japanese planes departed the burning planes and hangars at Clark Field around 1:30 p.m., they carried away MacArthur's hopes to control the skies above the U.S. military bases on Luzon. A workable defense of the Philippines against a full-scale invasion by Japan had always been problematic; the destruction of the planes and hangars at Clark Field made it nearly impossible.

With the Japanese onslaught, the immediate future of the American civilians in the Philippines became dependent on U.S. military success—or failure as it turned out. This would become more and more obvious to Selma Croft and her two children as they gathered around the radio the evening of December 8 and for several weeks afterward. Before going to bed that night, Patty took her wire-haired terrier, Suzy, out for their usual short walk. Chiquita had died the year before, so little Suzy was now her only pet. Patty kept their walk close to the apartment building that evening. Following the announced blackout for Manila, the neighborhood was pitch black. Fear of air attacks in coming weeks would shorten most of her trips outside the apartment.

Patty could not recall her mother speaking on the telephone with her estranged husband in Honolulu, but she remembered learning that he had escaped injury in the Japanese attack on Hickam Field where he worked. Telephone service in Manila would remain largely in service over the coming weeks, Patty remembered, providing her family with a vital lifeline to the outside world.

The next day brought only more terror to Patty, her mother, her brother, and their *amah* Tekay. The loyal nursemaid and housekeeper would remain with the Crofts through several frightening weeks before taking refuge in her *nipa* shack in Batangas on the southern end of Luzon. As dawn broke over Manila, Patty and her family were jolted awake by loud reverberations that shook their small apartment building. Japanese bombers were striking Fort McKinley and nearby Nichols Field, just a few miles east of Pasay. Patty remembered how her father had often flown in and out of Nichols Field in her childhood, an innocent time when she could never have imagined the air base under attack by an enemy air force.

Just after lunch the next day, December 10, the teenager heard distant explosions to the southwest of Pasay. Staring out some seven miles across Manila Bay from her apartment building, she could see the mighty U.S. Navy Yard at Cavite crumbling under Japanese bombs. She thought of the dinner she and her friends had enjoyed aboard the *USS Houston* just months earlier when it was docked at Cavite.

By the time of the attack on the navy base, the *USS Houston* and most of Admiral Hart's Asiatic Fleet had fled southward to avoid the fate of Brereton's idle warplanes at Clark Field. With no air protection from

Clark or Nichols Field, the naval facilities at Cavite were systematically destroyed by eighty Japanese bombers and fifty-two Zeros. The greatest damage came from the uncontrolled blaze that incinerated the support facilities and set fire to the cache of two hundred torpedoes, crippling the offensive capabilities of the submarines in Admiral Hart's fleet.[5]

Patty remembered great billows of smoke in the distance at Cavite. What she could not see were the hundreds of killed and wounded sailors from this attack. As an experienced nurse, her mother would soon begin treating military casualties from attacks and fighting from all parts of Luzon. "The casualties were mounting from Clark Field, Cavite and other military bases, and someone called my mother to help," Patty said. "Just a few days after the attacks began, all the nurses in the area were asked to report to Sternberg Hospital. It's the only place I remember my mother working during that time."

Patty vividly recalled the first day Selma came home after a long shift at Sternberg General Hospital, just a few miles north of Pasay. "She walked in with a gas mask and a helmet. That really impressed me." Selma and other civilian and military nurses worked frantically caring for the thousands of casualties streaming into hospitals throughout the Manila area. These caregivers' lives were also endangered by the Japanese air attacks. Patty's mother had the additional stress of worrying about the safety of her two children at home. She relied on Tekay to look after Patty and Bill, at least until their *amah's* departure around Christmas.

Night after night, Selma came home exhausted from her efforts and haunted by the horribly disfigured young sailors, soldiers and airmen under her care. "My mother told me that one of the guys she treated had his buttocks completely blown off," Patty recalled. "That always stayed with me. It was awful."

Ever the precocious teenager, Patty could not resist venturing out occasionally for a better view of some of the air action in the vicinity of her apartment building. "I remember going outside our apartment and watching two planes—an American and a Japanese—dogfighting, going back and forth. I could have been killed by a stray bullet. When you're a teenager, you do crazy things. I just wanted to see what all was going on."

Most of the time she stayed indoors with Bill and Tekay listening to the radio and trading phone calls with friends. With lights turned off in the evenings, sitting in the dark and listening to the radio became the norm. During this time she didn't recall anyone coming over to visit at her apartment. Most locals were too afraid of getting caught in a bombing attack. Pasay, however, would suffer only minimal damage from the attacks on nearby Fort McKinley and Nichols Field. Patty remembered no damage to any of the houses in the vicinity of her apartment.

As Patty watched the destruction of the Cavite Navy Yard the early afternoon of December 10, Admiral Hart trembled with rage as he, too, watched the debacle from the rooftop of the two-story Marsman Building near the Manila Hotel. Adding to Hart's despair that afternoon, a sailor brought news that the British battleship *Prince of Wales* and battlecruiser *Repulse* had been sunk by Japanese torpedo-bombers off Malaya. The loss of these two Allied vessels, the only two capital ships west of Hawaii, further strengthened Japanese control in the western Pacific. Hart resolved to move his headquarters southward to the Dutch East Indies and deploy his fleet outside dangerous Philippine waters.

Upset upon hearing the admiral's plans to leave the Philippines, MacArthur urged Hart to stay put and keep the sea-lanes open for the convoys of troops and supplies that would be needed for defense of the islands. But word came from Washington that Chief of Naval Operations Harold R. Stark agreed with Hart's plans. Stark believed attempts to save the Philippines were hopeless. Having lost much of his air power in the first days of the Japanese attack, MacArthur was now about to lose his naval support. He denounced this retreat, accusing Stark and navy brass of losing their nerve after Pearl Harbor and arguing that a seaborne relief effort to the Philippines could reverse the tide of defeat. MacArthur's calls for aid received no assurances from Washington.

Still, MacArthur clung to the illusion that the Japanese typhoon might be reversed. Counting on U.S. aircraft carriers to ferry warplanes to the Philippines, he ordered feverish construction of airfields on the central and southern islands. U.S. air commander Hap Arnold appeared to share the general's optimism, stating that MacArthur could regain air superiority if eighty B-17s and two hundred P-40s could be delivered. It was a big *if*.[6]

In the dark days of mid-December in the States, MacArthur emerged as a symbol of America's defiance of Japanese aggression. The general's jaunty demeanor, portrayed in newspaper and magazine articles, provided the hero the U.S. public so desperately needed after Pearl Harbor. At the same time this created a problem for President Roosevelt. After Germany declared war on the United States following the Japanese attacks, Roosevelt was committed to the earlier-planned "Hitler first" strategy and had no inclination to send scarce military resources to the staggering Philippine defense. The president maintained public support for MacArthur and his beleaguered defenders while at the same time refusing privately to push for a resource-draining rescue effort.

On December 11 several minor Japanese landings were made around Luzon. MacArthur correctly assessed these as feints and refused to commit his forces. "The basic principle in handling my troops is to hold them intact until the enemy commits himself in force," he explained in media reports. While this was sound strategy, the general would later be heavily criticized for getting distracted and delaying the more important consolidation of U.S. and Filipino troops on the Bataan peninsula. Instead of a quixotic attempt to drive the enemy from Philippine soil, critics would argue, MacArthur should have faced reality and began stockpiling supplies for an inevitable defensive stand on Bataan. But playing defense never sat well with the aggressive general.[7]

For the hundreds of thousands of Manila residents, the two weeks following the first devastating attacks on Clark Field and Cavite became an almost nonstop nightmare of Japanese bombings of local military installations, air raid sirens, conflicting news, and gnawing fear. Despite the devastation around them, the news on the airways and from local papers remained positive—and misleading—throughout the weeks following the first attacks.

High Commissioner Francis Sayre gave a radio speech from Manila on December 12 proclaiming "here on the firing line we have come to grips with reality." Yet the reality Sayre portrayed was of confidence in MacArthur's ability to fend off the invasion and anticipation of aid from American shores. "We on the front lines are fighting to the death," Sayre pronounced, "for we have abiding confidence in our cause and in our leader. We know that you back home will send us help and that you will not permit divided councils...or anything else to delay your getting effective help to us before it is too late....Come on America!"[8]

MacArthur released an upbeat communiqué of the first week's military operations on December 14 asserting that "the situation both on the ground and in the air [is] well in hand..." The report credited a Philippine army division with "smashing a Japanese landing at Lingayen" and U.S. bombers with sinking four Japanese troopships. Also reported was the sinking of the Japanese battleship *Haruna* in the waters north of Luzon, yet the Kongo-class warship was actually unscathed some 1,500 miles away in the Gulf of Siam. The release concluded with a statement that Japan had paid a high price in troop, plane and shipping losses in the first week. The beginning of the second week of the war, at least by MacArthur's account, saw Japanese landings on Luzon held in tight check. Actually, the Japanese landings in force were still a week away.[9]

What officials were saying about a successful defense of the Philippines and what the American civilians in Manila were seeing with their own eyes created what would later be called a "credibility gap" in a 1960s U.S. conflict in Southeast Asia. As one American civilian in Manila wrote: "We watched the systematic bombing of Cavite....The Cavite Naval installation was completely destroyed in several hours....Trucks drove down Dewey Boulevard loaded with dead bodies while we heard on the radio from the States, 'Cavite Naval Base was hit but there was little damage and no loss of life.'"[10]

No matter how upbeat the radio broadcasts and newspaper accounts in Manila, a different story was told by the daily smoke pillars at U.S. military facilities across Luzon. The constant air raid sirens and daily poundings from the sky testified to Japanese air superiority.

For two weeks after the first bombs fell on Luzon, MacArthur maintained a delusion of defeating the coming invasion on the beaches. On December 22, reality struck. More than 40,000 troops of General Masaharu Homma's 14th Army, seasoned veterans of the Chinese war, began an amphibious attack. The placid waters of Lingayen Gulf and its broad beaches made for an ideal landing zone. These were the same calm waters and scenic beaches that Patty Croft had viewed that peaceful Sunday afternoon just two weeks earlier as she and her teammates boarded the buses after their weekend in Baguio.

As the Japanese landed, most of the largely untrained, undisciplined Filipino troops fled inland and melted into the hills. Within hours of wading ashore, Japanese infantry were streaming southward toward Manila. By the next day, however, U.S. troops, Philippine Scouts, and some Filipino units began to slow the Japanese advance. But MacArthur soon received word of another major Japanese landing sixty miles southeast of Manila. The Japanese believed MacArthur would concentrate his troops around Manila to defend the city, so they planned to crush his forces between their northern and southern landings.

MacArthur could play into Japanese hands with a defense of Manila, or he could concentrate his forces on the more easily defended Bataan peninsula, just as the venerable War Plan Orange had envisioned decades earlier. The Orange defensive plan had always been distasteful to the offensive-minded general, but now he had little choice. MacArthur radioed his commanders with the directive: "WPO is in effect." Choosing not to defend Manila, on Christmas Eve MacArthur declared the Philippine capital an open city. "In order to spare Manila from any possible air or ground attacks," he announced, "consideration is being given by military authorities to declaring Manila an open city, as was done in the case of Paris, Brussels and Rome during this war."[11]

DURING THE WEEKS BEFORE CHRISTMAS, Patty and her family gave little thought to the upcoming holiday. Trying to get enough sleep dominated their daily life. Her mother faced near exhaustion with long days at the hospital and spotty rest at night. "It was hard to sleep with the sirens going off and the bombings going on," Patty said. "I don't know how my mother kept going. It was loud, and we had no shelter to go to."

Air raid shelters were practically nonexistent in Manila during these attacks, and Patty and her family could only stay inside and hope for the best. They were fortunate; the father of one of Patty's schoolmates was not. "Her name was Theodora Cowie. We called her 'Teedie.' She and her family had only been in Manila a short while before the war started. Her father was killed down by the piers in Manila harbor where he worked." As far as Patty could recall, he was the only American she personally knew who died in the Manila attacks. She believed there were others killed that she was acquainted with, but she never heard for certain.

As Christmas neared, Selma Croft began planning with a few friends and acquaintances to purchase a yacht and flee Manila by sea. No longer comforted by official pronouncements of their safety, a good number of civilians like Selma began weighing the pros and cons of fleeing westward across Manila Bay and southward to friendlier islands. "We had some friends, the Darrases," Patty said, "who were going in with us to buy one of these yachts tied up at the Yacht Club. That was a little before Christmas. There was going to be ten of us in all, including a newly married couple and three men."

On Christmas Eve, Selma and the Darras couple decided against fleeing in the yacht. Hearing the radio announcement of Manila's open-city status may have relieved some of their concern of being trapped in the city with U.S. and Japanese troops battling in the streets. "We got to thinking about leaving on that yacht and decided maybe it wasn't a smart idea to go," Patty remembered. "The other married couple went ahead, but we later learned they were picked up on Borneo and made prisoners. The group of men took another yacht."

Tragically, the three men fared the worst, she recalled. "We learned that they too were caught somewhere off the coast of Leyte. But they were all beheaded by the Japanese. So we were thankful that we didn't go."

For Patty and her family that year, Christmas Day passed without the usual exchange of gifts or special dinner. For Selma, it was another long day treating shattered and burned bodies at Sternberg General Hospital. With Tekay's departure for Batangas just before Christmas, Patty and Bill were now alone during the day. Before her departure, the housekeeper had ensured the Croft household was well stocked with food. Christmas 1941 would be one of the few holidays Patty could remember from her childhood without her beloved *amah* sharing the festivities.

Another aspect of that Christmas stands out for Patty: the stench in the air and the thick, black smoke covering the city. To keep stores of oil and refinery equipment out of Japanese hands, departing U.S. troops set fire to depots at several locations in the Pandacan district of central Manila. The Filipinos in Manila would later remember this holiday as the "Black Christmas" of 1941. One American civilian later wrote of this dismal holiday season: "Thunderous explosions and sky-high fountains of flame added to the taut sense of approaching disaster. Heavy black clouds formed a ceiling over the city which spotted the drying laundry and left a black, greasy film over everything." Patty remembered actual droplets of oil falling from the sky like rain.[12]

On Christmas morning some 150 members of the ad hoc American Coordinating Committee met in the high commissioner's office to discuss how U.S. civilians could best prepare for the impending Japanese occupation of Manila. The committee had been organized by American *Manileños* to deal with a Japanese invasion and occupation. A big issue was whether civilians should remain in their individual homes or assemble as a group. Most at the meeting favored staying in their homes and awaiting instructions from Japanese officials as the occupation began. Later that day, committee members dispersed throughout the city to meet with smaller groups of civilians and recommend their remaining in their homes.

Not all agreed to passively await the Japanese, and those at a large meeting at the Admiral Apartments considered chartering a large ship for

Americans who wanted to evacuate Manila by sea. The high commissioner's office discouraged the idea saying it would be impossible to arrange this on such short notice. American civilians later interned by the Japanese would point out that a large ship, the *Mactan*, was converted into a hospital ship and left Manila as late as December 31 with more than 200 wounded American and Filipino soldiers. Many of these interned Americans would characterize the official dismissal of their plan as another example of the U.S. government's disregard for the civilians' plight.

The use of the large University of Santo Tomás in central Manila as a potential internment site was discussed at subsequent meetings that week between key members of the American Coordinating Committee and Claude A. Buss, executive assistant to the high commissioner. Buss recommended Santo Tomás to the committee based on the advice of a Manila businessman in charge of army real estate transactions. The official had earlier told Buss that in the event of civilian internments by the Japanese, Santo Tomás offered a number of advantages for these purposes. The focus of these meetings was obviously shifting from escaping the Japanese to submitting to capture.[13]

The day after Christmas, Manila residents enjoyed a brief letup in bombing attacks. Instead, Japanese planes dropped leaflets addressed to Philippine soldiers. The message read: "Dear friends! Our aim is to destroy American force. We have no quarrel with you. Are we not all of the Far East? Drop your guns, return home to your loved ones." The Japanese appeals made little headway. Filipinos in the streets were openly derisive of this appeal.[14]

Despite Manila's designation as an open city, Japanese bombs began falling again on selected sites on December 28. The ancient Walled City was savagely attacked for more than three hours by Japanese bombers. The Santo Domingo Church, dating back to the 1500s, was almost completely destroyed. Also struck was the Intendencia Building, which housed the Philippine Treasury. Scores of deaths were reported and nearly 200 were wounded. Prior to this destruction, most of the Japanese attacks had been on purely military ground targets and ships in the harbor.[15]

Late on Christmas Eve, MacArthur, his family, and a hundred other military officers and government officials boarded the small inter-island steamer *Don Esteban* at a pier in Manila harbor. They crossed the waters of the bay to the heavily fortified island of Corregidor. President Quezon was aboard along with a few officials of the government of the commonwealth. It was a thirty-mile boat ride to the island. Looking back at the city, MacArthur's entourage viewed a wall of flames and a dense pall of smoke from the burning oil depots in Pandacan.

About four miles long by two miles wide, Corregidor had long competed with Singapore as the "Gibraltar of the East." The volcanic island, sometimes called The Rock, was terraced by three green layers named Topside, Middleside and Bottomside. Twenty miles of barbed wire ringed the island's shoreline, and the fortress bristled with coastal guns. Concrete trenches snaked across the landscape, and cable barriers and mines guarded the numerous little harbors along the shoreline. Key to the island's defense, an elaborate system of underground tunnels had been constructed connecting numerous personnel bunkers and a 1,000-bed hospital.

Although still a formidable defense, twentieth-century weaponry had made the island fortress more vulnerable. The 10,000 U.S. and Philippine troops and 2,000 civilians sheltering on Corregidor would be pounded with daily artillery barrages and more than three hundred bombing missions over the coming months.[16]

Hearing of Corregidor's new refugees, Patty and other American civilians felt a sense of betrayal. Many of these civilians now awaiting the arrival of Japanese troops had been led to believe that they too would be allowed refuge on the island. "The Americans were always talking about how the women and children would be taken to Corregidor if the Japanese attacked," Patty remembered, "but we never got over there. We all got pretty upset when we heard MacArthur left for Corregidor with his family—*and his Chinese amah!*"

As a child, Patty had enjoyed visits to Corregidor and strolls inside the elaborate tunnel complex. She remembered running up and down the concrete floors of the 830-foot Malinta Tunnel as a little girl. The tunnel was the main corridor connecting the various branches that honeycombed the underground labyrinth. A couple who lived on the island were friends of her mother, and Patty and her brothers would cross the bay waters to spend weekends with them. "They were of Swedish descent," she said, "and my mother would speak with them in Swedish. They became good friends. It was exciting to get to visit the island. The military was around, but they would let us tour the main tunnel."

By late December, Filipinos, American civilians and other foreign nationals in Manila were resigned to the imminent Japanese occupation. Japanese atrocities in China were still fresh memories for most *Manileños.*

Women tried to put away fears of sexual assault, but for many this concern was never far from mind. "It was tough thinking about it," Patty said. "We teenage girls were worried about getting raped. We had read about what happened in Nanking. I was not optimistic. I just felt that the Japanese were going to take over and that was it. Officials just weren't prepared for this attack on the Philippines."

As Manila readied for occupation, MacArthur's army completed its retreat onto Bataan peninsula. In military terminology this was a "retrograde maneuver," and it was complicated. Only a general like MacArthur—hunkered down on Corregidor but back to the decisive, even brilliant commander of old—could have pulled off this difficult consolidation of his forces on Bataan. Fighting a rearguard action against Homma's Lingayen landing force, the U.S. North Luzon Force of three divisions and a cavalry regiment coordinated their retreat with that of the U.S. South Luzon Force of one division and a regiment. These mostly Filipino troops of the northern and southern forces would converge on the strategic twin-spanned Calumpit Bridge, twenty miles north of Manila. The bridge would be the gateway westward to the Bataan peninsula and was scheduled to be demolished with explosives at dawn on New Year's Day just after the last units crossed.

The last two days of December saw a ten-mile traffic jam of U.S. and Philippine troops, trucks, tanks and artillery from the north and the south as they converged on the bridge. Expecting MacArthur's northern force to swing south for a decisive battle for Manila, the confused Japanese commanders let MacArthur's army escape across the bridge and onto the peninsula. At 6:15 a.m. on January 1, North Luzon Force commander Maj. Gen. Jonathan Wainwright ordered the bridge blown. An explosion of concrete, steel and smoke greeted the approaching Japanese troops, who saw all too late where the U.S. forces were headed.

MacArthur would now have 80,000 American and Filipino soldiers to defend Bataan and an additional 1,500 troops of the U.S. 4th Marine Regiment on Corregidor, just a few miles south of the peninsula. The withdrawal onto Bataan capped a brilliant series of maneuvers, but the lack of stored food and munitions would greatly diminish the fighting capabilities of the defenders. These troops would fight bravely and endure stoically for months awaiting a seaborne rescue from America that never came.[17]

On December 30, MacArthur had taken time away from directing the withdrawal onto Bataan to attend the second inauguration of Philippine

President Manuel Quezon at the mouth of Malinta Tunnel. Elected to a second six-year term in November, Quezon knew what was in store for the people of the Philippines as Japan tightened its grip. Speaking at the brief ceremony, MacArthur's longtime friend reassured the Americans of Filipino loyalty: "No matter what suffering and sacrifice this war may impose upon us, we shall stand by America with undaunted spirit..." Facing subjugation from imperial Japan, American civilians on Luzon could certainly use this reassurance from their Filipino neighbors.[18]

New Year's Eve saw little of the gaiety of past year-end celebrations in Manila. In a radio address Claude Buss of the high commissioner's office advised American civilians to dispose of all stores of liquor to deny them to approaching Japanese troops. Visions of drunken Japanese soldiers terrified many Americans. In one of Patty's few forays from her apartment at this time, she and her mother were driven by a friend down Dewey Boulevard along Manila Bay. "I saw them bringing out all those liquor supplies from the Army-Navy Club and the Elks Club," she said. "There were these big rocks by the bay. I saw men breaking all these bottles of liquor on those rocks."

She also saw Filipinos carrying off furniture, much of which had been stored by Americans in warehouses. Many of the locals were also raiding the *bodegas* for stores of food. In some cases, local authorities opened the warehouses to the public to carry off anything they wanted. Denying their goods to the approaching Japanese, some Chinese store owners invited people on the streets to help themselves to their merchandise. "You could see the Filipinos walking down the streets with all this stuff," Patty said. "I'll never forget that."[19]

The unusual scenes of smashed cases of liquor and open looting on the streets of Manila presaged even more remarkable scenes in the city. The Japanese troops were coming soon, but no one knew exactly when. Public information grew scarce as the local radio stations went off the air late on New Year's Eve. Army authorities had ordered the destruction of radio station transmitters to keep them from the Japanese. Copies of local newspapers became difficult to obtain after delivery services broke down.

Two days before the radio stations quit broadcasting, General MacArthur came on the airways to address the frightened American civilians. His message was grim but provided hope. "Do not follow the army to Bataan or Corregidor," he advised. "Get together in groups rather than be taken as individual families. Pour all intoxicating beverages down the sink. May

God be with you—I shall return."[20]

The evening of January 1, four staff members stood outside the front of the stately high commissioner's residence on Dewey Boulevard looking upward at the large U.S. flag. They knew they must act to keep it from the hands of Japanese occupiers. George Gray, who was an assistant to the commission's legal advisor, and three office secretaries lowered the flag and carefully spread it on the ground in the garden. They placed all of the office's smaller U.S. flags on top of it. Each of the four stood at a corner of the flag and solemnly recited the Pledge of Allegiance.

They next lit each of the corners and watched the flames consume the flags. Placing the ashes of the incinerated flags in a tin can, they enclosed a note: "We the undersigned, being American citizens do on this second [sic] day of January, 1942, solemnly and with reverence take it into our hands to burn the flag of the United States of America to prevent it from falling into the hands of the Japanese army, and to bury the ashes together with this record on the grounds of the High Commissioner's office."[21]

FRIDAY, JANUARY 2, DAWNED unusually dark and chilly for Manila. The thick pallor of smoke from the burning oil depots added to the gloom. The usually busy streets were mostly empty. The entire city seemed to be holding its breath. At noon a number of trucks began distributing free copies of the *Manila Daily Bulletin* containing a news release from the high commissioner's office: "Contact with the occupation forces has been established. While nothing can be guaranteed, it now appears that the occupation will be relatively small and that they will not enter the city until this afternoon or early this evening."[22]

That afternoon, Patty ventured outside her apartment and over to Taft Avenue, her curiosity outweighing her fears. She had heard from neighbors that the Japanese would be entering Manila and wanted to see for herself. "I just remember the tremendous tension in the air. You were afraid to go outside. It was scary. Fortunately, we had some American friends up above us in the apartment, so we could talk with them. The couple below were from Vienna, Austria, so they didn't need to worry about the Japanese. We just didn't know what to expect. It was a horrible feeling."

She saw the first of the Japanese occupation troops riding up Taft Avenue on bicycles. They were entering Manila from the south where they had been fighting with the South Luzon Force, which had retreated northward to join the North Luzon Force on Bataan. Cheering Japanese civilians lined the *sawali* (bamboo matting) fences along the avenue waving their "rising sun" flags and shouting "Banzai."

Patty noted that she was probably taller than most of the sloppy-looking, khaki-clad troops. Dirty and bedraggled from days of fighting, they pedaled down Taft with their long rifles strapped to their backs. "I just thought, *We're in for it now*. I didn't know if we would be killed or what. We just didn't know."

The next morning, few *Manileños* ventured from their homes, but those who did saw a ubiquitous Japanese flag, a red sun on white background. Where the Stars and Stripes had flown the day before—at the high commissioner's office, the Army-Navy Club, the Elks Club, the Manila Hotel, and dozens of other sites—it had been replaced by the flag of imperial Japan, now hanging in the smoke-filled air. A pair of Japanese sentries were posted at the city's main intersections and at the front of clubs, hotels and apartment buildings. Stores and businesses were closed.

On Sunday, a special, four-page edition of the Filipino-owned *Tribune* began circulating through the city with an announcement by the Japanese Imperial High Command. The message declared that U.S. sovereignty over the Philippines had "completely disappeared" and that the city was under martial law administered by the Japanese military. The Filipinos were now free from the "oppressive domination" of the United States, the announcement continued, and the Japanese goal was to establish the "Philippines for the Filipinos" as part of the Japanese orchestrated Co-Prosperity Sphere in Greater East Asia. Ominously, city residents were warned that rash behavior or rumormongering could result in severe punishment or death.

Although some American and British residents had been taken into custody by the Japanese as early as January 2, a systematic round-up of enemy civilians didn't begin until two days later on Sunday, January 4. Japanese officers accompanied by civilian interpreters, many of them local residents, canvassed homes, apartments, clubs and hotels. In most cases, Allied civilians were told to pack a bag or suitcase with personal items, bedding, and food for three days. They were to accompany the Japanese officer or report at designated locations for registration.[23]

Sheltered in their apartment, Patty and her family heard that civilians were being picked up in their neighborhood. They had no way of knowing when they would hear the knock at their door. It came about noon on January 6. "There were three Japanese soldiers," Patty said. "They had those rifles with the long bayonets on them. They said to pack clothing and food for three days. I think they gave us thirty minutes. *What do I pack?* I wondered."

Selma Croft gave terse instructions to her two children as they each stuffed a small suitcase with food and a change of clothing. A dozen silver spoons on her bedroom dresser caught Patty's eye. The spoons had been given to her as a child by an elderly American woman leaving the Philippines after her husband had died. The woman had grown fond of Patty and gave the spoons hoping the girl would remember her. The teenager threw six of the spoons in her suitcase, less from sentimentality than practicality—the utensils might be needed by her family while in captivity.

Leaving her room, she looked back at the bedroom furniture that she had received for her seventeenth birthday, just a little more than a month earlier. It upset her to be leaving it behind. In coming years she would realize how trivial this small loss was compared to the misery and grief she would endure.

Before accompanying the waiting Japanese to the truck outside the apartment building, Patty carried her terrier, Suzy, into the kitchen. She opened up several cans of dog food and filled numerous bowls with water. She cried as she hugged her pet and told her goodbye. "It was like putting a dog to sleep," she recalled. "But I closed the door and that was it." She would never know Suzy's fate.

Patty, her mom, and brother climbed into the back of what appeared to be a Japanese troop truck, which would transport them to nearby Rizal Stadium for registration. With no other civilian passengers aboard, the three stood alone in the truck bed holding onto the siding and looking out at the few Filipinos on the streets.

At the stadium they queued up in a disheartening, long line of mostly American and British civilians. It was the first of many such long queues they would endure in coming years. The civilians talked among themselves in low tones, and Patty recognized a few that she knew. It took nearly two hours for them to work their way to the front of the line, where they gave their full name, age, sex, nationality and marital status. With that, their registration was complete.

"There were a lot of people there," Patty said, "and everyone was scared. But it didn't do any good to cry. Then it was back on the truck, and they drove us through the city just like a bunch of cattle."

This time the truck carried a full load of civilian passengers. Word spread among the soon-to-be internees that they were being taken to the University of Santo Tomás just a couple of miles north of Rizal Stadium and near the center of Manila. "They paraded us around the city," Patty said. "The Filipinos were all looking at us." The status of the American and British civilians and the local Filipinos had been suddenly reversed. Those in the truck looked out with envy at many of the locals who had long worked for them as servants, laborers and clerks, but who could go back to their homes that evening unmolested by their Japanese occupiers—at least for the time being.

Late afternoon the truckload of new internees pulled up to the front of the Main Building of the sprawling University of Santo Tomás. Established in 1611 by Spanish Dominicans, the university had been the oldest in the world under an American flag until the recent Japanese occupation. With several large buildings and some fifty acres of campus, the school had a normal enrollment of 6,000 with a faculty of three hundred. Upon the recommendation of Claude Buss, the Japanese occupiers had approved the site for the internment camp of mostly American civilians trapped in the Philippine war zone.

The first large group of 300 men, women and children had arrived two days earlier on January 4. Patty would soon learn that her close friend and former basketball teammate Eileen Aaron had been among this first group of enemy civilians. Just a month earlier Eileen had been attending classes at the university, but the school had closed after the first Japanese bombing on December 8. Before being taken by the Japanese soldiers, Eileen, her sister Jean, and mother, Margaret—all British expatriates—had become separated from her father, John, and another sister, Madge. Two days later, they were relieved to learn that John and Madge were also at Santo Tomás.

Upon arrival, Eileen had taken comfort from the sight of a few of her school friends at the internment camp. She also still held hope that their internment at Santo Tomás would be brief. This was an optimistic belief held by most of the new internees. Eileen would have been distraught if she had known just how long her stay in the camp would be. Worse still, not all of her family would survive this ordeal. Eileen searched in vain among the first arrivals for her friend Patty Croft.[24]

The two friends were not reunited until several days later. Arriving late that afternoon of January 6, Patty and her family once again queued up for assignment to quarters. Following their captors' policy of segregating the internees by sex, Patty and her mother were assigned to a room with more

54

than thirty other civilian females on the first floor of the Main Building. Fourteen-year-old Bill would temporarily make do sleeping on a balcony connecting one level of the Main Building to another level.

Attached to the large front door of the Main Building was a terse Japanese notice: "INTERNEES IN THIS CAMP WILL BE RESPONSIBLE FOR FEEDING THEMSELVES." Each of the Crofts had packed enough food for a couple of days, but that was about it. *What then?* Patty wondered.[25]

"My mom and I were assigned to Room 6 on that first floor," Patty remembered. "It had been a classroom, but all the desks and furniture had been removed. We had no bedding or mosquito nets, so we and the others just had to lay out on the concrete floor."

Although most of the captives were unaware of it, the first civilian internee death at Santo Tomás had already occurred early that morning. At 2 a.m. a captive named W. G. Weaver made his way to the roof of the Main Building and leaped to his death. The few internees who witnessed the event were ordered to keep silent by their Japanese captors.[26]

No one in Room 6 slept much that first night. "The mosquitos were awful," Patty said, "and rats scampered around all night."

# CHAPTER 4

❧ ❧ ❧

# "Protective Custody" at Santo Tomás

ROOM 6 ON THE FIRST FLOOR was already buzzing when Patty Croft sat up the early morning of January 7 after a night of fitful sleep. Many of the more than thirty female civilians were chattering nervously, unsure of what lay ahead that day. Most had been part of the 500 distraught arrivals the day before bringing the internee population to about 1,200 after the first three days. Hundreds would continue to arrive daily.

Within a week the overflow from the Main Building would be sent to the one-story Domestic Science Building, soon rechristened the Annex. By the end of the first week, the Japanese camp commandant at the newly christened Santo Tomás Internment Camp, Lieutenant Hitoshi Tomayasu, restricted the Annex to women with children. That same day the university's large gymnasium began receiving internees, and the Education Building was soon opened to males. Within ten days more than 3,000 enemy aliens were being kept under "protective custody" by the Japanese, with about 70 percent of these Americans, about 25 percent British, and the rest from twelve other countries aligned against at least one of the Axis powers. Male internees outnumbered females almost two to one.[1]

Santo Tomás would be by far the largest of at least ten internment camps in the Philippines established by the Japanese to incarcerate expatriates of the Allied nations. More than 5,000 American civilians would languish in these camps during the war years. Proportionate to the percentage of non-American foreign nationals in Santo Tomás, around 2,000 expatriates from other Allied countries were interned in these camps.[2]

Both the Allied and Axis powers interned enemy aliens during the war. Ostensibly, the confinement of these civilians was not intended as a punishment. The foreign nationals were presumed to hold sympathies with an enemy's war objectives and thus could pose a threat to the security of the nation incarcerating them. The internees were generally given more privileges than military prisoners of war. With warring nations lacking diplomatic relations and suspicious of each other, repatriation of these captives was difficult.

The Japanese captors' use of the term protective custody to describe the incarceration of enemy aliens in the Philippines was a convenience to avoid the considerable responsibility of feeding and caring for this large group. Although the Japanese military guarded the internees, Santo Tomás was initially under Japanese civilian authority and would be administered differently from a POW camp for military prisoners of war. A key distinction of the Japanese internment camps would be that the captives would administer themselves and be responsible for their own food, healthcare, and other needs.

"Everyone was confused at first," Patty recalled, "but people were soon being assigned this and that job." The 17-year-old secured a job on the serving line for the central kitchen, quickly constructed in the rear of the first floor of the Main Building. With her valuable nursing experience, Selma began duty in the medical dispensary, also on the bottom floor.

The confusion initially experienced in the internment camp would quickly turn into a competently directed effort by mostly American internee leaders, who would display their talent for organization and self-government. With Japanese captors expecting the internees to provide for themselves, these civilians would organize, plan and administer a brand-new community under extraordinarily difficult conditions. Fortunately for their own welfare, a large number of these internees were well prepared for the challenging task at hand. Included among them were the teachers, healthcare providers, engineers and businessmen who had worked for decades to educate the Filipinos and develop the economy of the U.S. commonwealth. Many of these captives had been community leaders of cosmopolitan Manila.

Looking back many years later, Patty gave a more nationalist explanation for the success of these internees building and managing their township inside prison walls: "It was because we were Americans."

Americans, yes—but Americans undergoing a shameful ordeal. This was a humbling condition never experienced before in the proud history of their nation: a foreign power's mass incarceration of U.S. civilians deprived of the liberty and freedom that they considered their birthright. Their homes and businesses had been looted and destroyed. Most had little left but their lives. They had been shocked at how ineffectual the U.S. military had been at the outset of the invasion, and many felt betrayed by the failure of U.S. officials to warn them and aid them in their distress. It was all a hard pill to swallow.

Still, despite a deep disappointment in American officials, most of the internees maintained a profound and abiding faith in America itself. Almost every one believed that MacArthur's forces, supported by reinforcements from the mainland, would soon rally and vanquish these foolhardy Japanese. Was not America the leading industrial nation in the world and the arsenal for global democracy? Surely, their own government, surprised and knocked off balance by a deceitful Japan, would soon recover and right this grievous wrong. Their captivity would be short—months at most. (So they thought.)

Meanwhile, they would have to make the most of a challenging and frightening situation using American grit, ingenuity and self-sufficiency— traits that had served many of their pioneer ancestors on the frontier. Arriving with the first group on January 4, insurance executive L. Earl Carroll was chosen almost at random by Commandant Tomayasu to be the "general chairman" of an organization to administer the camp. Tomayasu had asked for a leader of these internees, and Carroll was pointed out as a prominent member of the now-defunct American Coordinating Committee. Forced into a role not of his choosing, the new chairman immediately appointed room leaders to account for and control the internees.

The next morning Carroll and the "room monitors," as they would be called, met to develop an organization for the feeding, care and control of the burgeoning internee population. They began the framework for what would develop into a complex organization over the coming weeks and months. The first leaders of the Central Committee—so named as they began meeting in the Central Office of Santo Tomás University—would be the aforesaid Earl Carroll, mining company executive A. F. Duggleby, and manufacturing executive F. N. Berry. Predisposed to republicanism as Americans, a discussion soon ensued over holding elections for key positions on the Central Committee. But, since the Japanese appeared satisfied with the current leadership, the decision was made to hold elections only for room and floor monitors. The internees hoped to maintain a semblance of autonomy over their newly established government.

By January 24 the Central Committee was renamed the Executive Committee with expanded membership to include a few British representatives. An Advisory Committee was established also with British members. Both of these committees' membership would change frequently over the months and years owing to internee transfers, releases, illnesses—and later deaths. But these two committees and the network of room monitors would provide the backbone of an ever-increasing organization administering the more than 3,000 captives at Santo Tomás Internment Camp.

This organization would soon include more than a dozen operating committees, which were considered working departments, responsible for and controlling the needs, infrastructure and activities of the camp. Among the most important departments were Medical Services, chaired by Dr. Charles N. Leach; Sanitation and Health; Work Assignment; and Building and Construction. In the first few months, the Philippine Red Cross provided the critical food supplies, medicines and bedding for the mushrooming community. Japanese overseers would later disrupt much of this local organization's work, but the group provided critical food and supplies in the opening months.

Considering the hostile origins of the camp and the immediacy of its needs, the new leaders of the internee community did a remarkable job of protecting the health and safety of the captives during the first year. Their task would become more difficult in coming years as food shortages developed and the harsh Japanese military increased its control of the camp, but doubtless many lives were saved by the courage, foresight and expertise of the various committee leaders.[3]

One of the Santo Tomás internees, A. V. H. Hartendorp, would later publish the most extensive chronicle of the inner workings of the camp's administration describing the high quality of those working on the committees. "Fortunately, the community was in many respects a select one," Hartendorp explains, "including many of the most prominent persons in the country—government officials, business executives, and professional men. Experts in almost every field of activity were among the population of Santo Tomás and the general level of intelligence and ability was high."[4]

Within a couple of weeks, the women of Room 6 were supplied with bedding and mosquito nets by the Philippine Red Cross, greatly improving the residents' living quality. "I was voted to be room monitor for a while," Patty recalled of her several weeks on the first floor. "I was one of the youngest in the room, so they stuck me with the job. I think my mother was room monitor for a while, too, but I'm not sure. But I wasn't in that room very long."

The primary duty of the room monitors was to keep track of the internees assigned to the room. The monitors maintained and updated a list of their room's occupants and called roll at least once daily. These room supervisors were held personally responsible for the internees in their charge. "They started doing this early on," Patty said. "If someone was missing, we were to turn them in. Some would be sick and go to the hospital. We had to account for all of them."

While a good part of the internee population came from the upper echelon of Manila society, some did not, including a smattering of prostitutes, gamblers and street hustlers. The camp was a great leveler of class. The common denominator was that they all were considered enemy aliens by their Japanese captors. And as captives, all would endure the same hardships and suffer the same indignities.

"We had many kinds of people in that room on the first floor," Patty said. "One of them was a Shanghai prostitute. She slept right next to me and my mother. In those days women wore panty girdles, and my mother had washed hers and laid it out to dry. After it turned up missing, she later saw the prostitute wearing it. She never even asked her about it because she sure didn't want it back."

After a month of incarceration, Patty was permanently assigned to the third floor of the Main Building in a room with young females, many of whom she knew from her years at the American School. It was a joyless reunion for these girls, but a comfort all the same. Patty was especially happy to take a bed next to her close friend and former teammate Eileen Aaron, who shared a bunk bed with her older sister, Jean.

"It was not a large room, just another converted classroom," Patty said. "I think we had thirty-six beds in the room. The beds were just one right up against another. You kept your clothes and a few personal items under the beds, along with any books you had. We sure didn't have any makeup or anything like that for long because we all ran out of it."

Personal space was at a premium in the crowded rooms of the Main Building with the average floor space per internee around 24 square feet.

A cot or wooden bed would have to fit into a space 6-feet by 4-feet with an internee's personal items stowed below, or above on the mosquito netting. No one was allowed to purchase or barter for extra space. This cramped personal space and lack of privacy upset many of the captives early on, but most learned to adapt and find a sense of solitude when they needed it.

Living in close quarters in the tropical climate promoted an unending parasitic torture: bedbugs. "We ran out of anything to kill them," Patty remembered. "They seemed to really love me. I had a constant ring around my stomach. They would really itch after biting." She carried her mattress down the three flights of stairs to try to wash out the bedbugs. After washing, the mattress would be left out in the sun all day. This process helped but never completely eliminated the tiny pests.

Each floor of the Main Building housed both men and women but always in separate rooms. Males numbered around 1,200 on the three floors, and women close to 1,000. The Japanese demanded segregation by sex in the rooms, but men and women internees frequently met in the hallways, dining areas, and outside. The gymnasium was soon restricted to male captives and reached a population of around 700. The Annex continued to house only women with their young children, and fluctuated around several hundred. A twelve-foot wall surrounded the entire campus of Santo Tomás acting as a deterrent to escape.

The growing population soon overwhelmed the available restroom facilities in these buildings, so the internees' Building and Construction Department swung into action with its cadre of experienced workers. The necessary replumbing and installation added toilets and shower facilities to all the buildings. The first floor of the Main Building, where Selma Croft would reside for several years, soon had five toilets and four showers for the approximately 260 women on the floor. Waiting in line was common at most of the women's facilities. The men's facilities were more sparsely equipped.[5]

The shower rooms offered no privacy, an inconvenience the women learned to live with. Some tried to maintain their modesty by showering in their underwear. The prying eyes of Japanese overseers added to the women's indignities. "The showers were all open," Patty recalled, "very degrading with all the people going in and out. But particularly degrading when the Japanese guards would come in to watch us girls shower. That was awful. We complained, but what could we really do about it. They had the upper hand."

Many of the women had a difficult time making the adjustment to the tight living quarters and frequent indignities, but overall morale remained high. Grace D. Oxnam, an appointed "House Mother" for the Main Building, much later reported her observations on these women captives. "They accepted the situation in Santo Tomás," she said, "the looting of their homes, everything, and said: 'Nothing matters except winning the war.'.... On the whole, I think the hardy pioneer spirit of our forebears was brought out in the women; the United States should be proud of its women in the Philippines."[6]

The myriad needs of the captive community provided numerous opportunities to keep the internees usefully occupied. Executive Committee members readily saw how assigning jobs to the camp's occupants would not only meet a need for labor, but also provide a purpose and routine for the nervous captives. The Work Assignment Committee ensured that able-bodied men and women were given jobs commensurate with their skills and abilities. An internee's previous social status in the Manila community had no bearing on his or her job assignment. A former vice president of a large electrical supply house in Manila took a role as a restroom attendant, solemnly passing out the four sheets of rationed toilet paper to those in need. A noted society lady of Manila washed out women's sanitary necessities.[7]

Like many of the younger women in camp, Patty took an assignment on the serving line outside the central kitchen. Within a few weeks of the camp's opening, a newly built and equipped kitchen began preparing and serving meager meals to some 2,500 to 3,000 per day. "Well, it really sounded like a good job," she said. "I thought I would be able to get extra food, but turned out I couldn't. I was too out in the open with guards and people watching me serve the food. I can still remember the kitchen workers yelling 'hot stuff' as they brought out more food to the serving line."

Diners queued up in four long lines outside the central kitchen, located near the rear hallway on the first floor of the Main Building. Patty was put in charge of her serving line, crewed by workers about her age. The internees filed past the serving counters and carried their plates of food to the long tables on the grounds outside. Meals were eaten outdoors for sanitary purposes. The camp was greatly, and justifiably, concerned with disease prevention.

Breakfast initially consisted of cracked-wheat porridge, a small roll and coffee. Dinner was usually a stew, a roll and a banana. The dinner fare was enhanced occasionally with a meat or chicken day. The Philippine Red Cross initially supplied what food was affordable and available in the Manila area. The first year at Santo Tomás saw no malnutrition among the internees, only a progressive weight loss. In the years afterward, the hungry and eventually starving captives would look back with longing for the scanty meals of that first year.[8]

"I think I weighed around 130 pounds when I entered the camp," Patty said. "My clothes started getting loose that first year, but without scales I never knew exactly how much weight I was losing. The first year wasn't really too bad. Much of the weight loss for those in camp was from not having the usual soft drinks, candy and alcohol. So those that were overweight seemed to be losing the fastest."

Just before the central kitchen began operation, an announcement of the beginning of "communal feeding" appeared in the first issue of the camp's tri-weekly newspaper, *Internews*. The letter-sized, two-page edition was edited by internee Russell Brines, an Associated Press journalist captured while covering the Japanese invasion of the Philippines. *Internews* stated its purpose in its first issue on January 24: "This little sheet is intended primarily to supply internees with news of their internal government and to report negotiations between camp officials and the Japanese authorities." Announcements published in the newsletters were to be considered "official." Brines strived to avoid antagonizing Japanese overseers by attempting only to "mirror a fragment of daily life" in the Santo Tomás Internment Camp and eschewing news about the outside world.[9]

The January 29 issue of *Internews* announced the first performance of a "floor show" that evening on the west patio of the Main Building. The makeshift stage for these open-air shows would be christened the Little Theater Under the Stars, and these infrequent variety shows would become a bright spot in the dull routine of internment life. Children in the camp usually sat directly in front of the stage, and many of the older internees watched from the windows of their rooms above. Sponsored by the Entertainment Committee, the improvised shows had their limitations but provided a small serving of joy to these captives enduring a bleak chapter in their lives.[10]

With her accordion skills in demand, Patty gamely performed in this first show, which started at 6:15 that Thursday evening. With Dave Harvey MacTurk (stage name of Dave Harvey) serving as master of ceremonies, the show also included performances by trumpet players, a tap dancer, a singer, and a sword swallower. Commandant Tomayasu was seen in attendance. "They were pretty hard up for entertainment," Patty said. "But the shows really helped break up the weeks. I was a little nervous that first evening, but not as nervous as when my German accordion teacher would take me out to play in front of two hundred GIs."

The teenage internee was fortunate to have had a Filipino outside the camp to retrieve her accordion from the Croft's abandoned and soon-looted apartment in Pasay. Her native friend had also been a student of the German instructor and performed with Patty at some of the U.S. military installations before the war started. He was one of thousands of native *Manileños* providing the internees with a critical link to the outside world. They brought food, personal items, messages and money to the captives at Santo Tomás. These pickups and deliveries were through a somewhat elaborate system that came to be known as the "package-line."

If not for this outside link, many of the internees would have faced starvation before the central kitchen became operational in late January. From the first days of incarceration, Filipino friends and servants of the internees, along with a smattering of native peddlers, gathered daily at the front of the university grounds passing food and bedding through the iron picket-fence to the desperate captives. This created a raucous social scene each day, and Japanese and German civilians passing by complained that the front of the university looked like a "picnic ground." After a few weeks the Japanese commandant banned these interactions.

Realizing how important this outside link was for the internees, Central Committee chairman Earl Carroll petitioned the commandant to restore the package-line. Carroll proposed the installation of a high *sawali* fence to screen this activity and to allow those bringing outside aid to enter through the front gate in an orderly fashion. Outsiders could drop off their parcels in a designated area for a later pickup or delivery, Carroll explained, with internees restricted to an area well behind the front fence. The commandant relented with the condition that deliveries be made during designated hours and carefully searched for contraband by Japanese guards. Also, internees would have to remain some 150 yards behind the drop-off area and would be prohibited from shouting or waving to those delivering the parcels.

At 8:30 each morning a large crowd of captives began to gather well behind the front gate in anticipation of arranged deliveries by a Filipino servant, friend or merchant. These morning hours became social time for the assembled captives, who could catch up on the latest news or rumors, or just indulge in idle conversation among themselves. News of the outside world was sometimes smuggled into camp in the delivered parcels. But if a Filipino was caught attempting this, he or she faced a humiliating hard slap in the face from one of the guards inspecting the delivery.[11]

The captives felt a deep sense of gratitude to the loyal Filipinos who faithfully continued to deliver—and sometimes pick up—messages, money, food and personal items at the package-line. The Japanese were confounded and irritated by the intense loyalty shown by many of the Filipinos. The Philippine natives should be glad to see the *Yanquis* occupiers in a reduced state, the Japanese reasoned, and certainly not so eager to provide them aid and comfort through the package-line. The loyalty to the Americans during these trying times said much about how the Filipinos viewed the previous decades of their country's occupation by U.S. military, officials, businessmen, and other professionals. They apparently considered the *Yanquis* more beneficial than malign.

"No matter what suffering and sacrifice this war may impose upon us, we shall stand by America with undaunted spirit...," President Quezon had pledged of the Philippine people at his second inauguration at the mouth of Malinta Tunnel. The loyal friends and faithful former servants of the Americans made good on that promise every time they delivered on that package-line at Santo Tomás.[12]

By the second week of February, life for the internees seemed to settle into a difficult but tolerable state. Patty and Selma met every day, usually when the teenager came down to the first floor to work the serving line. Now living in the all-male Education Building, Bill was assigned work distributing parcels brought to the package-line. He visited his family when time permitted. With Bill's fifteenth birthday approaching on Valentine's Day, Patty and her mother realized they could give him only the gift of their company. But a shocking chain of events in camp began on February 12 that overshadowed Bill's birthday and reminded the internees of their frightening and tenuous existence as captives of the Japanese.

Patty was outside the Main Building that afternoon when she saw three men, two Englishmen and an Australian, being beaten by a squad of Japanese soldiers as they were shoved into a barracks next to the commandant's office. She and many in the camp heard their cries inside the barracks as the Japanese continued beating the men with fists and gun straps. "It was awful," she said. "The Japanese wanted us to see and hear what would happen if we tried to escape."

About five o'clock the three erstwhile escapees were taken from the barracks and driven away in a police wagon. A few internees who witnessed the beaten men's departure said they had been barely able to walk to the vehicle. At roll call that evening the room monitors read a statement to the internees prepared by the Japanese commandant: "We regret very much to report that three men escaped from Santo Tomás last night at 8 o'clock. They were apprehended today by Japanese soldiers and returned to Santo Tomás where they were severely punished."[13]

Two days later on Valentine's Day, the camp was shocked to learn that a military court of the Japanese High Command had tried and condemned the men to death. The camp's Executive Committee sent a petition for clemency to Commandant Tomayasu, which he promised to deliver to the High Command. Despite the petition, the three condemned men were taken to Manila's Chinese Cemetery early the afternoon of February 15. Internees witnessing the executions included Carroll, interpreter and internee Ernest Stanley, the three men's room monitors, and a minister of the Church of England.

Ordered by the High Command to oversee the executions, Tomayasu expressed his condolences to Carroll as the three escapees smoked a final cigarette. The blindfolded men were then led to a freshly dug pit and ordered to sit on the edge with their legs dangling over the side. Three Japanese soldiers fired pistols from across the pit, hitting each of the men in the chest. The men slumped into the pit and the executioners fired into the groaning victims. Moans were still heard from the pit as the Japanese soldiers filled the common grave.[14]

The details of the men's deaths were not generally known in camp. The February 14 issue of *Internews* reported that the three escapees who had gone "over the wall" had been taken away from Santo Tomás, but nothing was said about their executions. The article also announced new restrictions on camp activities and a series of invasive room inspections. Commandant Tomayasu issued a separate statement warning that attempted escapes in the future would result in death for the escapees and reprisals on all in camp.[15]

Sincerely seeming to regret the whole affair, Tomayasu left Santo Tomás the day after the executions for a new assignment in Manila. He was succeeded by 55-year-old R. Tsurumi, a longtime official of the Japanese consular service. The new commandant had lived in Canada for eight years and spoke good English. He proved to be flexible in camp policies and considerate of the difficult position of the internees.[16]

The following month, Patty connected briefly with her formerly care-free life as a high school student when she and most of her senior class-mates from the American School were graduated in a "mock ceremony" in camp. The Education Department planned the outdoor ceremony for the twelve class of 1942 graduates on March 18, the same date set at the be-ginning of the school year in summer 1941—before these high schoolers had seen their world turned upside down by the Japanese invasion. Ameri-can School principal Lois Croft and class advisor C. F. Maynard, both now internees with their students, oversaw the austere ceremony without the white gowns, tuxedos and diplomas that would have been the norm.[17]

Subsequent graduating classes of internees in 1943 and 1944 would receive an official diploma at their ceremonies, which rankled Patty for many years to come. "I always thought some favoritism was shown by Mrs. Croft because her daughter graduated the year after I did," she said. "It seemed to me that she made sure that the class of 1943 received diplo-mas because her daughter was one of them. Oh, well, there was nothing I could do about it. At least I was officially, kind of, graduated from high school."

With 300 children between the ages of six and fifteen in camp, their continued education had become a priority in the first month of intern-ment. Within a week of the camp's opening, the Executive Committee was urged to begin organizing classes for these children. Under the guidance of the newly formed Education Department, 112 students from kindergar-ten to ninth grade were enrolled by mid-January. High school enrollments began shortly afterward. Classes soon started in the library atop the Main Building and in the open air behind the Education Building, an area shaded during the morning hours. Many of the teachers from the Manila schools were interned, so qualified instructors were plentiful. Although in short supply, textbooks were obtained from the now-closed schools in Manila.[18]

In addition to the interned professional teachers, a number of well-ed-ucated engineers, lawyers, accountants and other professionals at Santo Tomás added to the camp instructors. Even many adult captives enrolled in the wide range of classes available. Genuine progress was made by stu-dents of all ages despite the challenging conditions. For several years, the Education Department would do a laudable job at Santo Tomás instilling a spirit of education and discipline into the stressed youth of the internment camp. Efforts of the department ensured that, despite the hardships, these children continued to make academic progress. The classes also made a lasting contribution to the general quality of life in camp and intimated of a better day to come for the struggling captives.[19]

About the time Patty's reduced senior class held their graduation in mid-March, disconcerting news filtered through camp: Douglas MacArthur had fled Corregidor for Australia. With wild rumors the norm, many captives were justifiably suspicious of this latest report and nearly anything else they heard about the outside world. Yet the preponderance of news supported the stories of MacArthur's leaving Corregidor for safety in Australia. Written summaries of radio broadcasts from San Francisco or London were frequently smuggled into camp or thrown over the walls providing a quick and generally reliable means of keeping the internees informed of outside events.

Putting the best possible spin on MacArthur's flight, many internees said this was only strong evidence that the general felt certain that Bataan and Corregidor could hold off the Japanese without him. Many of the captives and Filipinos believed that as long as these strongholds continued to resist, they would be safe from Japanese depredations. And they maintained that MacArthur, of course, would quickly return with forces strong enough to vanquish the Japanese.[20]

Yet Patty said she was rattled by the news of MacArthur's flight. "It was scary but not devastating. Some of us just thought, *Well, we might be here a little longer than we thought.*"

DOUGLAS MACARTHUR HAD INDEED LEFT Corregidor at sunset on March 11, 1942, along with his wife, his son and their Chinese *amah*. It was not his decision. He fully expected to die on Corregidor. But George Marshall and Franklin Roosevelt came to realize they would need MacArthur to lead the protracted struggle taking back the western Pacific from the Japanese. Also, British Prime Minister Winston Churchill wanted to calm a nervous Australia, so he urged Roosevelt to name an American as the supreme commander in the southwest Pacific theater. MacArthur was unquestionably the most qualified. And as Churchill explained to the Americans, in 1940 he had ordered out the British commander at Dunkirk, Lord Gort, to deprive the Germans of a "needless triumph."[21]

Several weeks before his departure, MacArthur had sent a forlorn radiogram to the president urging aid for his decimated forces in the Philippines.

"After nine weeks of fighting not even a small amount of aid has reached us from the United States..." the general stated. "The British and American Navies, the two strongest fleets in existence, have seemingly pursued a strategy that excludes any attempt to bring aid to the Philippines. Consequently, while perfectly safe itself, the United States has practically doomed the Philippine nation to almost total extinction in order to secure a breathing space." Although not mentioned in MacArthur's criticism of the U.S.-British "Hitler First" strategy, this policy also ensured a lengthier internment of the civilian captives at Santo Tomás and other such camps in the Philippines.[22]

Roosevelt knew that he was "ordering the captain to be the first to leave the sinking ship," so he first directed MacArthur to leave Corregidor for Mindanao, in the southern Philippines, and from there plan a defense of these islands. With rumors of a great army assembling in Australia, MacArthur's staff asserted that he would be leading this force back to rescue Wainwright's troops on Bataan. In early March a cable from Washington urgently requested MacArthur's presence in Australia.

The general agonized over leaving Corregidor but in the end chose to obey the president. And once again, Roosevelt would prove less than forthright. In a last conversation with Wainwright, MacArthur emphasized he was leaving under protest and only after Roosevelt ordered him out. "If I get through to Australia you know I'll come back as soon as I can with as much as I can," he told the new U.S. commander in the Philippines. "In the meantime you've got to hold."[23]

MacArthur, his family, and key staff left for Mindanao on four PT boats on a 560-mile journey through enemy-held waters. Stormy weather turned the boats into "a combination of bucking bronco and wallowing tub," one of the passengers later wrote. MacArthur, his son, and their *amah* lay below in their boat, miserably seasick. After thirty-five hours of drama at sea, the party arrived at the Del Monte pineapple plantation on Mindanao. Delayed for several days while waiting for a plane to Australia, MacArthur sent a message to Manuel Quezon, telling his old friend that he hoped to leave Australia with a relief force before the situation deteriorated on Bataan.

After a harrowing plane ride from Mindanao through Japanese-patrolled skies, MacArthur's party was unable to land in Darwin in north Australia as the town was under attack. After diverting fifty miles farther south to Batchelor Field, MacArthur's party left for Adelaide by train. Stopping at a small station eighty miles from their destination, MacArthur's deputy chief of staff, Brig. Gen. Dick Marshall, boarded the train with startling news. He had just come from Melbourne, where MacArthur believed his newly assembled army awaited. Marshall told his superior that no such force existed. Even if formed into an army, the few, scattered Allied units in Australia would be wholly inadequate to turn the tide on Bataan. In fact, the Australians were concerned they might be unable to prevent the Japanese from invading their own land. Realizing the inadequacy of his new command "was the greatest shock and surprise of the whole war," MacArthur later wrote.[24]

MacArthur spoke with news reporters at the Adelaide train station nine days after departing Corregidor. "The President of the United States ordered me to break through the Japanese lines...," he said, "for the purpose, as I understand it, of organizing the American offensive against Japan, a primary object of which is the relief of the Philippines. I came through and I shall return." The general carefully considered the wording of his press statement, hoping to galvanize public support for prompt action by Washington. It was the last three words, however, that seized the public imagination and resonated over the years. The Office of War Information in Washington had tried to have MacArthur revise his statement with the words "we shall return." But he flatly refused, even against the advice of his own staff.[25]

The words did not emanate from the general's own considerable ego. The phrase was from Carlos Romulo, a Filipino journalist and close advisor to Manuel Quezon. "America has let us down and won't be trusted," Romulo told MacArthur's aides. "But the [Filipino] people still have confidence in MacArthur. If *he* says *he* is coming back, he will be believed." That MacArthur so strongly agreed with Romulo's phrasing and not that of Washington officials may have reflected his own growing mistrust of those leading the U.S. war effort. The Santo Tomás internees had also seen their faith in U.S. authority sorely tested since December 1941. Still, they never despaired. They, too, heard MacArthur's promise and continued to trust in America. But the captives could never have imagined how long it would take for MacArthur to make good on his pledge—nor the trials that lay ahead for them.[26]

The month after MacArthur left Corregidor, the American internees received another hammer blow with the surrender of U.S. and Philippine forces on Bataan. By late March the Japanese plans to overrun the

70

Philippines had been nearly two months behind schedule when General Homma launched a determined attack to break through the American and Philippine forces on the peninsula. On April 3, the Japanese commander suggested to Wainwright, now at Philippine defense headquarters on Corregidor, that he accept an "honorable surrender." Getting no response, Homma ordered the final offensive and succeeded in crossing Mount Samat near the center of the Bataan peninsula. By then nearly 80 percent of the exhausted defenders of Bataan suffered from malaria and dysentery. Surviving on less than 1,000 calories per day, a third of this force suffered from beriberi. On April 9, Maj. Gen. Edward King, who had replaced Wainwright on the peninsula, ordered the gallant defenders of Bataan to surrender.

The 76,000 U.S. and Philippine troops surrendered on Bataan were left to the whims of their Japanese victors, who considered surrendering soldiers dishonorable and undeserving of decent treatment. Some 10,000 American and 65,000 Filipino prisoners of Japan began the 65-mile Bataan Death March to imprisonment at Camp O'Donnell in central Luzon. Thousands of the starved, sickly captives died or were executed along the way.[27]

As the Bataan defenders succumbed, MacArthur attempted the first U.S. aerial counteroffensive against Japan, ordering the attack from his Melbourne headquarters. A special force of ten new B-25 medium bombers and three B-17s backtracked MacArthur's recent journey from Corregidor, hopping from Batchelor Field near Darwin to Del Monte on Mindanao. From April 12 through April 14, the U.S. planes attacked targets throughout the Philippines catching the Japanese by surprise. The air raids failed to accomplish much strategically, yet they deserved more recognition than they received. They were overshadowed in the media by the famous Doolittle raid on Tokyo on April 18.

MacArthur's air raid made a statement but did nothing to save Corregidor, still holding out in early May. In the three weeks following the surrender on Bataan, the island bastion was shelled incessantly. The morning of May 8 two Japanese assault battalions made separate landings on the narrow tip of the island. Remnants of the U.S. 4th Marine Regiment and a determined group of U.S. sailors, Philippine Scouts, and converted artillerymen beat back one of the landings, but the other gained a foothold. By the next day, the defenders had retreated to the opening of Malinta Tunnel. Many were out of ammunition, and water supplies were nearly exhausted.

Wainwright was forced to surrender Corregidor, sending a final message to Washington: "With profound regret and continued pride in my gallant troops, I go to meet the Japanese commander."[28]

The U.S. and Philippine forces on Luzon had held off the Japanese for 142 days following the air attacks on December 8, nearly triple the time estimated by enemy war planners.

FOR PATTY CROFT AND HER more than 3,000 fellow internees at Santo Tomás, the five months after the first Japanese attack had been shattering. They had never imagined American forces completely defeated or forced out of the Philippines. After the fall of Corregidor, they were compelled to accept this bitter and frightening realization. The American internees were now captives in Japanese-controlled Luzon without a U.S. military presence, except for troops lingering in POW camps worse than Santo Tomás.

"Corregidor's fall was very depressing," Patty remembered. "It was like the end of the world had come. We knew it was gonna be a long time before we were rescued. We would say, 'Maybe in the next six months.' Then after six months, we would say, 'Well, in another six months.' It just kept getting further and further out."

After the surrender of Corregidor, most in camp shared Patty's depression, which was coupled with fear for most. But many also shared the girl's continued faith that within six months or so America would come to their rescue. Meanwhile, as their British co-internees might have put it, they would "keep a stiff upper lip and get on with it," making their restricted existence as tolerable as possible.

Late the next month, internee leaders suddenly faced an initially appalling situation that would eventually work to the captives' benefit, at least for a while. Disaffiliated from the American Red Cross by Japanese decree in April, the reorganized and locally administered Philippine Red Cross had been providing the food and other supplies for the captives at Santo Tomás. On June 25 officials from the Philippine relief organization informed the Japanese commandant they had remaining funds to purchase food for only a few days. Other arrangements would be necessary to avoid starvation of the internees.

Calling in Executive Committee chairman Earl Carroll and his vice chairman, the commandant explained the situation and offered to negotiate with higher Japanese officials to supply the needed funds, but at a greatly reduced per diem rate for the now roughly 3,400 internees. After some dickering with Carroll, the commandant gained approval from the Japanese military to supply monthly payments at a per diem rate of 70 centavos (approximately 35 cents U.S.) for the captives. As part of the negotiations, the internees were to organize a committee to administer the funds including safekeeping of the monies, budgeting, and purchases from the local markets.

Reliance on the Japanese for this vital funding probably made the camp executives nervous, but they had little choice. Serendipitously, as it turned out, the new arrangements proved advantageous. The internee officials would now have more control over the camp's food supply and could plan the sparse menus accordingly. The last six months of 1942, the internees were fed on 48 centavos per day (approximately $4.47 in U.S. currency in 2023) with an additional 22 centavos per day ($2.05 U.S. in 2023) for miscellaneous supplies—toilet paper, soap, medicine and other needs.[29]

Underscoring their limited autonomy and penchant for self-government, in June the internees resolved to hold elections for a new Executive Committee, the chief policy-making group for the captives. Members for the committee had been chosen on an ad hoc basis in early January, and some of these same weary members supported the new elections. After a nominating committee provided fifteen American and six British candidates, internees age nineteen and older voted for seven of them to serve a six-month term. The top seven vote-getters formed the new Executive Committee, and Commandant Tsurumi chose one of the seven, Carroll C. Grinnell, as the new committee chairman.[30]

The undemocratic appointment of Grinnell by the commandant was a not-so-subtle reminder that the Japanese held ultimate authority over the camp. The allowance of limited self-government in camp showed only the Japanese's abdication of their responsibility for the internees' welfare rather than an approving nod to Western democracy. This abdication could cut both ways for the internees, but they would eventually come to view this policy as little short of abandonment.

Grinnell would become the leading figure in camp for the Santo Tomás internees for nearly all their remaining time in captivity. He had been the manager of the General Electric Company's operations in the Far East at the time of his internment and had conducted business with the Japanese for many years. His acquaintance with the Japanese language and their customs no doubt strongly influenced his selection as chairman by Commandant Tsurumi. Grinnell would prove an able and even benevolent leader for the camp. Despite his honest efforts and personal sacrifice in his difficult role as a mediator between the Japanese authorities and the internees, all would eventually end in tragedy for the American business executive.[31]

Grinnell and his family had been neighbors of Patty Croft's family when they lived in Santa Mesa in the early- and mid-1930s. His two sons had been the same age as Patty's brothers, so the boys strengthened a bond between the two families. The General Electric executive had only returned to Manila a short time before war broke out, and his wife and children were still in the States at the time of his capture by the Japanese.

"My mother and I talked to him a lot in camp," Patty recalled. "He was great and a big help to us. He was able to do us small favors, like if my mother needed to leave camp for a trip into Manila. He could usually arrange for a pass. He was wonderful and a really good administrator for the camp." While Patty knew Grinnell personally from their time as neighbors, the 17-year-old was often unaware of the internal politics and dire concerns burdening camp leaders like Grinnell.

A disturbing episode in camp that summer of 1942 threatened the teenager's life. Feeling sick one morning in July, she was soon beset with vomiting and diarrhea. The diarrhea became acute, and by the second day she was seriously ill. She was helped to the camp hospital, where she was diagnosed with both enteritis and amoebic dysentery, an outbreak in camp that was suspected to have originated in the central kitchen where she worked. These infectious diseases were serious even with the best of care. With the limited medical supplies at Santo Tomás, they could be fatal. "They thought I was gonna die there for a while it was so bad," she said. "I took five days in the hospital to get better."

The camp hospital where she was treated had been hastily established in January primarily through the efforts of Medical Services Committee chairman Charles Leach, a Rockefeller Foundation official who just happened to be in Manila when the war began. The physician had previously served in the Philippines as public health advisor to Governor-General Leonard Wood in the 1920s. Soon after their internment in early January, Leach and nurse Dorothy Davis started a clinic in one of the empty classrooms of the Main Building. After the Philippine Red Cross was unable to follow through on plans to provide a fully equipped medical unit, Leach converted the one-story Mining School Building into a makeshift hospital with room for eighty beds in four wards. Leach and another interned physician, Dr. L. Z. Fletcher, furnished the facility with a hodgepodge of equipment and bedding they purchased in Manila.[32]

By the time Patty was admitted to the hospital, Leach and Fletcher had the services of five other interned physicians. With Davis as nursing superintendent, the facility's staff was bolstered in March by twelve U.S. Navy nurses who had been stationed at the naval hospital at Cañacao when the war began. More medical help arrived in camp in early July with the internment of sixty-six U.S. Army nurses from Corregidor, who would be isolated at nearby Santa Catalina Convent for their first six weeks. The teenager remembered the navy nurses showing a poor bedside manner, forgivable considering the horrors they had seen since the war began. "They were pretty tough," she said. "With all the diarrhea I had I was having to go to the restroom constantly. At the peak of my illness I asked one of the nurses for help getting to the toilet. She said, 'No, you just get up and go.' I tried, but I passed out I was so weak."[33]

A number of Filipino doctors volunteered their services at the makeshift hospital, and it was one of these locals that may have saved the gravely ill teenager's life. "I couldn't eat anything without worsening the diarrhea," she said, "and I was getting pretty weak. The Filipino doctor told the staff to start feeding me only the water that rice was cooked in. They started me on that and gradually added a few kernels of cooked rice in each meal. This started building up my digestive tract. That's what helped me. It was the rice that did the trick."

Slowly recovering in bed after returning to her third-floor room, she remained too weak to work for a couple of weeks. But Patty would regain her health that summer, thanks to the volunteer Filipino doctor and the internees' Medical Services Committee that supported the health workers in the hospital and clinics on campus. She and many others in camp would continue to benefit from the committee's professionalism and dedication in the face of a chronic shortage of medicine and equipment.

By June 1942 it had become apparent that the cramped camp hospital would soon be inadequate. Dr. Leach negotiated to convert the nearby Santa Catalina Convent into a medical facility to meet the long-term needs of the camp. This large structure just beyond the east wall of Santo Tomás contained space suitable for hospital wards. After remodeling and installations, the old camp hospital's equipment was transferred to the new facility. From late August and for more than two years afterward, Santa Catalina Hospital provided vital medical services for the camp. Dr. Fletcher eventually became the medical director and many of the former U.S. Army and Navy nurses provided their services.[34]

For the first two years of the camp's operation, both the internees' Medical Services Committee and the Sanitation and Health Committee performed a near miracle in maintaining the overall health of the poorly fed internees living in dangerous, crowded conditions—and with no assistance from the Japanese authorities. The near miracle would not last. But while it did, it served as a testimony to the industry and resourcefulness of the still-proud Americans who organized and led the civilian captives at Santo Tomás Internment Camp in their struggle to survive the neglectful protective custody of their Japanese captors.

# CHAPTER 5

※ ※ ※

# A Miserable Routine

BY THE TIME PATTY CROFT recovered from her illness in summer 1942, much of the early drama in the first six months of Santo Tomás Internment Camp had ended. By July, life for the internees was being efficiently, although nervously, administered by the Executive Committee's seven elected officials and the various operating committees. Each of these working groups addressed a particular issue of daily life for the more than 3,000 struggling captives. As potentially life-threatening as conditions were, for the next year or so life in camp for most evolved into a kind of miserable tedium—with occasional frights and humiliations. To help cope with captivity, Patty began a hidden diary early in 1943 recording her frustrations and, more important, tracking the anticipated progress of America's return to the Philippines.

Completed in mid-July, a system of loudspeakers provided the sprawling campus a unifying medium, broadcasting information, instructions, and even music. Aside from special announcements, each evening a summary of camp news aided daily living and bestowed a sense of community. Subject to approval by the Executive Committee, these broadcasts avoided news on events outside the camp. The Music Committee arranged a schedule of light classics and popular music. Initially prohibited by Japanese authorities, jazz eventually found its way into the lineup of broadcast recordings.[1]

Sitting in groups while listening to music in the evenings improved the mood and morale of the captives. "We would listen to songs like 'Stardust' and 'Deep Purple' and some classical music," Patty recalled. "I would hang out with my girlfriends in the evenings trying to stay cool. God, it got hot there."

A grimmer aspect of daily life were the repetitious daily roll calls. Although the time of day and the frequency of roll calls depended on the mood of the Japanese authorities, Patty said she remembered these rituals as generally in the morning and sometimes in the evenings after curfew. "We would stand out in the hallway and the room monitors would call names from a roster. If a Japanese guard was present, you had to answer 'here' and bow to the guard. I never wanted to have to bow like that again."

The Japanese guards were particular about how the captives showed respect. "You were taught to bow down from the waist. The Japanese gave us lessons. If you didn't bow properly, you might get slapped. I was slapped one time when I didn't bow properly when a guard walked by me. I wasn't used to bowing from the waist. We all had to learn the hard way. It was an eye-opener." Despite the stinging humiliation, the 17-year-old held back the tears. She was careful after that.

The most important aspect of daily living for the hungry internees, naturally, were their servings of food. As the seasons passed, the captives would become more desperate over the adequacy and even the availability of these meals. But in 1942 and well into 1943, regular meals were rarely an issue, although the portion sizes and palatability were. The 48 centavos per diem provided by the Japanese military beginning in July 1942 allowed only spartan fare at best, but the internees' Finance and Supplies Committee made the most of the limited funding. Committee members were grateful to have control of the planning and necessary purchases for the meals at local markets.

As prices continued to rise in the war-torn Philippines, the captives sometimes received only two light meals per day. But this was enough to fend off starvation, and it was often supplemented by individual purchases and charitable contributions from outside the camp. The per diem for food would be increased to 62 centavos per day in June 1943 in a faltering attempt to keep pace with inflating prices.[2]

Another source of the camp's food came from the large garden planted and tended by internee volunteers. The three acres in the northeast corner of the university grounds had once served as a city dump, but with ingenuity and hard work, life-saving vegetables were wrested from this reclaimed land. Clearing the ground and laying out beds began in February 1942, and the first crop of talinum, a spinach-like plant, was harvested in April. The greens were donated to the camp's hospital patients.

In a rare show of support, Japanese officials encouraged the gardening efforts and allowed irrigation pipes and tools. Despite the blazing spring weather, the next crop of talinum was planted and harvested, providing 6,000 pounds of the leafy greens to the central kitchen in June. Another 9,500 pounds of vegetables were produced in July including a smattering of corn, eggplant and okra. By fall 1942 more than seventy men and women worked regularly in the garden.

Crop production was steady during the first four months of 1943 providing a supplement to meals served in the central kitchen and the smaller kitchens in the Annex and camp hospital. The transfer of many of the workers to the new Los Baños Internment Camp in May 1943 and a typhoon in July would combine to halt production for several months, but by the end of the year some 6,300 pounds of produce were harvested. With a decrease in purchased food supplies in 1944, the camp's gardening efforts took on increasing, even vital, importance. More than 63,000 pounds of talinum and camote (sweet potato) would supplement the skimpy food purchases and save lives in the camp's final desperate year.[3]

Between her serving-line duties in the central kitchen, Patty volunteered several hours each week in the garden. She pulled weeds, planted talinum, and harvested the edible leaves. Staying busy helped take her mind off the baleful conditions of life in a Japanese internment camp. She also took solace in playing her accordion in idle hours. As starved for entertainment as the captives, the Japanese guards often listened to her playing songs she knew by heart.

Outside one day with her accordion nearby, she was startled by a Japanese guard suddenly looming over her. With his long rifle and fixed bayonet, the soldier's abrupt presence frightened the teenager, who might have unthinkingly violated some camp rule. She stood and bowed respectfully to the guard, who gave a short, guttural command: *"Play songo!"*

Unsure of what he might want to hear, she quickly took up her accordion and broke into a rousing tango melody. From his broad smile, Patty felt relieved she had won over her audience. Music, the universal language, had spoken to the menacing guard.

Camp rumors provided ongoing entertainment for the internees and served as their chief intramural activity, especially so in the dark months following the fall of Corregidor. "Oh, the rumors going around camp," Patty recalled. "You wouldn't believe it. Incredible!"

Most of the rumors concerned the progress of the Allied war effort and the chances for an early ouster of the Japanese. The accounts were usually upbeat in 1942, which made the rumors more acceptable and improved the morale of the captives. Some of the more favored stories were that Formosa had fallen to the Allies and that fresh U.S. troop were landing in remote areas of the Philippines. Aggravating to their captors, the interned Americans maintained high spirits and refused to act like representatives of a beaten nation. None of the captives questioned whether America would win the war, it was just a question of when—and most of the rumors predicted very soon.

The upbeat tales emanating from camp likely bucked up Filipino morale and encouraged loyalty to the Americans. Thus the camp was seen by the Japanese as a dangerous hotbed of pro-American influence, and interaction was tightly restricted between the camp and Filipinos on the outside. As Japanese military setbacks accrued at Midway Atoll and Guadalcanal in 1942, the commandant warned against repetition of war news, and the Executive Committee dutifully repeated this admonition to the captives. This, of course, did little to stop the rumormongering.[4]

Late in July 1942, well-known American *Manileño* J. C. Cowper was arrested by the Japanese military police and charged with spreading false rumors. He was severely beaten and sentenced to fifteen years at hard labor. Making an example of him, the Japanese commandant ordered Cowper's sentencing broadcast over the camp's speaker system. He would die in New Bilibid Prison in Muntinlupa on the southern edge of metropolitan Manila.[5]

The Japanese dealt just as harshly with captives discovered making unauthorized contact with anyone outside the camp. One of the most prominent of the camp's internees, Fred H. Stevens, was suddenly arrested in October 1942 by two members of the Japanese secret service and taken to the infamous Fort Santiago prison in the ancient Walled City. Stevens had headed the American Coordinating Committee when the Japanese invaded Luzon.[6]

"My parents knew him well before the war," Patty said. "He was really a friend of our whole family. He was a thirty-third-degree Mason, very hard to get. My dad was a thirty-second-degree Mason. I think his wife had died, but we would visit with Fred at the Masonic Lodge in Manila." Continuing his role as a leader of the American expatriates during incarceration, Stevens developed a network to gather information and reported this news to the camp. "He could tell you exactly what was going on," Patty remembered.

His activism in camp led to his arrest by the Japanese. Under duress, he confessed only to coordinating outside funding to buy more food for the camp. He barely survived torture, starvation, and horrendous living conditions in the dungeons of old Fort Santiago before his return to Santo Tomás on Good Friday, 1943. Published in 1946 with a foreword by MacArthur, Stevens's limited-edition *Santo Tomás Internment Camp* provides an excellent eyewitness account of camp events from 1942 to 1945.[7]

The increasingly strict discipline at Santo Tomás from late summer 1942 and afterward partly resulted from the less friendly, new camp commandant, S. Kuroda, and co-Commandant Akira Kodaki. They replaced the relatively benevolent Tsurumi, who was recalled to Tokyo. A stern authoritarian, Kuroda would give the Executive Committee trouble until his replacement in 1943. A series of Japanese military police officials would command the camp in 1944 and into 1945, bringing even greater hardship.[8]

Demand for Selma Croft's nursing skills at the camp's main clinic turned her service into a full-time occupation. Patty remembered her mother frequently giving shots, but she also dressed wounds and gave advice to patients with minor aliments. Her skill at giving immunizations was renowned among internees. "Everyone always wanted to get into the line where my mother was giving shots," Patty said. "She was at the clinic most of the day."

Dropping by the clinic to chat with her busy mother, she remembered visiting with a friendly orderly named Carl Mydans, who was often seen mopping floors for Selma. Mydans had been a noted photographer for *Life* magazine covering the war when he was swept up by the Japanese. He was among a handful of fortunate American internees to be repatriated in 1942. Mydans would return to the Pacific war zone in 1944 photographing iconic scenes of MacArthur's return to the Philippines and the liberation of civilian internees.[9]

Repatriation was only a fond hope for most of those at Santo Tomás. An agreement between Japan and the Allied nations allowed for repatriation of selected internees through an exchange program, but only a few hundred from Santo Tomás ever returned home through this arrangement. In the first exchange in September 1942, Mydans and several other journalists were selected to join a little more than one hundred American and British internees from Santo Tomás. They were initially transported from Manila to Shanghai and later returned to their homelands aboard the Swedish ocean liner *Gripsholm*.[10]

Patty saw several friends from the American School repatriated through the exchange program in 1943. But this reprieve never happened for her family, nor for the overwhelming majority of internees in camp. "It took a little pull to get repatriated," she said. "Or you had to be really sick like some of them were."

In fall 1942 one of the returning women created a stir in the U.S. media by providing the names of 900 Americans interned at Santo Tomás. The anonymous repatriate left the list of internees with a friend in Los Angeles, who gave the information to the media with the caveat that the returned woman's identity would not be revealed. Forbidden to leave camp with a written list, the woman had painstakingly committed the names to memory after learning she would be repatriated. For many in the United States, this was their first news of friends or relatives missing in the Philippines since the first month of the war.[11]

A complicated aspect of camp life concerned the social interaction between men and women internees. Living quarters were segregated by sex, and husbands and wives were officially denied private relations. The Japanese prohibited any physical contact between the sexes in public, such as holding hands. From the camp's beginning the Executive Committee was ordered by the commandant to adopt rules to discourage all physical contact between the sexes. But in the end, of course, human nature would prevail, especially with several hundred married couples at Santo Tomás.[12]

While their diet and living conditions were adequate in 1942 and most of 1943, Patty and her teenage girlfriends quite naturally eyed some of the young men in camp, although social contact was restricted. Returning to the serving line after her recovery from dysentery, the 17-year-old began furtive attempts to socialize with a new internee who had caught her eye.

"I was standing outside one day with some girlfriends when this truck came in," she said. "There were a bunch of new internees standing in the truck, and I saw one of them with blond hair that really stood out. I told my friends that he looked like Sterling Hayden, the [1930s] movie star. 'He's mine,' I told them. 'You can have all the rest of them.'"

The handsome captive came through her food line for the next two weeks, and Patty furtively added a little extra to his servings and attempted to flirt with him. Then one Sunday morning, one of her coworkers approached with some news. "She said to me, 'Guess who said mass this morning at the Catholic church,'" Patty recalled. "I asked who, and she said, *'Your Sterling Hayden!'* Boy, after that he got cut off from any extra food from me."

By fall 1942, food prices in Manila had dramatically increased due to the war, greatly concerning the Executive Committee. The 48 centavos per day allotted for each internee would be stretched to the maximum. Sugar prices had doubled by November, so thereafter this would be a luxury for the camp. Patty's eighteenth birthday on November 25 passed without a cake to celebrate it. On this milestone birthday, she thought of how different her angst-ridden captivity in a Japanese internment camp was compared to what she had planned a year earlier—attending college in California and working toward a nursing degree.[13]

In contrast with her dull birthday, just two days later on the fourth Thursday of November, the captives celebrated the Thanksgiving holiday about as well as could be managed in a prison camp. The internees were treated to a real turkey dinner that day. Somehow extra funds had been scraped together to purchase these birds at the local market. The day's festivities were topped off with a football game dubbed the Talinum Bowl. In the hard years ahead, Thanksgiving 1942 would be warmly remembered by the increasingly hungry internees.[14]

The extra effort that went into this Thanksgiving celebration was probably as much a show of patriotism as a display of gratitude to the Almighty. As the newly embattled America girded for the years of struggle ahead, in late December 1941 Congress had passed a joint resolution officially declaring the fourth Thursday of November as Thanksgiving Day. This ended years of confusion and various state celebrations on different dates. The struggling internees at Santo Tomás likely intended to make a point of celebrating this now-officially designated U.S. holiday despite their captivity by an enemy nation. Observing this day both connected them to their homeland and emphasized their allegiance.

As Christmas and the end of 1942 neared, most of the internees were astounded that they had not yet been liberated. They were still struggling to adjust to the reality of their situation. The Executive Committee recognized that the holiday season might be especially depressing for the captives and called for an all-out effort to boost morale.

Several weeks before Christmas, a special committee solicited hundreds of internees to make dolls, wooden toys, and a variety of Christmas novelties for the children of the camp. More than 1,400 of these handmade gifts were distributed to the excited children on Christmas afternoon under a decorated Baguio pine tree near the Annex. Other standing committees put together a program of various holiday entertainments, including the first movie shown at the camp, "The Feminine Touch," a 1941 Hollywood production starring Rosalind Russell, Don Ameche and Kay Francis. The audience first had to endure a Japanese propaganda film, but probably considered it a small price to pay for the opportunity to view the U.S.-made movie with its scenes of an America they could only dream of.[15]

The package-line set a record for deliveries on Christmas Day, with some 6,000 deliveries of gifts, roast turkeys, and whole-roasted pigs *lechon*-style (spit roasted). Much of this fare was purchased by captives who still had access to money, and some was sent as gifts from friendly Filipinos in Manila. Many skipped the regular meal at the central kitchen, feasting instead on the delicacies brought into camp. Included in these holiday treats were Red Cross kits from South Africa that had arrived in Manila just before Christmas. The kits included canned goods, condensed milk, tomatoes, cheese, pudding, chocolate cake and a piece of soap. In addition, each internee was given four eight-ounce cans of corned beef from the Red Cross shipment.[16]

Patty said she remembered getting some of the delicacies from a partial kit that Christmas, and she savored the rich treats. "But I sure didn't get any roast pig or anything like that," she said. "They did let us go to church services on Christmas Day at the Catholic church next to the camp. And I remember making my mother a little pincushion heart with her name embroidered on it. It had a little lace around it that I got from somebody. It turned out cute."

Christmas 1942 at Santo Tomás was as good as could be expected under the circumstances, another bright spot to be remembered in the harder times ahead. In contrast, New Year's Eve passed with little fanfare. The thought of beginning another year in captivity may have been just too depressing for the camp. On December 31, lights went out as usual at 10:30 in the captives' quarters. At midnight a solitary siren from downtown could be heard. Only a few of the internees stayed up to see the new year begin. Patty and a few of her friends were among those.[17]

Probably as a means of recording her progress toward a life outside

Santo Tomás Internment Camp, the 18-year-old began a diary with the first entry on January 1, 1943. Written personal accounts of life in captivity were strictly forbidden by Japanese authorities, so she was taking a great risk. She began taking stenography classes in camp at the time, so by February most of her nearly daily entries were in Gregg shorthand—the most popular form of handwritten stenography in the first half of the twentieth century. If her diary were discovered by the Japanese, the entries in shorthand might have given her some protection. Still, this blatant defiance of Japanese policy put her at risk of death—a risk she was willing to take to help cope with the endless grind of captivity.

She still believed America was coming soon to rescue her and her fellow inmates, yet the wait seemed unbearable. As miserable a condition as her life had devolved into by early 1943, she had no way of knowing how long this would last or that it would turn into a desperate struggle to survive. "I think I would have shot myself," she later said, "if I had known that I still had more than two years left in internment."

Her first-year diary entries in 1943 usually focused on the banal wretchedness of everyday life as a captive and a daily summary of Allied progress in the war. Some of the war news received in camp was reliable, but of course this was interspersed with the ever-constant rumors, usually sensational, of impending rescue or dramatic Allied victories. With the camp rumors generally unreliable, Patty and her mother depended on news from the American Jesuit priest known throughout Santo Tomás as Father Hurley. The interned priest had solid news sources from the outside, some transcribed from the Spanish newspaper *La Vanguardia*. With Spain maintaining neutrality during the war, the Japanese allowed circulation of this newspaper in Manila. Although radios were banned in camp, typed summaries of radio broadcasts from northern California's KGEI radio station were also smuggled into camp. Patty's diary makes several references to this source.[18]

Understanding that her liberation rested on American victories, the teenager's nearly daily entries were filled with news of Allied progress in both the European and Pacific theaters. Like many of the internees, Patty understood that military efforts in the Pacific would be dependent on success against Germany in Europe. In an entry on Friday, January 8, 1943, she celebrated Allied victories in both theaters: "Germans retreating on all fronts in Russia....9 or 10 ships sunk near Solomon Islands." But her frustration with the daily drudgery of life in an internment camp is obvious.

"Same old routine!" begins a diary entry that same week. "Am I getting sick of it!! Very little news. People just haven't had any time to think up any rumors."[19]

Patty's January 8 diary reference to the Solomon Islands highlights one of the few bright spots in the Allied efforts in the southwest Pacific in early 1943. The August 1942 landing of U.S. Marines on the island of Guadalcanal in the Solomons marked the first U.S. land offensive of the war against the Japanese empire. The decision by the Japanese to begin withdrawing troops from the island in December put them on the defensive and gave the U.S. a base of operations to begin the long slog northward and the eventual return to the Philippines. Patty and her fellow captives now pinned all their hopes on MacArthur's pledge to return to the Philippines.

GENERAL MACARTHUR TOOK HIS FIRST STEP toward fulfilling his pledge in July 1942 when he moved his Melbourne headquarters northward to Brisbane, Australia, some 1,200 miles closer to the war front, and closer to the Philippines. On the eastern coast of Australia, Brisbane was still far southeast of Japanese attacks along the northern coast, but MacArthur's move was intended to strengthen Australian morale. Top Australian commanders at the time were in favor of ceding territory north of Brisbane to the Japanese and concentrating their forces in southern Australia in a passive defense of the country. MacArthur vehemently opposed this defensive strategy, and relocating his command staff closer to the front underscored his calls for offensive action.[20]

As U.S. Marines struggled in the jungles of Guadalcanal and Tulagi in the eastern Solomons in late August, additional Japanese forces moved southward with an amphibious assault on Port Moresby in southeastern Papua New Guinea, only a few hundred miles from the northern tip of Australia. Anticipating this action, MacArthur and the Seventh Australian Division were ready. In a ferocious ten-day battle, the Japanese force was destroyed marking the first time Japanese troops were forced to retreat after establishing a beachhead.

Undeterred, enemy forces regrouped to take Port Moresby from the north by marching over the formidable Owen Stanley Range separating southern Papua from the northern coastline. Committed to defense of the port city, MacArthur made a fateful decision. "We'll defend Australia in New Guinea," he declared to his staff. In a tour de force of a press conference in Brisbane, the general outlined his plans emphasizing that Australia would be saved in Papua New Guinea. "We must attack, attack, attack!" he told a spellbound group of journalists.[21]

With the meager Allied forces at his command, MacArthur's own staff was as astonished at this strategy as the Australian high command. The general had concluded that if the Japanese established an army in southern New Guinea, they could easily land in force in northern Australia. The Allies had too few troops and weapons to stop an enemy force from sweeping across the Australian plains. Thus, he maintained, the Japanese must be stopped in New Guinea. This offensive strategy also surprised the enemy.

After the war, a senior staff officer of the Japanese Imperial Fleet at Rabaul—the strategic New Britain port and enemy bastion between the Solomons and New Guinea—testified that the Japanese commanders reasoned that MacArthur's troop shortage would keep him on the defensive in Australia. "The Japanese did not think that General MacArthur would establish himself in New Guinea and defend Australia from that position," Captain Toshikazu Ohmae said. "They also did not believe he would be able to use New Guinea as a base for offensive operations against them." MacArthur proved them wrong on both counts.[22]

After considerable squabbling between MacArthur and U.S. Navy commanders, the southwestern Pacific offensive, code-named Watchtower, was finally agreed on. The first phase of this strategy was the establishment of air bases on Guadalcanal and Tulagi in the eastern Solomons, underway by U.S. Marines by late summer 1942. Airfields on these islands would protect the buildup of troops and supplies flowing from the United States to Australia. The second phase would be MacArthur's securing Port Moresby as a base of operation in the region and expelling the Japanese from Papua. The final phase entailed amphibious landings from Papua onto New Britain and the destruction of the strategic Japanese stronghold at Rabaul. MacArthur would have responsibility for the second and third of these offensive thrusts.

As MacArthur's new air force chief, 52-year-old Lt. Gen. George C. Kenney would provide invaluable support to MacArthur's offensive in Papua and further advances thereafter in the southwest Pacific theater. Kenney's first task would be transporting the troops and supplies over the six hundred miles from the Australian coastline across the Coral Sea to reinforce Port Moresby. The air commander told MacArthur he could rapidly transport 26,000 troops with his C-47 air transports to the seaport and supply them with all the supplies and equipment necessary to drive the Japanese from Papua. "Give me five days and I'll ship the whole damn U.S. Army to New Guinea by air," he boasted. Although he had often been at odds with air corps leaders, MacArthur was won over by the pugnacious Kenney and affectionately nicknamed him "Buccaneer."[23]

By October, the Japanese attack on Port Moresby had been repelled, thanks to Kenney's air transports and a tenacious effort by mostly Australian troops. MacArthur ordered an offensive thrust to the north coast of Papua and an advance along the north coast to secure the rest of Papua in the coming year. In November 1942, MacArthur moved his advance base from Brisbane to Port Moresby, another 1,500 miles closer to the Philippines. In a theatrical appeal to avenge the U.S. humiliation on Luzon, the general conjured up the ghost of Corregidor: "[It] symbolizes within itself that priceless, deathless thing, the honor of a nation," he stated. "Until we lift our flag from its dust, we stand unredeemed before mankind....There lies our Holy Grail."[24]

Moving across Papua to the northern coastline, Allied forces stalled before the stubborn Japanese garrison at the port city of Buna. To break the stalemate, MacArthur ordered to the front two of his senior officers, Lt. Gen. Robert L. Eichelberger and his chief of staff Clovis E. Byers. "If you don't take Buna," he told Eichelberger with all seriousness, "I want to hear that you and Byers are buried there." By December 1942, after bitter fighting and heavy Allied casualties, Buna and the nearby coastal village of Gona fell to Allied troops. The Japanese threat to Australia had ended.[25]

By 1943, the grand strategy for Allied efforts in the Pacific emerged. The U.S. Navy would move across the central Pacific using marines to seize key islands, while MacArthur would continue northwestward along the slanting northern coastline of Papua New Guinea. From the Papuan coast, the general would coordinate the conquest of the island of New Britain and its stronghold at Rabaul, northeast of Papua. MacArthur would then continue to direct his forces northwestward along the lengthy New Guinea coastline. The Allied land and sea offensives would converge on the Philippines. A decision would then be made—although it was already made in MacArthur's thinking—whether to retake all of the American commonwealth or leapfrog to Formosa, closer to the Japanese homeland.

Hand in hand with this strategy, the Allies were perfecting new means of warfare. MacArthur recognized these innovations, and the heavy use of his air force bombers was one of these. The commander began to see these warplanes as a more mobile extension of artillery firepower. He also recognized the war in the vast Pacific as a struggle to supply the far-flung outposts at the front and saw his air force as invaluable in the protection of his supply lines and the destruction of the enemy's. "Victory," he said, "depends on the advancement of the bomber line." He ensured that newly constructed airfields for Kenney's bombers accompanied the progress of his ground troops. His warplanes would not only protect his supplies and diminish the enemy's, but also serve as a striking force when needed in battle.[26]

Ironically, another innovation in the Allied efforts developed from a collaboration between Admiral William F. "Bull" Halsey and MacArthur, who, predictably, had often quarreled with U.S. naval commanders. Halsey may have been the first to advocate bypassing certain enemy strongholds and leaving them behind "to wither on the vine" without resupply or purpose. But MacArthur soon endorsed and adopted this advancement in Pacific war fighting. This "island hopping," or "leapfrogging" as MacArthur preferred to call it, was dramatically illustrated by Halsey's recommendation to bypass the Japanese fortress at Rabaul.

With the ferocious effort required to take Buna fresh on MacArthur's mind, he told his staff that taking all the Japanese strongholds in the southwest Pacific in a step-by-step offensive would delay the reconquest of the Philippines by ten years and cost untold lives. "I don't see how we can take these strongpoints with our limited forces," he said proposing the new approach at a war council of Allied commanders in the Pacific. "Well, let's just say we don't take them....[We] incapacitate them."[27]

After the war, MacArthur elaborated on this island-hopping strategy, describing it as "the adaptation of modern instrumentalities of war to a concept as ancient as war itself...the classic strategy of envelopment." In fact, the Japanese had applied this same strategy when they had blockaded and temporarily bypassed the Philippines in the early months of the war, moving southward to seize the resource-rich islands of the Dutch East Indies. It proved an effective strategy for both sides, but the Allies would ultimately ride this approach to victory in the Pacific, reducing to irrelevance many heavily manned and fortified Japanese strongholds—and saving countless lives on both sides.[28]

The highest-level Allied war conferences of 1943 provided little to encourage the thousands of interned American expatriates in the Philippines. These sessions maintained the focus on defeating Germany first, and the majority of troops and supplies from America would be so directed. Whether the Philippines would be bypassed by advancing U.S. troops was yet to be resolved in Washington. But not in the mind of General Douglas MacArthur. His rhetoric continued to focus on the Philippines as the primary objective in the larger goal of defeating Japan. Although many of the American internees at Santo Tomás felt deserted by MacArthur when he fled Corregidor early in 1942, as 1943 drew to a close they still had a highly influential friend at the head of the Allied efforts in the Pacific. Whether that friendship would bring relief in time to save these captives was still an open question.

PATTY CROFT'S DIARY ENTRIES early in 1943 noted her first anniversary at Santo Tomás on January 6 and celebrated the distribution of additional goods from the British and Canadian Red Cross shipments in December. "Comfort kits were distributed," she wrote. "Imagine—a candy bar, sugar, butter, cheese, etc." It would be hard to overestimate how welcome these treats would be for internees like Patty with their usual bland, skimpy diet bolstered with sweet potato and the spinach-like talinum. A few days later on January 10, she noted another dietary triumph when a friend of her family in Manila sent a shipment of steaks and chicken. "Did it taste good!!" the hungry captive wrote in an understatement.

The welcomed food had been sent by Hilton Carson, a 66-year-old widower hospitalized in Manila. Carson and his wife had been friends of the Croft family in pre-war Manila. "Hilton and his wife always liked me as a girl," Patty recalled. "They never had any children of their own. I remember them paying my way to summer camp in Baguio one year."

Because of his illness, Carson had not been interned with the other American *Manileños* at the time of Japanese occupation. Selma Croft had secured passes from the commandant's office on several occasions in 1942 to leave camp and provide aid to the hospitalized Carson. By January 1943 he was deemed well enough to be discharged from the hospital and sent to Santo Tomás. Carson had managed to bring some of his money with him at internment, and his generosity would provide much-needed aid to Patty and her penniless family.

"Uncle Hilton [Carson] came in at eight. What a surprise!!" Patty's diary entry recorded on January 11. "Cigarettes were issued at roll call," she continued. "I drew a package of Old Gold. Mother got Sweet Corporal [Caporal]." Neither Patty nor her mother smoked, but the valuable cigarettes could be sold or traded with other internees growing increasingly desperate for tobacco products.

Carson's internment soon contributed to an upgrade in quality of life for Patty and her family with the new arrival's funding of the construction of a "shanty," one of the more than 600 one-room *nipa* shacks with *sawali* walls crowded around the buildings of Santo Tomás. These huts allowed residents a respite from the noisy, congested living quarters in the buildings. Patty, her mom and brother spent much of their free time during the day and evenings of 1943 and 1944 in the privacy of Carson's hut. "It was a nice little shanty," she recalled. "At first no one was allowed to spend the night in the shanties, but later on the men could. Women were not allowed to sleep in them at night. It was a good way to get away from all the people in the rooms during the day."

In pre-war Manila, shanties like these were associated with poverty and squalor, but in the upside-down world of wartime internment, shacks like Carson's symbolized aristocracy. Residents could lounge in privacy, read books, or prepare their own meals with foods obtained through the package-line. The various enclaves of huts were given descriptive names like Glamourville, Froggy Bottom, Jungletown and Garden Court. The communities of shacks elected mayors to coordinate policies and enforce camp rules.

Upsetting to the Japanese authorities, the numerous shanties posed a problem for the enforcement of the campus-wide prohibition on sexual relations among the internees. The same month Carson's shack was built near the Education Building, Japanese officials sentenced four male internees to thirty days in jail for impregnating their wives. As more internees were brought in and conditions became even more crowded early in 1944, Japanese authorities allowed married couples to live full-time in the shanties. As nature would have it, even in the harsh, underfed conditions of camp life, by late summer 1944 some 140 captives would be pregnant. For most of the parents-to-be, these pregnancies were not seen as joyful occasions. The care of these women and the nurturing of these stressed newborns in the camp's life-threatening final stages would become heartrending.[29]

The four husbands jailed in January 1943 served their thirty-day sentences in the new detention center at the southwest end of the campus. Resembling a monkey cage, the new 11-by-26-foot jail would house a steady flow of prisoners in the camp's final two years. Besides fathers-to-be, many of the incarcerated were miscreants sentenced by the internees'

Discipline Committee for drunkenness or theft. Some of the captives became quite innovative at manufacturing alcoholic beverages to relieve the boredom and stress of camp life. Patty said she rarely saw a drunken internee in the camp, but she knew they were around and often heard stories about them. "Some of the men fermented coconuts and pineapples and stuff," she said. "This was always done outside in the shanties."[30]

The strengthened attempt to prevent sexual relations between married couples represented just one aspect of Commandant Kuroda's hardening attitude toward the captives early in 1943. Other punitive measures soon followed including Kuroda's cancellation of the election of new members to the Executive Committee in January. The commandant appeared upset that his personal choice, incumbent chairman Carroll Grinnell, received too few votes in the primary to qualify for the final election. The commandant's edict ending democratic elections of key committee members was read over the camp loudspeakers on January 19: "[T]he holding of an election in this camp at this time is not in accordance with our wishes and it is hereby ordered that the election be suspended indefinitely." The Japanese-favored Grinnell would thus continue to head the Executive Committee by decree of the commandant.[31]

Grinnell had served ably as an administrator and was obviously preferred by the Japanese, probably owing to his speaking Japanese and familiarity with their customs. Yet his fellow internees, as democracy-minded Americans are wont to do, decided he had served long enough as committee chairman. The Japanese commandant's suppression of the democratic process in camp was bitterly resented by the captives, a Western reaction likely perplexing to the authoritarian Kuroda. His heavy-handed action boded ill for the captives in the many months ahead as their privileges continued to shrink.

Immediately following this incident, Kuroda ended the camp newsletter. Started in early 1942 as *Internews*, the publication's name had been changed to *STIC-Gazette* later in the year but continued to provide a unifying medium with its announcements and articles about everyday life in camp. The commandant decreed that all news and announcements for the camp would be broadcast over the loudspeakers. The captives viewed this mid-January directive as punishment for the final newsletter's printing of the vote tallies showing Grinnell's failure to be renominated as chairman.[32]

On January 30, Patty's diary entry recognized President Roosevelt's sixty-first birthday, a remembrance some internees likely made to connect

Pioneer aviator Alfred J. Croft left his English homeland before World War I to seek opportunities in America's burgeoning aviation industry. He came to the Philippines after World War I to help develop an air service in the U.S. territory, where he soon married nurse Selma M. Bergstrom and was honored by Governor-General Leonard Wood for saving an American flag from a fire at the famed Manila Carnival. *Photo courtesy of Patty Kelly Stevens*

The second of Alfred and Selma Croft's three children, Patty Gene Croft was born in Honolulu but came to Manila with her parents and older brother soon after her first birthday. She visited the States with her family about every five years while growing up but became so accustomed to living in the Philippines that she felt like a foreign visitor on her trips to America. *Photo courtesy of Patty Kelly Stevens*

Living in the Santa Mesa district of Manila in the 1930s, the Crofts were a part of the several thousand U.S. expatriates living in and around the cosmopolitan tropical city. From left, William, Selma, Patty, Alfred and Al Jr. *Photo courtesy of Patty Kelly Stevens*

The Polo Club, Elks Club, and Army and Navy Club (above) were centers of social life for Americans in 1930s Manila. *Photo from National Archives*

Renamed Pedro Gil Street in 1965, Calle Herran meandered through pre-war Manila and typified the wide, shaded streets in the tropical city called the Pearl of the Orient. *Photo from National Archives*

Dressed in the white suits of Manila businessmen, Maj. Gen. Douglas MacArthur and his chief aide, Maj. Dwight Eisenhower, came to the Philippines in 1935 to bolster Philippine defenses against a Japanese invasion. *Photo from National Archives*

This luncheon in Manila in fall 1939 was given by Philippine President Manuel Quezon (center right) to honor departing Lt. Col. Dwight Eisenhower and his wife, Mamie. MacArthur and Eisenhower are smiling in the photo, but their long relationship had been difficult for the general's aide, who asked his commanding officer for a transfer when war began in Europe. *Photo from National Archives*

Aerial view of the internment camp at Santo Tomás University in the heart of Manila. A high wall surrounded the campus making escape difficult. *Photo courtesy of Manila Nostalgia website*

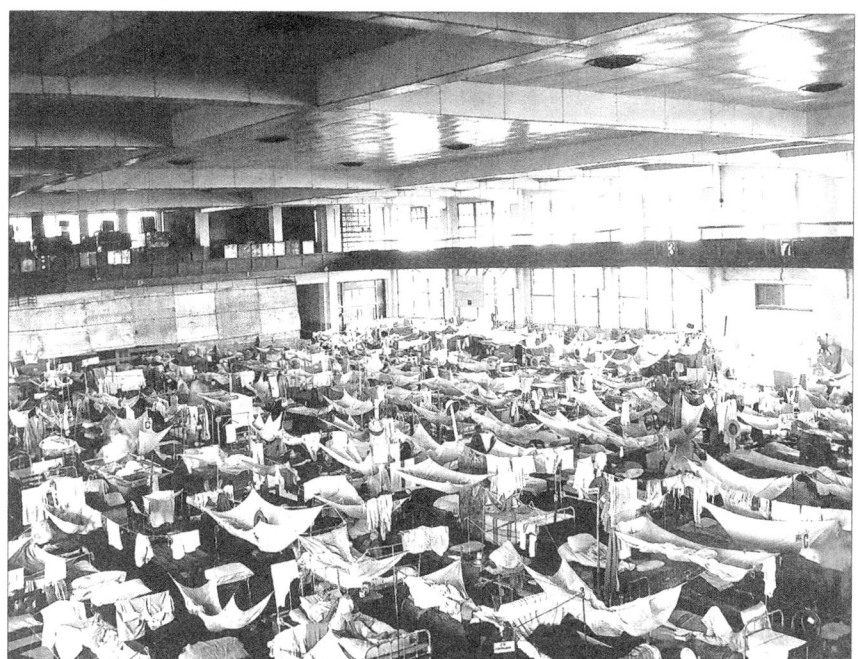

Civilian internees were crowded into the Santo Tomás University gymnasium (above) and in similar fashion in other buildings on campus. The small bed space for the captives was also used to store their meager personal belongings. *Photo from National Archives*

Many of the better-off captives at Santo Tomás constructed shacks around the campus with *sawali* siding and *nipa* roofs to escape the tight quarters in the various buildings. Note in the background the high wall surrounding the campus. *Photo from National Archives*

To firm up plans for the final stages of the war in the Pacific, MacArthur met with President Roosevelt, Admiral William Leahy, and Admiral Chester Nimitz (with map pointer) on a July evening in 1944 in Honolulu. MacArthur argued strongly for a landing on Luzon to liberate Manila, but Nimitz proposed bypassing the northern Philippines. *Photo from National Archives*

With their khaki trousers still wet from wading the surf onto the beach at Leyte, MacArthur (third from left with trademark corncob pipe) and his entourage proceed inland just behind the troops. *Photo from National Archives*

This magnificent photo (also on book cover) captures the exuberance of newly liberated captives at Santo Tomás Internment Camp as they unfurl the Stars and Stripes for the first time after three years of captivity. Advance elements of the First Cavalry Division had stormed the camp two days earlier on Feb. 3, 1945, but the celebration was delayed pending the surrender of holdout Japanese guards in one of the buildings. *Photo from National Archives*

Starved Santo Tomás captives show the effects of malnutrition from the months before their liberation in February 1945. *Photo courtesy of Manila Nostalgia website*

Selma Croft (sitting on amtrac below standing soldier at right) is evacuated Feb. 23, 1945, with other freed Los Baños captives in the Water Buffalo amtracs of the 672nd Amphibian Tractor Battalion. *Photo courtesy of Manila Nostalgia website*

Eleventh Airborne commander Maj. General Joseph Swing (in jeep on left) and Eighth Army commander Lt. Gen. Robert Eichelberger confer just outside Manila in early 1945. *Photo from National Archives*

Liberated captives from Los Baños disembark amtracs after their dramatic rescue on Feb. 23, 1945, by troopers from the 511 Parachute Infantry Regiment, Eleventh Airborne Division. *Photo from National Archives*

After their rescue from Los Baños, Bertha Palmer and her sons, John and Ronald, eat their first full meal in many months the evening of Feb. 23, 1945, at their temporary quarters at New Bilibid Prison. *Photo from National Archives*

Band members of the U.S. 37th Infantry Division entertain convalescing former captives at Santo Tomás several weeks after the camp's liberation. *Photo from National Archives*

General MacArthur (center) accompanies a 37th Infantry Division patrol to the Manila Hotel, where he had lived on the top-floor penthouse before the war. Before he could retrieve his personal items, the penthouse was set ablaze by retreating Japanese troops. *Photo from National Archives*

The center of Manila was gutted before Japanese troops were finally expelled in March 1945. This aerial photo looks southwesterly across the Pasig River with downed Santa Cruz Bridge in center. *Photo from National Archives*

Former internees from Santo Tomás and Los Baños board a California-bound transport docked at a Manila pier in April 1945. *Photo from National Archives*

Patty Croft and Paul Kelly were married in Oklahoma City on Feb. 24, 1946, one year and a day after her liberation from Los Baños with 2,145 other captive civilians. Recently discharged from the U.S. Army, Paul wore his uniform as a lieutenant in the First Cavalry Division, units of which had liberated the internment camp at Santo Tomás. *Photo courtesy of Patty Kelly Stevens*

with an America now far removed, but still a homeland to which they longed to return. "Let's hope we can go to his Birthday Ball next year!!!!" the 18-year-old added hopefully. An entry on February 3 spoke to the increasing scarcity of personal items in camp. "No more soap can be gotten from the camp supply house," she groused. "This morning I stood in line for a small cake of cheap yellow soap which cost forty centavos. What a price!!"

An early-February diary entry revealed some of the tension doubtless building among the internees in the tedious, crowded conditions. Working mostly full-time in the camp clinic and feeling the stress of trying to protect her two children, Selma Croft's short temper would have been understandable. "Mother is in the doghouse," Patty wrote. "Billy and I walked out on her after she cracked my elbow with a glass cup which broke and cut me. Always something for excitement!"[33]

The first official death of an internee on the Santo Tomás campus occurred on February 20 with the passing of Elizabeth G. Pond in the camp hospital. Nearly 100 internees had died before Pond's death, but they had died after being discharged to hospitals or care outside the camp. The purported death of a recently discharged internee followed just two days later, one closer to Patty and her family. Her diary entry for February 23 reported on a rumor later disproved: "Roy Bennett died."[34]

The 54-year-old Bennett had been an editor at the *Manila Daily Bulletin* before the war and had called Selma Croft in the early morning hours of December 8 to break the frightening news of the Japanese attack on Pearl Harbor. He had also been the family friend who had suggested the name Chiquita for Patty's new wire-haired terrier on the Crofts's return voyage to Manila early in 1936. Recording his rumored death, the 18-year-old remembered that happier time aboard ship just seven years earlier—but it felt like a far distant world and long, long ago.

Patty's 1943 diary entries noted many significant American holidays, even listing February 22 as Washington's birthday and March 17 as Saint Patrick's Day. These connections to life in the United States continued to take on new significance to her and other internees. Movie night on April 24 received a lengthy recitation in her diary, no doubt because of the film's transporting her and the other Americans in the audience back to a distant land they now pined for. The moviegoers were once again forced to watch a Japanese propaganda film before the feature, she complained. The featured movie was a comic satire released by Hollywood in 1941. "The main picture...was 'Sullivan's Travels,'" she wrote, "with Veronica Lake and Joel McRae. It sure was wonderful!"[35]

After several sentences on May 5 updating Allied progress both in Europe and the Pacific, she ended the day's news roundup with a terse statement: "Rumor is that we're going to Los Baños." As events unfolded, this would be more than just speculation, and it would have dire, potentially fatal, implications for Patty and other internees. Named after the thermal springs at the base of Mount Makiling, the small, bucolic town of Los Baños hosted an agricultural college about thirty miles south of downtown Manila.[36]

Sunday evening, May 7, a statement by co-Commandant Kodaki, announced the proposed new internment camp at Los Baños over the camp loudspeakers—repeated to ensure the message was understood by all. The announcement explained that an expansive internment camp at Los Baños was to replace the facility at Santo Tomás. A larger facility was needed to house the 2,000 "enemy nationals" in Manila not presently interned, many of mixed ethnicity. Calling the new location an "ideal health resort" with fresh air and access to fresh meat and vegetables, Kodaki said much of their food could be cultivated by the internees. "In carrying out the above plan," the commandant continued, "the first group of eight hundred men to be selected from the present internees, which will constitute the core for the new camp, will be dispatched to Los Baños on the fourteenth of this month."[37]

The news caused an uproar among the internees. Life was far from ideal at Santo Tomás, but much had been accomplished by the captives to make daily life grudgingly tolerable. Now the devil they knew at Santo Tomás was to be traded for the devil they didn't know at Los Baños. And the move to a distant location outside cosmopolitan Manila would only further isolate the internees from America and the international community. The captives partially, and unfairly, blamed the Executive Committee for failing to prevent this action, and they singly criticized the increasingly unpopular Chairman Grinnell, who many suspected knew well in advance of the impending relocation.[38]

"We didn't want to go," Patty said. "No one knew much about this area around Los Baños. There was fear of the unknown, and we at least had a building to sleep in at Santo Tomás. But, of course, what could we do about it?"

On May 10 a special committee of three internees accompanied the

newly appointed Los Baños Internment Camp commandant, a Lieutenant Colonel Naruzawa of the religious section of the Japanese military, to
inspect the proposed site. Returning that evening, the internee inspectors
reported to the Executive Committee their apprehensions about the unsuit-
ability of this location. Their biggest concern was the inadequacy of the
water supply, but they also worried about a recent outbreak of malaria in
the area. They urged a postponement of any large groups to the site until
better planning and preparation were completed.[39]

A protest letter was sent to the Santo Tomás commandant urging this
delay. It was rebuffed. The able-bodied transferees, made up of volunteers
and conscripts, prepared to leave as required on the morning of May 14.
After an early breakfast, the 786 male and twelve female captives lined up
for roll call before leaving. Patty noted the event in her diary entry later
that day: "At 5:00 three alarm clocks all went off. We were allowed to go
out to the shanties at 5:30 a.m. At 5:30 they played the Bugle Call Rag.
What swing! There were 20 trucks. It took two loads to take them out.
Twelve navy nurses left with them. When they were leaving, they played
'Anchors Away' [sic]."[40]

The eighteen-year-old seemed to enjoy the spectacle, the catchy marching song of the U.S. Navy, and especially the uplifting "Bugle Call Rag"—
whose jazzy rendition had been popularized in the States by Benny Good-
man and Glenn Miller. A more somber song blaring over the camp loudspeakers that May morning was "Onward Christian Soldiers," played as
the trucks with the 798 captive pioneers departed for Manila's Tutuban
station for the train ride to Los Baños.[41]

With internees worried about more transfers to Los Baños, on July 30
the Executive Committee sent a letter of protest to the director general
of the Japanese Military Administration in the Philippines. The message
stressed concern over the health of those forced to relocate to the new
camp and requested a postponement of future transfers until minimum living conditions could be ensured. Following a two-week visit to Los Baños
by Commandant Kodaki in August, it was announced that Santo Tomás
would be kept open and the population of Los Baños would be capped at
3,000. The Santo Tomás captives breathed an uneasy sigh of relief, and
their chief concern returned to food, their constant worry.[42]

The menu in the main kitchen for the month of June provided meager
yet adequate nutrition for the ever-thinning captives. Daily fare included
a ladle of cornmeal mush with a tea substitute for breakfast; a plate of

mongo beans for lunch; and dinner of a vegetable and beef stew, a banana, and a cup of tea substitute. A sparse diet, but life sustaining—if it could be maintained. "The cornmeal mush was much like a cereal," Patty remembered. "The tea sure wasn't Lipton's. The three meals a day was sometimes just two. Soon after this it was always just two."[43]

With the announcement by Japanese authorities of another repatriation scheduled for September, the Executive Committee began wrangling with the issue of which internees in camp should be recommended for exchange and a return to their countries. Ordered by the Japanese to operate in secrecy, internee leaders began preparing a list of recommended repatriates but were bedeviled by accusations of bias and insider dealing. At any rate, only 127 mostly American captives from Santo Tomás ultimately boarded the *Teia Maru* in September. They were to be joined by twenty-four members of the American consular staff for the voyage to Goa on the southwestern coast of India, where they would transfer to an exchange ship.[44]

In a speech to the assembled internees at a farewell gathering, Commandant Kodaki said that the Executive Committee had no role in the selection of the returnees and that it was the captives' own governments that determined the final list. Kodaki also used the occasion to warn those departing to "be careful to take no action or say anything that might antagonize the interests of those who remain behind"—an unveiled threat by the Japanese that group punishment of the captives might result if conditions at Santo Tomás were reported in an unfavorable light.[45]

Those departing were forbidden to take any written accounts or papers with them, but several memorized a report by the Executive Committee on the harsh conditions at Santo Tomás. This description of the "serious problems" faced by the internees included the following: "(1) Food increasingly difficult, diets lack meat, sugar, fats, vitamins. (2) Many medical supplies including specifics and anaesthetics (sic) nearly exhausted, unobtainable, no medical relief shipments received. (3) Medical staff advises internees health deteriorating, vitality diminishing, physical nervous strain due to congestion, difficult living conditions undermining general health...." The memorized text was to be reported to the U.S. government, and various American officials were likely informed.[46]

Sent along on the *Teia Maru* were several thousand written messages from the internees to relatives or friends in their home countries. For the first time since their capture nearly two years earlier, the internees were allowed to send correspondence outside the Philippines. They were well aware that the contents would be carefully censored by the Japanese. Still, it must have greatly relieved many in America and elsewhere to receive word that a beloved relative or friend was still alive.[47]

Patty never held much hope that she or her family members would be selected for the September repatriation. She knew some who made the list for the exchange ship, and she viewed their selection as largely a result of personal or political connections. "It took *pull* to get repatriated," she explained. "The father of one of the American School students I knew had taught a Japanese officer in Tokyo before the war. He got on the ship. My family just didn't have any pull."

She was not even sure her short letter made the voyage on the *Teia Maru*. "I remember writing to my aunt in California. I never knew if she received it, but I turned it in to be sent. I'd be surprised if she got it. We did get one message from my aunt after that, but I can't remember what it said. They were limited by the number of words they could write, just like we were."

As if the captives didn't have enough trouble in the confines of camp, in mid-November a tremendous typhoon upended their lives. Twenty-seven inches of rain inundated Santo Tomás over four days, and the shanties not blown down by the powerful winds soon flooded. "We've gone through hell for the last five days," Patty noted in her November 19 diary entry. She wrote of wading through waist-deep water and the camp's going without electricity, gas or piped water for several days. Yet her youthful spirit shines through in this otherwise fraught entry. At the height of the typhoon, she and some friends decided to venture outside the Main Building to defy the storm's fury. "At three o'clock [in the morning] Eileen, Betty and I took a walk around the building. It was more fun!! Men and children were being brought in from their shacks & they had no place to sleep."[48]

On December 3, twenty-seven of the men sent to Los Baños Internment Camp in May were returned to Santo Tomás. They gave the first detailed reports of conditions at the new camp, confirming the earlier concerns of the Executive Committee that much work lay ahead preparing this facility for additional occupancy. The *nipa-sawali*, wooden-framed barracks being constructed were flimsy, and four of them had been wrecked by the November typhoon. The returnees reported more barracks were to be constructed and the Japanese at Los Baños had indicated additional transfers from Santo Tomás were planned.[49]

Patty's younger brother, now sixteen, volunteered for a second group transfer to the growing new camp south of Manila. "Bill wanted to go to Los Baños," she remembered. "Some of his younger friends from the Education Building rooms were going. They were told it was a better environment and that the food was better. My mother tried to talk him out of it, but he went anyway. She didn't want any of us to go to Los Baños at that time."

This second group of internees were transferred on December 10 and included 177 women and thirty men. Many of these were wives of those in the first group sent in May. The women had petitioned the Executive Committee to be reunited with their husbands, even if it meant an unsettling move from the familiar drudgery of Santo Tomás Internment Camp. The Japanese readily obliged their requests. Bill's separation from his mother and sister added to his continued aloofness and isolation from his family, the start of an emotional wound from which Patty says her youngest brother never fully recovered. "It was sad," she remembered. "They wouldn't have taken him at that age if he hadn't volunteered."[50]

The captives who remained at Santo Tomás took grudging satisfaction from the distribution of a bounty of treats in Red Cross relief kits beginning on December 16. To celebrate Christmas, the internees planned a series of events much like the memorable festivities the year before. A chorus of 150 presented Handel's oratorio "The Messiah" on December 21; a movie was shown on December 22; and a Christmas concert was held on December 24. Christmas Day was celebrated with a special noon meal in the central kitchen followed by the presentation of children's gifts in the afternoon.[51]

Patty, recently turned nineteen, noted the holiday festivities in her diary with a lengthy description of the New Year's activities, starting on December 30 with a showing of the 1941 black-and-white movie "Honky Tonk," starring Clark Gable and Lana Turner. It was followed by "Dumbo," a movie about a circus elephant "in technicolor by Walt Disney," the entry reported.

She spent New Year's Eve with friends watching the camp's live production of "Cinderella" in the open-air Little Theater Under the Stars. "Eileen, Evelyn and I stayed up until 2:00," she noted in her diary. "There sure were a lot of drunks around. We had a little party consisting of us three and had toasted cheese sandwiches and coffee. There wasn't much excitement."

The second year of internment had ended on a relatively positive note for the captives of Santo Tomás as they awaited relief from an America seemingly more concerned with the war in Europe. Yet it was noted by internee leaders that morale was still high at the end of 1943 despite a distracted America and the camp's grinding "same old routine" that so dispirited the youthful Patty. This tedium was about to come to an end with a series of frightening changes for the internees beginning early in 1944—changes that would leave them yearning for a return to that same old miserable routine.

# CHAPTER 6

※ ※ ※

# The Starving Time

FOR PATTY CROFT AND OTHER INTERNEES at Santo Tomás, the months of 1943 had passed much like those of 1942 but without the initial shock of confinement as a prisoner of Japan. Many of the teenager's 1943 diary entries had been less about privations in camp, to which she had become accustomed, and more about Allied progress in Europe and the Pacific. Patty viewed Allied victories as an indicator of how soon American forces might liberate the camp. But daily life at Santo Tomás would change dramatically in 1944, and her private journal began tracking the life-threatening changes in her and her fellow captives' their third year of captivity. They grew increasingly desperate awaiting the return of U.S. forces to Luzon.

The beginning of Patty's third year of confinement on January 6 passed unnoted in her diary. Moreover, she failed to make a single entry for January until the final days, summarizing the month mostly with details of a Red Cross relief supply distributed to internees on January 25. She listed a new pair of shoes as one of her prizes, which could replace her *bakyâs*, the wooden clogs now worn by many of the captives.

Significantly, her diary entry of February 1 recorded the first of the frightening changes ahead for internees at Santo Tomás in 1944: "The gate is to be closed on Monday....No more outside communication with people. We're now prisoners of war....Today was the first day of Japanese food." These new policies resulted from the Japanese authorities transferring supervision of the camp to the Japanese Army's War Prisoners Department. This move had been intimated by co-Commandant Kodaki several months earlier in a discussion with several of the internees' leaders. "That would be bad for you," the seemingly sympathetic commandant had relayed to the Americans in what would prove a monumental understatement.[1]

On January 14 the camp's loudspeakers announced this takeover by the Japanese army, but the implications of this change were downplayed at the time. "In principle, there will be no radical changes in the operation of this camp, nor that of the Los Baños and Baguio camps," the internees were told by their temporary new commandant, Kitaro Kato of the Japanese consular service. "Even though it is anticipated that at some future date the military authorities will undertake to furnish supplies instead of cash to the camp..." Whereas the Japanese army had been providing funds, albeit inadequately, to the internees to purchase their food and other supplies in the local markets, the new policy meant the army would be furnishing these provisions directly. If the supplies were maintained at the same level, the camp's rations would be no worse off. Yet as the war turned against the Japanese military throughout 1944, the army's increasingly inadequate food rations for the camp—sometimes unavoidable, oftentimes spiteful—condemned the captives to slow starvation.[2]

That the Japanese were losing the war by early 1944 was becomingly joyfully obvious to the internees at Santo Tomás Internment Camp. A columnist in a January 23 issue of the *Manila Daily Bulletin* newspaper—the Japanese occupiers' heavily censored mouthpiece distributed in camp—inadvertently admitted as much with editorial advice to *Manileños*: "There is not a spot on the globe which is absolutely safe from air raids. If our psychology is normalized, it should give us enough commonsense not to let anything we must do for our safety left undone." The writer was attempting to downplay the implications of Japanese plans to construct air raid shelters around the city. The captives in Santo Tomás had no problem reading between the lines of this article, and they *welcomed* these Allied air attacks as a harbinger of their long-sought liberation.[3]

Yet the approaching Allied invasion proved to be a two-edged sword for the vulnerable internees. It could ultimately allow their rescue from the hands of a ruthless and determined captor, but in the interim bring frightening reprisals as the Japanese army resolved to turn back the Allied onslaught. The survival of the captives would become a race against time, with the internees praying for the arrival of their liberators before death by starvation, disease or execution.

The previously announced "future date" for the Japanese military to begin supplying the camp's food came quickly on February 1, just two weeks after the January notice was broadcast. The official daily ration for each adult captive was to be 716 grams of food: rice (200 grams), corn (200 grams), fish (50 grams), vegetables (200 grams), miscellaneous (66 grams). Children twelve and under were to get half this amount. For perspective, three cups of white, long-grain rice weighs about 716 grams. This would provide roughly 1,200 calories of nutrition—bordering on starvation level for adults. As meager as this was, from the beginning the Japanese would fall short of providing this promised ration.[4]

The package-line had been a steady source of supplemental food since internment at Santo Tomás began, but the Japanese military permanently closed this resource on February 7. This was a key part of the Japanese army's new plans to isolate the camp, and it was a body blow to the internees. Many of the captives receiving outside funds had been purchasing a big part of their food from the local markets and receiving this through the package-line. They sometimes shared their surplus with less fortunate fellow captives. With the camp's population peaking at just under 4,000 by January 1944, the food lines in the central kitchen increased dramatically with the closure of the package-line.[5]

"Closing the package-line went over pretty bad in camp," Patty remembered. "Many people had to start eating what little the Japanese gave them, not what their servants brought them." Patty and her mother never had much money to purchase food from the outside, so they felt less affected by this new policy.

But the 19-year-old food-line server did suffer from the increased pressure put on the central kitchen from the closing of the package-line and the lower quality of food supplied by the Japanese. "The lines got much longer," she said, "and lots of times I wasn't liked very much on the serving line. One time I had to give out crummy-looking bananas. One guy took it and threw it back at me even though I had no control over the food quality." She remembered that the captive's temper tantrum was later punished. "He had to spend a few days working with some of the little old ladies picking out worms and weevils from the rice that we cooked."

With the de facto ban on outside food purchases by individual internees, additional nutrition would have to come chiefly from reserves stockpiled by the captives' Finance and Supplies Department. Anticipating this kind of crisis, internee officials had stored more than 30,000 pounds of dried beans during better times in the past. These beans would provide a much-needed substitute for animal protein before the exhaustion of this hoard in July. The foresight of camp leaders to build this and other smaller stockpiles of food doubtless saved many lives as conditions worsened throughout 1944. Besides these reserves, some additional foods for the camp were requisitioned by the Finance and Supplies Department and purchased for the camp by the Japanese at local markets. These purchases were funded by international relief organizations and from drafts on outside businesses by employees interned at Santo Tomás.[6]

Ensuring an adequate food supply for the internees had been at the forefront of the civilian leaders' concerns since the early days of internment, but these apprehensions reached a crisis in the last six months of 1944. This period of slow starvation began with the camp's population already malnourished. A physical examination of the internees by doctors at Santo Tomás in summer 1944 revealed an already dramatic weight loss over their thirty months of incarceration. The weight of the average male captive was recorded at 140 pounds in late July, a 31-pound average loss since January 1942. For women captives during this same period, the average weight was down to 114 pounds, an 18-pound drop. Already in a depleted state with no excess body fat, the captives would suffer continual reductions in their daily calories in the months afterward.[7]

Changes to the camp brought by Japanese army oversight extended beyond the internees' diet, as troubling as the reduced rations were. The new overseers quickly replaced the captives' long-standing and mostly elected Executive Committee with a Japanese-appointed Internee Administrative Committee. This streamlined executive body would consist of only three members: Carroll Grinnell, Earl Carroll and Samuel Lloyd. The captives' self-administration and minimal direct contact with their captors were coming to a sudden end. Santo Tomás would no longer resemble a small, largely self-administering American community operating with some interference by Japanese authorities; it would hereafter be a camp of beleaguered prisoners at the mercy of increasingly hostile captors.[8]

Some of the troubling new policies were instigated by Sadaaki Konishi, a sadistic 28-year-old army lieutenant who sometimes implemented repressive measures without approval of the camp commandant. One of the first of Konishi's actions was his ban on the cooking of meals in the camp's numerous shanties. Many of these shanty dwellers had stored food over the months before closure of the package-line. Their private meals were a vital source of nutrition—even more important with the meager fare now available in the central kitchen. After a protest from the new Internee Administrative Committee, the commandant offered a compromise allowing group cooking in the shanty enclaves. It appeared Konishi had suffered a setback.[9]

Relentlessly vindictive, the Japanese lieutenant next limited the purchase orders for supplying the camp's canteen and some of the supplemental food used in the central kitchen. The Japanese were purchasing this supplemental food on the local market with money from the internees' general funds, most of it supplied by outside sources. Konishi's limitation cut further into the camp's overall food supply and forced more dependence on the Japanese.[10]

Aggravating to the weary captives, twice-daily roll calls by Japanese soldiers began on March 1. Previously, internee room monitors had handled these line-ups, which in some months had been only once daily. The 8 a.m. and 6:30 p.m. roll calls were now formal affairs with submissive respect shown to the Japanese soldiers. This included a new emphasis on "correct" bowing by the captives.[11]

"They were going to keep better track of us with these roll calls," Patty recalled, "and of course we would have to show more respect with proper bows from the waist down. They would always have a couple of guards with bayonets watching us during these roll calls."

The 19-year-old captive had little remembrance of Lieutenant Konishi or his machinations at Santo Tomás, but she would later get well acquainted with him and his sadistic manner in a different setting. In late March the abusive Japanese lieutenant took a lengthy leave of absence to treat a chronic health condition, but he may have left a parting gift—a dramatic raid on the captives' quarters.

The raid began when some fifty Japanese soldiers surrounded the Main Building at 12:20 a.m. March 31. The sleepy captives were commanded to remain in their assigned rooms with the lights on. As the soldiers went from room to room, the half-dressed internees were ordered to line up as their quarters were searched. The exercise was not concluded until 11:00 that morning. It was rumored that the Japanese had hoped to find some kind of radio broadcasting apparatus hidden in one of the rooms. Although the fruitless search resulted in no punishments, this heavy-handed action typified the new harassment experienced throughout 1944.[12]

To reduce overcrowding at Santo Tomás, in late March the camp commandant ordered 500 more internees to Los Baños. Even with the two large transfers from the previous year, the population at Santo Tomás now hovered around 4,000 with Allied nationals rounded up from Mindanao and other islands in the Philippines continuing to arrive. Among those selected for the early-April transfer to Los Baños was Hilton Carson, whose shanty provided a refuge for Patty and her mother during the day.[13]

Carson was being forced to leave the relative comfort of his shack, likely to labor in the construction of new barracks at the growing internment camp. He shared his distress over his transfer with Patty and her mother. The teenager's April 3 diary entry records the news: "Hilton's name was drawn for Los Baños. He sure is *vexed*."[14]

Carson was certainly not the only internee "vexed" at being transferred to the new camp. To tamp down dissent before the transfers on April 7, the Japanese attempted to ban conversation in the shanties. "For the past few days, we have not been allowed to talk in our shanties," Patty records in her April 4 diary entry. "We had to talk in front of the education building in the hot sun....It all seems so silly."[15]

The morning of April 6, the Japanese broadcast a list of sixteen men to precede the larger group's departure for Los Baños Internment Camp. These early deportees would unload and carry the 500 transferees' baggage to their new barracks. The larger group would be transported in two truck convoys beginning the next day. Hilton Carson's unlucky streak continued when his name was broadcast among the baggage handlers. With just hours before his forced transfer, he bade a hasty farewell to Patty and her mother, bequeathing his shanty for their use during the day. The baggage detachment left at 1 p.m. that same afternoon.

The first group of 360 transferees left at 5 a.m. the next day, Patty noted in her diary. Much of the camp assembled at 3 a.m. when the music started to blare. The remaining captives gave their fellow internees a send off as they crowded onto the trucks. The second group would leave the next day. "There are no trains so they all have to go up by truck," Patty recorded. "Rumor is that the [train] bridges have all been blown by guerillas."[16]

Her diary reference to Filipino guerillas underscored the increasing activity of the Philippine resistance movement as the war turned against the Japanese occupiers. These guerrillas were particularly active around Los Baños. Former students from the agricultural college's Philippine Reserve Officer Training Corps (ROTC) formed the nucleus of a resistance force after the Japanese invasion. A number of these paramilitary units operated in the area, but one in particular, Hunters ROTC, exhibited a marked degree of military professionalism. This group would later provide invaluable support to U.S. forces operating south of Manila.[17]

Three days after Carson's departure, Patty and her mother moved most of their possessions from their rooms in the Main Building to the shanty. Although they had already spent many hours in the shack since Carson had it built in January, they now had it all to themselves during the day. They would return to their rooms in the evenings as the Japanese prohibited single women from staying in the shanties at night. "And it was safer in the buildings at night," Patty recalled. "In the daytime it was nice and quiet in the shanty. Inside the buildings you could always hear the constant chatter and the sound of *bakyâs* [wooden shoes] always slapping up and down the halls."

In late April, Patty recorded a number of events in camp that highlighted the heightened control by Japanese authorities. "A lot has happened the last few weeks," she wrote. "We have changed Commandants. We have now a colonel from the Japanese army. They say he's tough, but he can't be much worse than the last one." The new commandant was a Lieutenant Colonel Yoshie, who would prove somewhat eccentric and display a disarming affection for the internees' baseball games.[18]

Her diary's roundup of April events included the new commandant's heavy-handed action requiring the relocation of shanties that were less than sixty feet from the outer wall. This new policy was intended to prevent escape attempts and further isolate the internees from local Filipinos, who occasionally threw written messages over the wall. "250 shacks have to be moved," Patty wrote. "What a job it has been for these poor men."[19]

Also troubling was a new directive by the Japanese requiring all captives to sign an oath by the end of April pledging "not, under any circumstances, [to] attempt to escape or conspire directly or indirectly against the Japanese Military Authorities, as long as...in their custody." Patty recorded in her diary the internees' resistance to this new directive: "Japanese have given us an oath to sign saying that we will not do anything against the Japanese army and that we will not attempt to go over the wall. Everyone refused to sign the oath and we're now waiting for further report from the Internee Committee."[20]

Responding to the internees' disobedience, the Japanese commandant sent a written order to the Internee Administrative Committee demanding all internees sign by April 30. Committee members responded in a clear and courageous letter to the commandant explaining the internees' noncompliance. Following Japanese threats that anyone refusing to sign would "lose his status as a civilian internee," all but one of the nearly 4,000 captives eventually signed the oath. The one holdout, a Chinese-American named Lee Tun Yen, would spend the rest of his time at Santo Tomás in the camp jail. "The oath didn't bother me," Patty said. "I eventually signed it. I couldn't climb the wall anyway. And they would shoot us if we tried to leave through the front gate."[21]

About this same time, another entry in the 19-year-old's diary noted a disconcerting report from Los Baños: "Rumor this morning is that Betty Lou Gewald has died from an appendix operation. I sure hope it isn't true." But the rumor proved accurate. "She was about five years older than me," Patty recalled. "I also knew her parents and her brother, who was a friend of my older brother. Betty had a nice family."[22]

The 24-year-old Gewald's death resulted from the shortage of medical drugs in the civilian internment camps. She had earlier reported to the Los Baños camp hospital with pain and swelling in her excessively thin lower abdomen. Navy nurse Dorothy Still was horrified when she recognized the familiar symptoms of appendicitis. The experienced nurse knew that without postoperative antibiotics to kill the infection the young woman was doomed. Nonetheless, the operation to remove the diseased appendix was dutifully performed by Dr. Dana Nance, who had earlier been transferred from Baguio Internment Camp. Despite heroic efforts to drain the infection coursing through Gewald's underfed body, she succumbed in late April. Nurse Still could only weep over this tragedy, so easily prevented with drug therapy. This kind of heartbreak grew depressingly common at both Los Baños and Santo Tomás later in 1944 and into 1945.[23]

Patty witnessed a similar but closer tragedy in early June when her best friend Eileen Aaron's mother died of breast cancer in the camp hospital. Margaret Aaron had suffered from the cancer before the war, but it seemed to have gone into remission. Perhaps owing to poor diet and the harsh camp conditions, by late 1943 the disease had returned. Patty worried with and then grieved with Eileen, whose bed had been next to hers on the third floor of the Main Building since early in 1942. "I had been over to see her mother in the camp hospital a week or so before she died," she recalled. "I was on my way walking toward our shanty when I saw her mother's body go by. A little horse was pulling a small wagon with her body in a box. It was all really sad."[24]

Patty's diary entry on June 7 recorded the Japanese-controlled *Manila Daily Bulletin's* version of the D-Day landings by the Allies on June 6 in Normandy, France. Despite the spin, the perceptive captive grasped the significance of the event. "Today's newspaper said all our troops wiped out in Normandy," she wrote. "Otherwise, the second front has started." At last, Allied troops were thrusting into mainland Europe and soon toward the heartland of Germany. Patty and the other internees clearly understood how the Allies' "Hitler First" strategy had slowed American advances in the Pacific and delayed their eventual liberation. The opening of this second front in Europe provided hope for a rapid German defeat and a return of American forces to the Philippines.[25]

This hope would be sorely needed in the months ahead as conditions worsened at Santo Tomás following the recall of Lieutenant Colonel Yoshie to Japan. Acting Commandant S. Onozaki announced in late June that the camp was not operating under rules established by the Geneva Convention of 1929—the international agreement promoting the humane treatment of war prisoners. Instead, the camp was being run under a set of regulations determined by the Japanese government, which applied retroactively to the start of the Japanese army's oversight of the camp on February 1. No written summary of these regulations, however, would be available for internee leaders. Under this new edict, camp rules would apparently be whatever the Japanese authorities decreed.[26]

As the dispiriting rainy season began in July, camp morale was raised somewhat by ongoing war news filtering into camp—the fall of Japanese Prime Minister Hideki Tojo's government, the recapture of Guam by U.S. forces, and Hitler's injuries from an assassination attempt. The morning of July 16, a distant explosion shook the buildings in camp and electrified the captives. One excited internee leaped from her bed and shouted, "Oh, boy! They are here!" But the long-sought U.S. return was not at hand. The explosion was later attributed to the sabotage of a tanker in Manila Bay.

The night of July 25-26, a practice black-out of the camp was ordered, a tacit admission of Japanese concerns about Allied air raids. About this same time, a rumor spread through camp that a government official in America had announced an impending attack on the Philippines. The song "Someday He'll Come Back to Me" from the opera *Madame Butterfly* was added to the evening concert program. At reveille the next morning the camp heard Al Jolson's recording of "Just Around the Corner." Patty remembered the sense of anticipation that permeated the camp by summer 1944. "We could see heat lightning out there at a distance from the camp," she said describing the faint flashes from thunderstorms too distant to hear. "When we'd see these flashes of light, people in camp would say, 'Maybe they've landed. Maybe they're coming.'"[27]

Yet the captives' anticipated liberation failed to arrive. By the end of July an alarming food shortage stalked the camp. In mid-July the Japanese had announced the substitution of 100 grams of coconut milk in lieu of the earlier-authorized daily ration of 300 grams of camote. This meant a reduction of approximately 300 calories per day from the internees' already inadequate ration of 1,200 calories per day. Rising food prices in the Manila market put further pressure on the captives' diet, decreasing the supplemental foods purchased with internee funds. Captives scavenging through discarded vegetable cans became commonplace.[28]

Camp official Earl Carroll addressed the food crisis in a speech to internees the evening of July 26. With the central kitchen's daily fare now inadequate, Carroll said that the camp's reserves of canned meats—corned beef, Vienna sausage, and pork and beans—would be tapped to supplement the Japanese army's daily allotment. Prudently, camp leaders had built up this store from past Red Cross shipments in anticipation of a future food crisis like the one now at hand. The decision to use these emergency reserves was urged by the camp's doctors, who were seeing firsthand the detrimental effects of the internees' poor diet. In a letter to the Internee Administrative Committee, the doctors called the reduced Japanese ration "grossly deficient" and the cause of slow "starvation" of the captives.[29]

Patty also remembered a less-threatening hardship at that time, a kind of insult on top of injury. In August the commandant informed the captives that no toilet paper remained anywhere in the Philippine Islands. The Japanese would attempt to supply the camp with newsprint. "Oh, that was awful!" Patty said. "I remember some Sears and Roebuck catalogs, but there wasn't enough newsprint to go around. We would use leaves."

With camp officials having delayed distribution of the emergency food reserves as long as possible, the first issue of the canned meat to the nearly 4,000 half-starved internees began on September 6. Twice per week, one 12-ounce can of corned beef was distributed among groups of four captives. After the corned beef reserve was consumed, plans were to periodically issue servings of the Vienna sausage and pork and beans in 4-ounce quantities to each captive. Camp leaders knew that even with this careful rationing the food reserves would be exhausted by the end of October.[30]

Patty clearly remembered the constant, gnawing hunger she felt at the time. "You just feel like you're not gonna make it," she said. "You're very weak. You get dizzy. It's even hard to sleep. We all thought about food all the time." She had no memory of receiving an allocation of corned beef in September or October 1944. "But I do remember that a can of corned beef would sell on the black market for around seventy-five dollars American at the time," she said. "Some people would write checks for stuff like that." Acceptance of these checks for food was obviously highly speculative.

Nearly to the point of despair as summer ended, Patty and the Santo Tomás internees were suddenly granted a glorious feast for their eyes in the skies above. In one of the longest entries of her wartime diary, she recorded the day's events:

> Today was one of the most exciting days I've ever experienced and which I will never forget. Sept. 21 at 9:20 was the first time since February 1942 that American planes have flown over Manila. Before the planes came over, the Japanese had between seven to 14 of their own planes up and they were practicing shooting at them, which they've been doing for the last three days with each plane carrying a balloon for a target....I heard the sound of plane motors and ran out of the shack to see them, and lo and behold, they were American planes. They just seemed to drop out of the clouds. There were three waves that came from different directions. The wave I saw at first had about 60 to 100 planes. I said right away that they were American planes but Mother just sort of laughed. Then the Japanese started firing up at them and then the siren went off. Of course, after that we were positive.[31]

The diary entry goes on to describe the U.S. Navy's raid on Nichols Field, Camp Murphy, and several other sites around Manila. She and her mother watched from their shanty as the U.S. planes dived at their targets. The diary entry continues:

> I had a chance to see the whole show. There were Japanese guards all over the place. One was posted right out

*in front of our shack with fixed bayonet ready to poke anyone if they happened to come along. During the air raids, we were not allowed to go out of our shanties. For one reason: they didn't want us to see what was going on. These planes came over three times. There was another raid at 2:30 in the afternoon. They bombed ammunition dumps in the port. It was over with at 5:00.[32]*

"Oh, it was a big day," Patty remembered fondly. "Those planes must have come from a ship. I remember one plane was hit, and I followed it all the way down. I often wondered what ever happened to the pilot. Some days still when I see a plane flying overhead, I think of that day." Her memory of the damaged U.S. plane going down in flames did little to diminish her elation at what she and her fellow internees believed this raid meant: *America was soon to return to the Philippines!*

THE ECSTATIC CAPTIVES HOPED THE U.S. warplanes had launched their attack from land bases near the Philippines, or perhaps from one of the southern islands. The increasingly isolated internees at Santo Tomás often lacked details about U.S. military progress in the region. *Could the raid be a prelude to landings on Luzon?* In fact, it was—but not nearly as soon as the beleaguered internees fervently wished and desperately needed. The navy planes were from aircraft carriers in Admiral William Halsey's famous Third Fleet (Task Force 38), at the time some forty miles off the east coast of Luzon and 150 miles from Manila.

Halsey wrote of this raid following the war: "We hit them four times on the twenty-first and expected to hit them four times the next day, but the approach of foul weather and the dearth of suitable targets influenced Pete Mitscher (Vice Adm. Marc A. Mitscher) to recommend that I cancel the last two strikes. I did."[33]

Halsey's ability to position his fast carriers so close to Luzon by September 1944 owed much to MacArthur's determined march ever closer to the Philippine archipelago throughout 1943 and into 1944. The Japanese outer perimeter had drastically receded before the near-constant advance of MacArthur's vaunted bomber-line across the southwest Pacific. The general's brilliant leadership enhanced this progress. And certainly the U.S. Navy's advance through the islands of the central Pacific also contributed mightily to U.S. forces threatening to recapture the Philippines by late 1944.

Just nine months before Halsey's air raid, the Allies' frontline had been 2,000 miles southeast of Luzon, and U.S. strategists had not determined whether the Philippines would even be retaken on the long slog to Tokyo. Some in Washington argued for bypassing much of the Philippines and capturing the island of Formosa (Taiwan) before mounting the invasion of the Japanese home islands. MacArthur, of course, never wavered in his insistence on the U.S. reconquest of the Philippines—and as soon as practicable. With the northeast coastline of New Guinea secured by early 1944, the general's forces moved north across the Bismarck Sea to secure the Admiralty Islands and cut off the Japanese fortress at Rabaul to the south.

By April, MacArthur's forces were moving farther northwestward along the New Guinea coast in a line toward the distant Philippines. The port city of Hollandia, the rear supply base for the Japanese on New Guinea, was taken by May. Air commander George Kenney's pilots from the bomber-line destroyed some 300 Japanese planes protecting the strategic site. MacArthur would soon establish his headquarters at Hollandia to stay close to the front.

"The Philippines didn't look anywhere near as far as they did a few months before," Kenney later said after the occupation of Hollandia. But the air commander's eagerness to retake the Philippines was not shared by all of MacArthur's senior officers. Their objections, of course, mattered little to the Allied ground commander in the Pacific. MacArthur was hell-bent on returning to the Philippines and destroying or bypassing all Japanese forces between him and his goal. And in directing this campaign he was "performing as a virtuoso..." his preeminent biographer William Manchester describes, "pivoting from one island or coastal base to another, avoiding the foe's troop concentrations, caroming from airfield to airfield, using Nipponese rigidity to break Nippon's back, shielding his flanks and avoiding bloodlettings like Buna and Tarawa."[34]

After securing Hollandia, the tempo picked up markedly for the Allied advance along the New Guinea-Philippines axis. In August, the capture of Sansapoor at the northwest tip of New Guinea marked the end of the campaign in this region. The spearhead of MacArthur's forces now pointed toward the Philippines with the archipelago's second largest island, Mindanao, only 600 miles distant. The general had overseen a remarkable turnaround since fleeing to Australia early in 1942, drawing some 1,200 miles closer to the Philippines and destroying two Japanese armies along the way. He also left behind a quarter of a million enemy troops cut off from support and withering on the vine.[35]

In summer 1944, leaders in Washington turned attention to both the upcoming presidential election and where next to strike Japan. The two seemingly unrelated events would prove more closely connected than most would ever know. Although MacArthur denied any interest in politics, many in the States encouraged him to run for president against Roosevelt in 1944. This prospect made Roosevelt uneasy, but after assurances the general would not be a candidate, FDR decided to meet with him to discuss strategy for Japan's downfall. George Marshall ordered MacArthur to rendezvous with the president and Admiral Chester W. Nimitz, Commander-in-Chief Pacific Ocean, in late July at Hickam Field outside Honolulu. Fleet Admiral William D. Leahy accompanied Roosevelt to the top-secret discussion.

Regardless of MacArthur's unwavering plan to take back all of the Philippines, Roosevelt's key military advisers were divided on whether this strategy provided the optimal route to Japan's defeat. Washington-based Chief of Naval Operations Ernest J. King, who replaced Stark in 1942, argued for bypassing the northern Philippine islands almost as strongly as MacArthur proposed retaking them. Positions of other top brass in Washington were spread along a continuum somewhere between MacArthur and King's positions. Roosevelt withheld his opinion and hoped to move closer to a decision after his meeting with MacArthur and Nimitz.[36]

After social pleasantries and a motorcade through downtown Honolulu, MacArthur, Nimitz and Roosevelt got down to business after dinner in a mansion overlooking Waikiki's picturesque beach. "Well, Douglas," Roosevelt opened, "where do we go from here." MacArthur replied unequivocally: "Mindanao, Mr. President, then Leyte—and then Luzon." The general's already well-known cards lay on the table.[37]

Arguing the position of his superior in Washington, Nimitz laid out Admiral King's case for leapfrogging the northern Philippine islands, including Luzon, and moving on to Formosa. The debate went back and forth for several hours with the president acting as a neutral moderator. MacArthur's argument went beyond military strategy, urging Roosevelt to uphold U.S. honor as the Filipinos had been betrayed by America's failure to defend the islands. "Promises must be kept," he declared believing his pledge to return to the Philippines had committed America. The Filipinos would never forgive a second betrayal, he warned.[38]

MacArthur later said that in a private moment with Roosevelt during the discussions he had warned that Admiral King's plans to bypass the main island of Luzon would not go over well with U.S. voters. "I dare say that the American people would be so aroused," he told the president, "that they would register most complete resentment against you at the polls this fall." The meeting ended around midnight with Roosevelt keeping his opinion to himself. But before going to bed that evening, the president asked his physician for an aspirin and requested another be left for the next morning. The general's reference to the political impact of bypassing the northern Philippines may have given the ever-political FDR a headache.[39]

Upon MacArthur's return to his headquarters in Hollandia, he told his staff that he had won the president over. Before Roosevelt left Hawaii, the president told reporters "we are going to get the Philippines back, and without question General MacArthur will take a part in it." Returning to the States, the president told newsmen that he and MacArthur were in "complete accord." If Patty Croft and her fellow prisoners at Santo Tomás had been privy to the outcome of the meeting in Hawaii, they might have felt some relief despite their gnawing hunger and fear.[40]

Roosevelt's statements to the press notwithstanding, the Joint Chiefs of Staff in Washington continued the Luzon-versus-Formosa debate through September. All agreed to taking the southernmost Philippine island of Mindanao followed by an amphibious landing at Leyte, the south-central island in the Philippines some 350 miles southwest of Luzon. Admiral King, however, did not acquiesce to the retaking of Luzon until the last week of September. Finally withdrawing his objection to MacArthur's plans, the acerbic naval commander groused that the Luzon invasion might be more about the general's redemption of his pledge than military strategy.

MacArthur's staff made plans for taking Mindanao on November 15 followed by a landing in Leyte on December 20. Yet these plans changed quickly. The week before Admiral Halsey's warplanes made their air raid on Manila on September 21, the aggressive Third Fleet commander made a critical observation—the island of Leyte held far fewer Japanese troops than estimated by U.S. military intelligence. He suggested bypassing the southernmost island of Mindanao and swiftly seizing Leyte instead. With Leyte even closer to Luzon than Mindanao, the aggressive MacArthur quickly responded. "In view of COM3rdFLT's latest report on carrier operations in the Philippine Islands area," came the general's coded reply, "I am prepared to move immediately to execution of King II [Leyte invasion] with target date of 20 Oct 44." Unbeknownst to the emaciated captives at Santo Tomás and Los Baños, this changed timetable gained them two months in their race against starvation.[41]

The Leyte operation was bold and difficult. The Joint Chiefs' approval came just thirty-four days before the landing on October 20, and the assault was 500 miles from MacArthur's bomber-line. Beyond the range of land-based fighter cover, the navy was needed to provide air support. Ground forces for the operation consisted of X Corps and XXIV Corps troops, both a part of the Sixth Army commanded by Lt. Gen. Walter Krueger. The 63-year-old Pacific veteran had commanded the Sixth Army since its activation in January 1943.[42]

The morning of October 20, the largest assembly of naval assault craft and warships ever concentrated in the Pacific entered Leyte Gulf. Troop landings on the east coast of the island rapidly secured a beachhead along an eighteen-mile front just south of Tacloban, MacArthur's first duty station after graduation from West Point forty-one years earlier. Hours after the initial landings, MacArthur waded ashore and fulfilled his pledge. "People of the Philippines: I have returned....," the general announced over a portable radio set. "Rally to me. Let the indomitable spirit of Bataan and Corregidor lead on...."[43]

MacArthur had been eager to put his feet on Philippine soil, and early that afternoon an army photographer recorded the general's presumedly determined countenance as he took the forty strides from his barge onto Red Beach. Actually, the photo's famous, jut-jawed MacArthur scowl reflected the general's disgust at having to wade through the knee-deep surf. But when the image-conscious general saw the photo, he immediately recognized its publicity value. As MacArthur and the photographer made history at Leyte, Patty and her fellow captives at Santo Tomás grew more desperate with each day. General MacArthur may have returned to Philippine soil, but his army was still hundreds of miles from Luzon and the thousands of starving Allied civilians.[44]

BUOYED BY HALSEY'S AIR RAIDS on September 21-22, the high spirits of Santo Tomás internees led to a wave of over-optimism in camp. Some predicted the captives would be liberated by the end of October. But with the raids soon diminishing, some disillusionment settled on the camp by the first of October. "People feel kind of down," Patty recorded in her diary on October 1, "but one can't expect them to come over here all the time, especially when we know things are moving here all the time....There's also a rumor around that we've made landings in Tacloban in Leyte, also that there are 500 to 1,000 ships headed to this paradise." The camp rumor about the landing at Leyte was about three weeks premature but amazingly prescient.[45]

October brought near constant air-raid alerts to the camp and an occasional bombing distant from the camp but clearly heard by the captives. Patty's diary entries in late October make no mention of MacArthur's actual landing at Leyte on the 20th, but the news certainly would have filtered through camp. In fact, a radio in the Main Building had been assembled from spare parts and began receiving news broadcasts from the outside world long before the Leyte landing. The radio's existence and location were tightly guarded secrets, but a select few internees had access and cautiously shared some of the information gleaned from the news broadcasts.[46]

The Allied air raids and landings in the Philippines brought new restrictions and reprisals to the camp. On October 30, the commandant discontinued the camp's loudspeaker system, a source of unity and entertainment for the captives. "It was probably just another way to punish us," Patty said. "They knew we liked listening to the music at night. I remember some Japanese politician talking to us in camp earlier, and he said, 'We can be generous to you while we are victorious.' So they were losing the war by then, so they just wanted to punish us."[47]

That same day the commandant's office issued an order strictly enforcing the requirements and correctness of the internees' bowing protocol for showing respect to the Japanese: "Every morning and every night, each monitor shall see that his group practices bowing" the order stated. "This is to include men, women and children....bowing should be from the waist."[48]

The weary, starving captives must not have shown the proper spirit regarding this new order. The commandant soon set aside three days devoted to the custom of bowing. Each morning and evening room monitors and shanty-area supervisors were to demonstrate the proper method of bowing and have the internees practice this technique. "The Japanese are getting meaner," Patty noted in her diary entry of November 5. "We had to bow to them three times during roll call."[49]

As the Thanksgiving holiday approached, the camp showed little of the festive spirit shown in the previous two years. Memories of the servings of turkey in November 1942 seemed distant and dream-like to the starving captives by 1944. Still, Patty had a poignant memory of how her resourceful mother managed to serve an ersatz pumpkin pie on that singular American holiday. Selma had been approached by an internee who knew where some wild pumpkins were growing. He said he could scrounge a couple of eggs and some sugar, and asked her if she could use the wild pumpkins to bake a pie.

"My mom ground up some cassava root," Patty remembered fondly, "and we got a coconut. I grated the coconut and squeezed out the milk. But what would we use for lard? 'Well, mom, I have a jar of Abolene Cold Cream from one of the Red Cross kits,' I told her. 'Let's use that for lard.'" Surprisingly, the artificial pumpkin pie turned out well providing a sumptuous treat for the ravenous captives.

Two days later on November 25, Patty's twentieth birthday, she received a welcome gift. "Had an air raid for my birthday," she gamely recorded in her diary. "Two waves of planes flew over. It was the first time I was able to see the insignia. Lots of oil was destroyed." Considering her circumstances, she could hardly have asked for a better birthday present. Yet these occasional air raids were the only sign of an oncoming America. In the three weeks following MacArthur's October landing on Leyte, no news of further American advances in the Philippines reached Santo Tomás Internment Camp.[50]

By December, the steady decrease in daily calories throughout 1944 showed in the haggard faces and listless behavior of the captives. Of the nearly 4,000 stooped, scrawny internees at Santo Tomás, only a few maintained a normal physical appearance. Increasingly common, the swollen feet and ankles of beriberi sufferers attested to the deficiency of thiamine (vitamin B-1) in the camp's diet. This condition can cause a potentially lethal buildup of fluids around the heart and in the lower extremities. By November both Patty and her mother were showing signs of the disease. "My legs were starting to swell," she recalled. "People were starting to die from malnutrition."[51]

The numerous pigeons normally seen around the Main Building vanished in the cook pots of the starving. Leaves and roots of unnamed plants growing wild around the campus became ingredients for improvised salads and stews. Discarded peelings from camotes and other vegetables outside the central kitchen were scavenged by women and children. One of the saddest scenes of all was the pathetic group of children loitering outside the camp's food processing shed hoping for a stray scrap.[52]

Six months after the July medical examinations of the already-thin captives, the men now weighed an average of 121 pounds, a further loss of 19 pounds. The women were down to an average of 100 pounds, an additional loss of 14 pounds. This kind of weight loss was associated with an expected increase in inmate deaths, with the 7.3 average deaths per month in the first thirty-four months doubling to 16 deaths per month in the last two months of 1944. The Japanese ordered camp doctors to avoid use of the words "malnutrition" and "starvation" on the internee death certificates. Refusing this directive, one brave physician was locked up in the camp jail.[53]

In the midst of these lethal conditions at Santo Tomás, on November 28 the Japanese announced the impending transfer of an additional 150 captives to Los Baños Internment Camp. Volunteers were welcome. The three previous transfers from the camp and the steady incarceration of additional civilian prisoners from across Luzon had swelled Los Baños to nearly 2,000 captives by late 1944. But the construction of new barracks continued to provide shelter for more captives. After the announcement of this fourth transfer, Patty and her mother began weighing their options. They could volunteer for this move and hope for improved conditions. Or they could remain at Santo Tomás and continue their physical decline. It was a difficult decision with life-or-death implications.

"Having a hard time trying to decide if we should go to Los Baños or not," Patty wrote in her diary on December 2. "Mother wants to go, but I don't want to." Patty's desire to stay at Santo Tomás was influenced by her close association with a number of school friends from pre-war Manila. Selma's inclination to transfer stemmed largely from her motherly instinct to care for her youngest child, Bill, who had been at Los Baños and separated from his family since December 1943.[54]

Patty's former music teacher at the American School, Grace Nash, had faced this same dilemma earlier in the year. She and her husband heard reports of better living conditions and food supplies at Los Baños. The area around the camp south of Manila was said to be at the heart of coconut and banana plantations. They also hoped to get away from Lt. Konishi, the sadistic Japanese officer tormenting the captives at Santo Tomás early in 1944. In April, Nash and her family volunteered for Los Baños. Shortly after the April transfer, the Nashes sent a brief written message back to Santo Tomás: "We are doing better here in partitioned barracks and garden space, family groups living in units."[55]

Although the Nashes' improved conditions would prove short-lived, this message may have influenced Selma Croft's decision, especially the part about "family groups living in units." "My mother said we needed to go be with Bill," Patty said. "And if we didn't get out of Santo Tomás, something bad was going to happen to us. She had that feeling. She always had premonition feelings. We also heard there was more food there."

On December 3, Patty and her mother began packing their meager possessions for the transfer to Los Baños. One of the Japanese officers prevented their taking much of what they hoped to carry with them. "Abiko would only let us take three packages with us instead of seven," Patty defiantly wrote in her diary that evening. "We'll get even with him yet."[56]

The 150 transferees gathered with their belongings in the pre-dawn hours of December 5. Included in Patty's baggage was her precious accordion, a comforting reminder of better times before the war. Selma hoped to take a small chest with her, but the troublesome Japanese officer objected. A dispute erupted that could have ended badly for Patty. "I remember Lieutenant Abiko got angry at my mother," Patty recalled, "and we all got into it. He turned on me, and I ran away. He started to chase me. I ran around the back of the Main Building to an entrance and got lost inside. I was scared to death. I don't know what he would have done to me if he caught me."

Following this drama, the transferees were loaded onto trucks for the brief ride to a train station in downtown Manila. A long, trying day lay ahead for Patty and Selma. December 5, 1944, would mark Patty Croft's first step outside the walls of the Santo Tomás Internment Camp since January 6, 1942, two years and eleven months earlier. It was impossible to know whether the transfer to Los Baños would improve the fortunes of Patty, her mother, and the weak, starving captives leaving with them.

# CHAPTER 7

### ✤ ✤ ✤

# Desperation at Los Baños

HERDED INTO A BOXCAR at the train station in Manila, Patty and Selma Croft sat on their personal belongings with twenty-three other women and children in the predawn hours of December 5, 1944. Around 125 male transferees from Santo Tomás were jammed into several other stifling boxcars of the Manila Railroad Company. "We only had about forty miles to go by train to Los Baños," Patty said, "but they put us in there and made us wait a long time. And it got hot! Whew! It was awful!"

At 4:30 a.m., the train lurched away from the station making its way southward. The tropical sun would soon beat down on the train and its human cargo all morning. "They would go a little bit and stop," Patty remembered. "Then they'd start up again and stop. Seemed like they were doing this to aggravate us."

Just after noon they finally arrived at the railroad station for the town of Los Baños and the nearby Los Baños College of Agriculture, which had closed during the war. The station was a short distance from the center of town but more than two miles from the college campus, adjacent to which the internees would be incarcerated in Los Baños Internment Camp. The weakened captives trekked uphill carrying their belongings under the midday sun.

"It was way up this hill," Patty said, "and my mother was so sick and weak. Halfway up we had to sit down. The Japanese guards came around with their bayonets, grunting and poking at us to keep moving. I was scared to death they were going to bayonet my mother. But she finally got to her feet. It was awful dragging her up that hill in that heat."

The internment camp lay southeast of the town of Los Baños with its 10,000 residents near the south shore of Laguna de Bay. With a surface area of 350 square miles, Laguna de Bay was the largest lake in the Philippines. Looming southwest of the internment camp, the dormant volcano Mount Makiling rose nearly 3,600 feet above sea level. Los Baños was a farming and fishing community with a variety of fruits and vegetables growing in the hilly countryside. The frequent rains in the region kept the fields and grounds muddy, another aggravation for the captives at the internment camp.

More than twenty barracks had been constructed at the 25-acre Los Baños Internment Camp since its start-up early in 1943. Situated on a plateau next to the agricultural school, these billets were single-story, elongated structures about 150 feet long and 25 feet wide with *nipa* roofs and *sawali* siding. Each held around 100 internees. A dirt corridor bisected each of the barracks, providing a hallway down the center. *Sawali* walls partitioned these quarters into wooden-floored cubicles of eight to ten captives. This provided a little more privacy than the large, crowded rooms at the Santo Tomás camp. The two dozen or so barracks were laid out in pairs roughly in a long column. Each pair of barracks was connected in the middle with crude showers and toilet facilities. The unplumbed toilets were no more than communal outhouses that drained into cement septic tanks.[1]

The entire camp was surrounded by an inner and outer barbed-wire fence. The rickety main gate was on the north end of camp and opened to a roadway angling toward the town of Los Baños to the northwest. A few smaller gates provided openings in the fences at several locations. The fenced camp was not as secure as the walled Santo Tomás campus.[2]

Patty and her ill mother were directed to a barracks next to a chapel near the camp's southeast corner. The billet quartered mostly missionaries and nuns from the various religious groups the Japanese had rounded up in the islands and interned at Los Baños during the past year. Only women were housed in this barracks as all of the living quarters were segregated by sex. When Patty and her mother arrived, they met with the head of the billet, a missionary of the Seventh-day Adventist Church. Selma Croft had once worked with the woman at a Manila hospital.

"I could see she had a little portable burner," Patty said, "and I happened to have a couple of little tea bags from our Red Cross kits earlier in the year. I asked her if she would heat up a little water so I could give my mom a cup of tea. 'No, I can't do that,' she said. 'If I did it for you, I'd have to do it for everyone else.' Here she was a former RN who had worked in a hospital with my mother—and she was so nasty! It turned me against Seventh-day Adventists."

Their rude welcome to Los Baños Internment Camp was somewhat assuaged by a passable meal that evening. "We ate mungo beans and camote for dinner," Patty recorded in her diary entry that night. This barely adequate meal would prove an exception to the rule at their new camp. Patty and her mother soon discovered that the captives at Los Baños were no better off than those starving at Santo Tomás. Despite the close proximity of fruits and vegetables in the surrounding fields, the captives were purposely being deprived of food. A few days after their arrival, Patty and Selma had an emotional reunion with younger brother, Bill, and family friend Hilton Carson. The two veterans of the camp confirmed the dire food conditions at Los Baños.[3]

The chief instigator of their slow starvation was Lieutenant Sadaaki Konishi, who had tormented the captives at Santo Tomás before health issues forced him to leave at the end of March. Soon after Konishi left, music teacher Grace Nash and her family had transferred from Santo Tomás to Los Baños. Later in the year, Nash was horrified to see Konishi report to his new duty station at Los Baños. The sadistic officer moved quickly cutting food rations and devising petty persecutions.[4]

As newcomers to the camp, Patty and her mother had fewer duties than at Santo Tomás. Mere survival occupied the biggest part of their day. Most of the required jobs had been filled by earlier arrivals, so Patty volunteered to labor a few hours a day in the camp garden. Working in the early morning hours, she could hear the distant train whistles from the railway station in Los Baños. She became good friends with another internee who tended the crops, Margie Whitaker, who had transferred to Los Baños with her family at the same time as Patty and her mother.

Two years younger than Patty, Margie had been a sophomore at Manila's Central High School when the Japanese overran Luzon. Margie and her mother, Evalyn, were quartered near Patty and Selma in an enclave known as "Vatican City," so named for the hundreds of Catholic nuns and priests in this southeastern section of the camp. When walking alone, Patty, Margie and some of the younger women worried about sexual abuse by the Japanese soldiers. They agreed to always walk in pairs when crossing isolated areas of the camp.[5]

Much like Santo Tomás, Los Baños Internment Camp was self-administered by the internees with the Executive Committee organizing and overseeing various operating committees. At the camp's inception in 1943, former Manila banker Alex D. Calhoun and several prominent camp leaders from Santo Tomás had been appointed to the new Executive Committee. Late in 1943 the internees lobbied to elect their camp leaders. The new members of the Executive Committee took up their duties early in 1944 with 53-year-old clergyman Harry Fonger replacing Calhoun as committee head. Although the internees had been administering their new community, the camp suffered under the new authoritarian policies of the Japanese army, just as at Santo Tomás.[6]

Commandant Yasuaka Iwanaka showed little interest in overseeing the camp. He was an older reserve officer in the Japanese army, and many of the Americans thought him lacking in intelligence and mostly interested in gardening, painting and writing haiku. Iwanaka's aloofness enabled sadistic Lieutenant Konishi's role as de facto head of Los Baños. Konishi's racist contempt for Caucasians energized his harsh policies harassing and starving the captives. His first official acts at Los Baños were to cut food rations in the camp by 20 percent and to prohibit local Filipinos from selling food to the internees.[7]

Just before Patty and the new group of 150 transferees arrived at Los Baños, Konishi had denied the camp a delivery of Red Cross kits with their life-saving cans of food. Outraged camp leaders descended on Konishi's office to protest this latest cruelty. The Japanese lieutenant sent them away contemptuously, warning as they left, "Before I'm done, you'll be eating dirt."[8]

By fall 1944, camp medical director Dana Nance reported the daily ration at the food kitchen was down to 881 calories, a 65 percent decline from earlier in the year. Cases of beriberi were common by this time. The frail captives' inadequate diet also increased fatalities from dysentery, anemia, and intestinal parasites. The overworked Dr. Nance and his navy nurses had few medications to treat these diseases. The death rate at Los Baños ultimately averaged around seven captives per week, exhausting the camp's malnourished internee gravediggers.[9]

The desperate captives searched the grounds for wild greens to supplement their two meals per day—mostly servings of *lugao*, a thin rice mush rife with worms, mouse droppings and unidentifiable debris. Foraged from around camp, a mixture of leaves, vines and edible weeds simmered in the captives' cook pots. Patty often picked grass and pigweed as a dietary supplement. She remembered a sign that read: KEEP OFF THE GRASS. WE EAT IT. "Pigweed grew everywhere," she said, "and we cooked it for greens. It wasn't much to eat, but at least it was something. It was tasteless. We were eating a lot of pigweed and canna lily bulbs. The bulbs weren't very good, but we were hungry enough to eat them."[10]

Some of the captives cooked the occasional slugs slithering around the barracks, a repulsive dietary supplement that Patty never tried. "But I ate plenty of worms," she recalled. "They were protein. We had women picking out the worms before we cooked the meals at Santo Tomás. But toward the end at Los Baños, we just ate the worms, too."

As Christmas neared, internee conversations were dominated by food cravings and speculations on when American troops would arrive. As much anticipated as the return of U.S. troops was, the captives focused even more on their ceaseless, gnawing hunger. This yearning for food tapped into distant memories of favorite dishes and drove a kind of recipe madness in camp. The captives obsessed on the preparation of past culinary delights, swapping recipes and pictures of these dishes. Discussions about delicious meals remembered from past holidays dominated conversations. "Oh, we were writing recipes all the time," Patty remembered. "When we had magazines, if there was anything about food, we would cut it out and put it on the wall. We would dream about food. Isn't that awful. We were kind of crazy."[11]

Christmas 1944 came to Los Baños with none of the festivities or programs of past holiday seasons at Santo Tomás. Starvation threw a heavy gloom over everything. "We just didn't celebrate it much that year," Patty said. "We had a little Catholic church service, and that's about it."

Shortly after their arrival, Patty and her mother had been moved to a section of their barracks dominated by Catholic nuns. The nuns both irritated and fascinated Patty. She found them aloof and unwilling to share some of the food they had saved. Patty especially craved some of the peanuts the nuns rudely munched in her presence. "And I was dying to see the nuns with their habits off," she said, "but I never did. They kept their heads covered with a blanket when they got up to go to the bathroom outside."

After more than three weeks without a diary entry, she resumed writing on January 1, 1945. "We had a nice dinner for nourishment today consisting of camote, kidney beans and greens," she recorded of the holiday meal. "It sure tasted good!!" The bland New Year's Day meal had obviously been a welcome change from the usual, tasteless *lugao*. Another highlight on New Year's Day was the flight of U.S. heavy bombers spied by the captives. "Today was the first time we've ever seen any four motor, land based planes fly over. There were 22 besides some P-38 fighters. It was a glorious sight." Despite the overall dismal conditions in camp, the flights gave the captives a good start to the new year.[12]

The plane formations continued through the first week of January. "The planes constantly fly over in the same flight of the previous 22," Patty's diary entry for January 2 reads. "Today 24 more." A similar entry follows the next day: "There were 25 B-24s plus 6 B-25s." The camp sensed U.S. ground forces were ever closer to Luzon, and they desperately clung to this prospect.[13]

On January 4 the camp came alive when they heard another flight of planes overhead and a burst of gunfire. The captives initially assumed the Japanese were shooting at the warplanes but soon realized the U.S. planes were firing their machine guns in a pattern: three quick bursts followed by a longer one. *Da-da-da-duumm*. A wave of exaltation swept the internees when they recognized the opening notes of Beethoven's Fifth Symphony—the Allied victory signal! Not only were U.S. forces coming to Luzon, they felt certain, but their rescuers also knew of the camp at Los Baños and were signaling to the starved captives. *They had not been forgotten!* Surely a troop landing on Luzon was just ahead.[14]

"Three years ago today, wow," Patty wrote in her January 6 entry, marking the third anniversary of her incarceration. "Gosh, it seems like forever. There's been a lot of activity all day. 25 B-24s, some B-25s, P-38s and fighters. Everyone expects landings."[15]

The drama at Los Baños continued to build the same evening of Patty's third anniversary. New Executive Committee chairman Murray Heichert, who had replaced Harry Fonger in the new year, was awakened around midnight with an odd demand by the Japanese to send all the camp's shovels to the commandant's office immediately. Heichert roused Arkansas engineer Jan H. "Pat" Hell, who oversaw the camp's gardening efforts, and by 1 a.m. the dozens of shovels were piled around Major Iwanaka's office. The nearly one hundred Japanese guards were milling around the front gate where a dozen troop trucks awaited.

Heichert and former high commission official George Gray, now a member of the Executive Committee, knocked on Commandant Iwanaka's office door to ask about the unusual events of the evening. Upon entering and bowing, they were dismayed at the sight of a disheveled Lt. Konishi sitting at the commandant's desk with a half-empty bottle of whisky. Upon Iwanaka's arrival minutes later, Konishi translated the commandant's bombshell announcement that the Japanese were deserting the camp and turning over responsibility for the captives to the Executive Committee. The Japanese were leaving food, and committee members were to keep the internees inside the camp. "That is all we have to say," Konishi barked to Heichert and Gray. "Now go!"[16]

Early the morning of January 7, the Japanese garrison drove away in the trucks, seemingly abandoning the internees. "I remember being awakened in the early morning hours," Patty said. "There was all this yelling going on, people running back and forth in front of our barracks. I heard shouting: 'We're free! We're free!'"

Patty and her mother stepped outside their barracks to investigate the commotion. Despite her weakened state from beriberi, Patty soon joined in the celebration with the other internees. She had experienced a lifetime of fear, anguish and suffering during the previous three of her barely twenty years of living. But now she and her fellow captives were free of their Japanese persecutors—as best they could tell.

The tropical sun over the east horizon would be the only "rising sun" saluted in camp that day. "We all had decided to have a little ceremony around sunup," Patty recalled, "and someone asked if anyone had an American or British flag. That's when my mother came up with the flag." Patty was as astounded as the others in camp when Selma produced the decades-old U.S. flag. She would never learn where her mother had been hiding the banner presented to Alfred Croft nearly twenty-five years earlier. The Croft family heirloom was joyfully hauled up the bamboo flagpole. Large and badly wrinkled, the Stars and Stripes that Selma had kept at risk of her life would be the first American flag to fly over Luzon since the fall of Corregidor nearly three years earlier. One of the British internees brought out a Union Jack to raise alongside the U.S. flag.

A recording of "The Star-Spangled Banner" blared over the sprawling camp's loudspeakers. Singing the national anthem for the first time in years, American internees, young and old, wept openly. This was followed by the British Royal Marine Band's recording of "God Save the King." Next, a voice on the speakers declared the internment camp would now be called "Camp Freedom." The flag raisings and singing of the national anthems became vivid lifelong memories for Patty. "It was all such a thrill," she said. "We were all crying—but laughing, too."

After the ceremony the flags were lowered out of caution, and everyone turned attention to relieving their intense hunger. Patty went with a group to loot the Japanese *bodega*. "That's what we called it. It was a little warehouse where the guards kept their food. We got into the rice and all the other stuff." Before long many of the camp's residents became ill, their shrunken stomachs unable to handle the bounty of food.

A committee of internees tried to keep order and urged the suddenly freed prisoners to stay inside the camp's fences until more was known about conditions in the area. Yet many could not resist leaving the camp to barter with the Filipinos in the nearby town of Los Baños. Writing pens, articles of clothing, and other personal items were traded for eggs, sugar, salt—even liquor.[17]

Patty's diary entry the evening of January 7 is one of her most exuberant:

> *Today is the most wonderful day in the history of mankind. Wow. Awakened at 3:30 by a lot of people screaming, "We're free." I immediately got up and expected that the troops had arrived. It appeared that the Japanese had left the camp and left the committee members in charge of us. We only had to sleep. Lee Campbell and Tony Montgomery got out their coffee and sugar, which they had just traded for, and we started a fire. Imagine at 3:30 Eddie, Hilton, Odie, Nick and the rest of us all got to go in the cubicle and drink coffee....We immediately got our American flag out. Eddie took it down to the office. At 6:30, the first American flag was raised on Luzon and in the Los Banos Internment Camp. It was raised with the British flag. It was a very impressive ceremony. The Japanese had left all the food behind except for a few sacks of rice and they also left a radio. At 5:00 pm the Voice of Freedom was picked up and transmitted to us by loud speaker. At 6:00 pm we listened to KGEX from San Francisco.[18]*

The second day at Camp Freedom, the prisoners thrilled to the optimistic voice of President Franklin Roosevelt on the loudspeakers telling of a large battle between Allied and German troops in the Ardennes Forest of Belgium and Luxembourg. This was followed by a variety show, whose first tune seemed miraculously directed at the camp's eager listeners. It was the 1930s Cole Porter song, "Don't Fence Me In," a recent hit by crooner Bing Crosby and the Andrews Sisters. The song's lyrics took on a special poignancy for the internees, who boisterously sang along: "Oh, give me land, lots of land, under starry skies above..."[19]

Ominously, Patty noted in her January 8 diary entry, "There are still about five Japanese left in camp. The poor fellows don't know why or where." Speculation was that these soldiers were left to prevent contact between the internees and the local Filipinos. If true, this proved futile. As Patty noted in her diary entry, these soldiers were only guarding the main gate. The captives controlled the other four.[20]

On January 10, the camp's fourth day of freedom, the evening radio broadcast electrified the camp. "This morning, January 9, 1945 [January 10 in the Philippines], General MacArthur led 68,000 men of the U.S. Sixth Army in a landing at Lingayen Gulf, 100 miles northwest of Manila. There was only light opposition from Japanese forces. The battle for Luzon has begun!" This was the news the captives had waited so long to hear. As he had promised, *MacArthur had returned! America had returned!* The news couldn't get much better.[21]

As Patty savored these wondrous events at bedtime, she thought back to that Sunday morning, December 7, 1941, when she had looked out over the placid waters of the Lingayen Gulf before boarding the bus back to Manila with her basketball teammates. Now, just over three years later, these same waters were teeming with U.S. warships and more troops waiting to land. How much her world—the entire world—had changed in those three years. "The news is wonderful today," she wrote in her diary that evening. "At 7:00, the broadcast came true. We have made landings on Lingayen with a convoy of 800 ships 70 miles long."[22]

On and on went the celebration. "We were eating like kings and queens," Patty said. The feasting was relative, of course. For the starved internees, a meal of rice, vegetables and a banana was as delectable as prime rib or filet mignon in their former lives. Bill Croft traded some blue denim, probably looted from the Japanese supplies, with a local Filipino for a chicken, six eggs and two dozen bananas. Patty recorded in her diary the evening of January 12 that she had eaten chicken for the first time in a year.[23]

Yet, despite all the wonderful news and full stomachs for the first time in at least a year, the captives' suffering was not yet at an end. Three days after news of MacArthur's landing in northern Luzon, trucks were heard arriving at the camp in the middle of the night. Hoping to greet American troops officially liberating Los Baños, many of the captives ran to the gate to cheer. But their newly uplifted spirits were crushed by a shocking site. The Japanese garrison and the vengeful Konishi had returned!

Commandant Iwanaka had earlier been ordered to bring his garrison to Manila, but inexplicably received new orders a few days later to return to Los Baños. Angry guards soon began searching the barracks for the American and British flags raised in their absence. Fortunately for Patty and Selma, the internees had rehidden them after the first day's celebration.[24]

As the Japanese soldiers rifled through the captives' meager belongings and bedding, Patty sat outside her billet in agony. "The Japs searched our barracks three or four times trying to find those flags," she recalled. "I remember sitting outside the barracks when they searched and getting so upset. My mother kept telling me, 'Don't get all worked up, Patty, don't get all worked up. They won't find it.' They would have killed us if they found that American flag."

THE LANDING OF MACARTHUR'S Sixth Army on January 10 at Lingayen Gulf came less than three months after U.S. troops first landed in the Philippines on the beaches of Leyte. Lightning speed considering Japanese resistance on Leyte and the logistics of invading Luzon.

As the U.S. invasion of the Philippines had become imminent, the Japanese transferred Lt. Gen. Tomoyuki Yamashita, the legendary "Tiger of Malaya," to Manila to defend the archipelago. He arrived at his post just ten days before the Leyte landing and MacArthur's dramatic splash through the surf on October 20. For his headquarters on Leyte, MacArthur chose a stucco-and-concrete mansion in Tacloban owned by American businessman Walter Price, an internee at Santo Tomás. Once MacArthur's forces were committed to the Leyte invasion, the Japanese navy made a dramatic move to smash the U.S. beachheads. The Japanese main fleet under Vice Admiral Takeo Kurita raced up from Singapore and divided into two striking forces to converge on the freshly landed U.S. troops. This ferocious collision of Japanese and U.S. naval forces would be recorded as the Battle of Leyte Gulf, the largest naval engagement in world history.

Attempting to approach Leyte through the Surigao Strait, the smaller Japanese southern force was destroyed by the U.S. Navy the night of

October 24-25. But the northern force commanded by Kurita improbably sailed through the San Bernardino Strait the evening of October 25 and was just off the eastern shore of Samar Island the early morning hours of October 26. The strait had been left unguarded when Admiral Halsey had famously "taken the bait" and scurried northward and away from Leyte in pursuit of a decoy force of Japanese carriers. Only an outgunned task force of U.S. jeep carriers, destroyers and escorts stood between Kurita's battlewagons and the vulnerable transports of MacArthur's invasion fleet. But the fog of war prevented Kurita from realizing he was routing his enemy and could wreak havoc on the Leyte landings. With Kurita's timid withdrawal, the wide-ranging Battle of Leyte Gulf ended with the Japanese navy a spent force. Increasingly desperate, the Japanese would turn to *kamikaze* suicide flights, terrifying but largely ineffective. [25]

General Yamashita had planned to concentrate his troops on Luzon, but reluctantly reinforced the garrison on Leyte on orders from Tokyo. By November 15 the Japanese general knew Leyte was a lost cause, radioing the island's commander: "IN THE EVENT THAT FURTHER TROOP SHIPMENTS CANNOT BE SENT, LUZON WILL BECOME THE MAIN THEATER OF FUTURE OPERATIONS IN THE PHILIPPINES." Although endless rains had prevented MacArthur from establishing air bases on Leyte to support his troops, by December 26 he declared victory and announced the Leyte campaign closed. Withdrawing Krueger's Sixth Army from the front lines to prepare for the Luzon campaign, the "mopping up" on Leyte was left to the newly activated Eighth Army led by Lt. Gen. Robert Eichelberger. MacArthur had prematurely announced the end of the Leyte campaign as Eichelberger's troops would kill another 27,000 Japanese troops over several more weeks of bitter struggle. The Eighth Army commander called this closing action "bitter, exhausting, rugged fighting—physically, the most terrible we were ever to know." MacArthur had been eager to get on with the Luzon campaign.[26]

Needing the island of Mindoro to establish airfields within fighter range of Luzon, MacArthur's forces easily overran this 4,000-square-mile stepping stone in December. Lying just two hundred miles southwest of Manila and three hundred miles from Lingayen Gulf, the island had been far more lightly defended than nearly everyone but MacArthur predicted. The stage was set for America's return to Luzon, the center of the Philippine economy and government—and where around 5,000 American and 2,000 other Allied civilians languished near death in internment camps.[27]

The first week of January 1945, MacArthur boarded the light cruiser *USS Boise*, his flagship in the thousand-ship armada sailing to Lingayen Gulf. His force of 280,000 men and three-thousand landing craft—some of these boats redeployed after earlier service at Normandy on D-Day—were transported up the west coast of Luzon, close enough for MacArthur to see the familiar outline of Manila, Corregidor and Bataan. He later wrote movingly of seeing those landmarks on the voyage north: "At the sight of those never-to-be-forgotten scenes of my family's past, I felt an indescribable sense of loss, of sorrow, of loneliness, and of solemn consecration."[28]

Japanese commander Yamashita waited for MacArthur on Luzon with 275,000 troops, the largest enemy concentration U.S. forces would face in the Pacific theater. Yamashita knew MacArthur would land at Lingayen— the only approach to the central Luzon plane where U.S. tanks could maneuver. But before MacArthur's arrival, Yamashita had decided not to oppose him on the beaches. Firepower from the naval taskforce could obliterate Japanese defenses along the shoreline. Virtually without air support, the Japanese commander also had little confidence of defeating MacArthur's army inland. He planned only to prolong the struggle and buy time for Japan to strengthen its home defenses.[29]

When MacArthur's 1,000-ship navy dropped anchors the morning of January 10, the placid waters of Lingayen Gulf were ideal for landings. General Krueger's four divisions filled the beaches on a broad front before the day was done. Recreating the landing scene at Leyte, MacArthur waded ashore after stepping out of a Higgins boat just behind the first troop landings. The photographer recording the general's determined look as he splashed ashore was former Santo Tomás internee Carl Mydans, who had mopped floors for nurse Selma Croft in a camp clinic. Repatriated later in 1942, Mydans had been eager to return to his work documenting the war for *Life* magazine. Adding to the theatrics at MacArthur's landing, a small group of Filipinos cheered his arrival. The avenging general had returned not just to another island of the Philippines, but to Luzon, the site of his only—and America's greatest—military defeat.[30]

On January 12, MacArthur moved his headquarters to a schoolhouse in the town of Santa Barbara, twelve miles east of the gulf. Ten days later, the general made an audacious move to Hacienda Luisita, thirty miles closer to the front than Sixth Army commander Krueger's command post. Dismayed at what he considered plodding advances by General Krueger, MacArthur's forward movement was intended to goad the Sixth Army's commander into bolder action.[31]

MacArthur's rapid push to get into Manila was aided by General Ya-mashita's decision not to defend the city, strategically worthless in the Japanese commander's view. The Japanese main force moved to the mountains east of Manila. "I was fighting on ground that had witnessed... my own campaigns at the beginning of the war," MacArthur later wrote. "I knew every wrinkle of the terrain, every foot of topography." Putting this knowledge to use, the general made several dazzling thrusts, landing a corps at Subic Bay above Bataan and putting a regiment ashore at Mariveles on the lower tip of the peninsula. Meanwhile, the Eleventh Airborne Division had been inserted at Nasugbu, about 50 miles southwest of Manila. Even George Marshall, never keen on MacArthur, effusively praised the general's moves from Washington.[32]

By late January, MacArthur correctly reasoned that a "flying column" of heavily armed troops could smash through to the center of Manila. He was greatly concerned that the civilian internees at Santo Tomás—many of whom he remembered from his years in Manila before the war—might be killed by their Japanese captors as U.S. forces closed in.

Fears over American military and civilian prisoners being executed by their Japanese captors were well founded. MacArthur had been appalled when Japanese troops in mid-December 1944 tried to incinerate some 150 American POWs held on the Philippine island of Palawan just southeast of Mindoro. Most were burned alive, but four miraculously lived to tell the gruesome story. It would never be clear if the Japanese had a deliberate policy to execute all U.S. POWs and civilian internees on Luzon, but after Palawan, MacArthur chose to act as if they did.[33]

The first of the raids to rescue POWs and civilians on Luzon was undertaken by a U.S. Ranger battalion assisted by nearly 300 Filipino guerillas on January 28 at Pangatian, near Cabanatuan and just north of Manila. Most of the 200 starving U.S. POWs were barely able to walk when their rescuers reached them, but almost all were brought safely back to American lines. MacArthur was sickened by the abuse suffered by the rescued POWs but heartened by the success of the raid.[34]

Just after the Cabanatuan rescue, MacArthur called on the First Cavalry Division to mount a similar operation for the civilian prisoners at Santo Tomás. At the time, the division was seventy miles north of Manila and facing crumbling resistance from Japanese troops. "Go to Manila," MacArthur told First Cavalry commander Maj. Gen. Vernon Mudge. "Go around the Nips, bounce off the Nips, but go to Manila. Free the internees at Santo Tomás."[35]

On February 3, two 700-man cavalry squadrons, a tank company, and a battalion of 105-mm howitzers reached speeds of thirty-miles-per-hour racing down the eastern edge of the Luzon plains. Marine fighter planes guarded the column's charge into Manila, and one of these planes swooped low over Santo Tomás dropping a pair of pilot's goggles with a note attached for the internees. It read: "Roll out the barrel."[36]

Guided by Filipino guerillas, the troopers smashed through the main gate at Santo Tomás at 9 p.m. that evening. After initial resistance by the Japanese and some lengthy, tense negotiations, the camp was surrendered. The nearly 3,800 starving men, women and children were fed a delicious, full meal of stew the day after the First Cavalry's dramatic arrival. Although enemy casualties were light, one of the Japanese soldiers killed by the U.S. troopers was Lieutenant Abiko, who had chased Patty Croft into the Main Building the day she and her mother left for Los Baños.[37]

General MacArthur visited the freed captives a few days after Santo Tomás Internment Camp was liberated. "I cannot recall, even in a life filled with emotional scenes, a more moving spectacle than my first visit to the Santo Thomas [sic] camp," the general later wrote. "It was a wonderful never-to-be forgotten moment—to be a life saver, not a life taker."[38]

On the grounds of Santo Tomás sometime later, the internees presented representatives of the liberating units with a specially engraved silver cup. The presentation was made at a ceremony honoring these liberators and expressing the former captives' gratitude. "The internees as they looked upon the embarrassed faces of the representatives of the First Cavalry Division...," former prisoner Fred Stevens later wrote, "knew in their hearts that no silver cup, no eulogizing, would ever convey to these men one-half of the sincere thanks and how much their hearts overflowed with gratitude. Through them, they knew their country had not forgotten them."[39]

MacArthur was doubtless encouraged by the successful liberation of Santo Tomás, but the day before this emotional event he had already assigned responsibility for the rescue of the starving civilians at Los Baños Internment Camp. "TAKE NECESSARY ACTION TO ASSIGN ONE OF YOUR UNITS MISSION LIBERATING LOS BANOS INTERNMENT CAMP PLANNING SHOULD BE STARTED IMMEDIATELY SCAP [Supreme Commander Allied Powers]," the February 2 message to Lieutenant General Eichelberger read. Eichelberger delegated the liberation of this second-largest internment camp in the Philippines to the Eleventh Airborne Division on February 4. Commanded by Maj. Gen. Joseph M. Swing, the division was driving toward Manila from the south after its amphibious landing at Nasugbu, southwest of the capital city, and a coordinated parachute assault on nearby Tagaytay Ridge.[40]

MacArthur knew the liberation of Los Baños would be far more difficult than the earlier rescues. The camp was deep behind enemy lines with thousands of Japanese troops nearby. After the Japanese guards were eliminated, the two thousand or more debilitated captives would need a rapid evacuation to safety. Planning and logistics for this feat were daunting. "I knew that many of those half-starved and ill-treated people would die unless we rescued them promptly," MacArthur later said. "The thought of their destruction with deliverance so near was deeply repellent to me."[41]

Fortunately for all concerned with this mission, the Eleventh Airborne's brilliant, young intelligence officer (G-2 in military parlance), Henry J. Muller, had been gathering information about Los Baños since December. As the Eleventh Airborne mopped up Japanese resistance on Leyte, the 27-year-old lieutenant colonel heard about the internment camp while preparing for the division's scheduled redeployment in southern Luzon. Questioning a Filipino grower who had recently traveled through the area, Muller was stunned to hear of the 2,000 or more civilians imprisoned at Los Baños—1,600 of those Americans, 300 British, and the rest from other Allied countries.

Muller immediately informed his division commander, General Swing. The general told his G-2 to send a report about the camp up military channels, but otherwise concentrate his efforts on the division's upcoming operations west of Los Baños.

Although told by the intimidating Swing not to concern himself further with the internment camp, Muller kept hearing the words of the Filipino grower describing the civilians: "They are in pitiful shape. They're dying." Without Swing's knowledge, the intelligence officer resolved to gather any related information he could.[42]

Following the Eleventh Airborne's amphibious landing on January 31 at Nasugbu, Muller met with Maj. Jay Vanderpool, who had spent the last several months behind Japanese lines on Luzon gathering intelligence and meeting with Filipino guerilla groups, including Hunters ROTC near Los Baños. After briefing Muller on Japanese strength in southern Luzon, Vanderpool was asked about the internment camp. He confirmed everything that Muller had heard from the Filipino farmer. The G-2 directed Vander-pool to continue collecting information on the internment camp during future liaisons with the guerillas.[43]

When Swing was formally assigned the Los Baños mission in early February, he asked for and received a delay until he could spare some of his troops, heavily engaged at the time in the attack on Manila. The resourceful Lieutenant Colonel Muller, however, immediately focused on the difficult task of rescuing the captives. Pulling out the maps and gue-rilla reports quietly gathered from Vanderpool over more than a month, he pondered the intricacies of this ultimately epic operation—which in 1993 would be called by Chairman, Joint Chiefs of Staff Colin Powell "the text-book airborne operation for all ages and all armies."[44]

PATTY CROFT BREATHED EASIER after the Japanese search for her mother's U.S. flag proved futile. But she and the other internees soon felt the full wrath of the newly returned Lieutenant Konishi after their brief taste of freedom. Furious over losing face, Konishi demanded the captives return the food and other supplies taken from the *bodega*. Since the captives had already devoured much of the food, little could be done.[45]

The Japanese were especially determined to get back Commandant Iwanaka's looted radio. After repeated searches and threats, the captives eventually turned over a radio. Iwanaka grew even angrier when he dis-covered the radio offered was not his. What the captives couldn't say was that the commandant's radio had already been traded to a Filipino for food. Upon learning that the captives had been hiding another radio all along, Iwanaka likely became concerned that he might be punished by his supe-riors for his negligence. The matter about the radio was dropped, but daily rations were cut to a mere handful of rice.[46]

Few in camp knew it at the time, but another radio in one of the men's barracks would continue to receive nightly news broadcasts. It had been built by an ingenious internee named Gerald Sams, who had been working as a civilian radar expert at Cavite Navy Yard when the Japanese invaded. After listening to the news each evening, he dismantled the homemade radio and hid its various components. To keep up camp morale, he leaked "rumors" about progress in the war from the newscasts. Only a few trusted associates ever saw Sams's radio.[47]

"Everyone is down today because old Konishi returned," Patty wrote in her diary on January 14. "He immediately took over the food bodega and kitchen. Contact has been stopped with the Filipinos." She also wrote about standing for roll call in the middle of the afternoon under the tropical sun. The Japanese had assembled the entire camp for this roll call while they searched the captives' barracks for the radio, food and supplies taken during the guards' absence.[48]

Still, the internees took heart after seeing their captors' recent flight and knowing that U.S. troops were now on Luzon. Surely, they reasoned, the Japanese must know their authority over the internees was about to end. To protest Konishi's cut in daily rations, nearly 100 women from Barracks 22 boldly marched to the commandant's office demanding more food. Patty Croft joined the rowdy group as they trooped by her barracks. "I was with them, too," she recalled. "You bet I was. These were mostly younger women. We were pounding on his desk. He was really mad at us."

They showed Konishi none of his required respect, crowding his office and making threats. Discombobulated by the mob of angry women, the normally imperious lieutenant appeared to give in, agreeing to add a noon meal of rice to the daily rations. That evening, men in camp hid the bags of rice that had been taken from the Japanese *bodega* during the Japanese absence.

The next day, however, additional troops reinforced the camp guards, and Konishi demanded the return of the pilfered rice. The kitchen supervisor was threatened with execution, and Executive Committee members were placed under guard without food. With the captives' brief insurrection at an end, some of the healthier men returned the heavy bags of rice to the *bodega*.[49]

Further dismaying to the captives, the first shooting of an internee by a guard at Los Baños occurred the day after the rice had been returned. Missouri-born Pat Hell had been working as a mining engineer when interned by the Japanese in 1942. Sent to Los Baños with the first group of nearly 800 men in May 1943, the 34-year-old Hell began oversight of the meager garden at the camp. Angered by the Japanese confiscation of the captives' lifesaving vegetables after their recent return, he left camp in the night and planned to sneak back in with food obtained from nearby Filipinos.

Late the next afternoon, several rifle shots reverberated through camp. Hell's lifeless body was found in a ravine just outside the camp's double fencing. His nearby knapsack was filled with coconuts and bananas. In tribute the next morning, several internees covered his grave with red cannas, white phlox and blue cornflowers—a patriotic salute to a brave

American buried on foreign soil.[50]

"Also, the fellow by the name of Pat Hell I knew from the garden was shot trying to get over the fence," Patty recorded in her diary the evening of January 16. "This has been the first person killed in camp. That, of course, upset everyone."[51]

A few days after the mob of women captives had browbeat Konishi into agreeing to increase the daily rations, he reneged. Exacerbating the food shortage, he also prohibited the Filipinos' donation of fruits and vegetables to the camp. During the Japanese absence a number of internees had left camp and testified to the abundance of edibles growing in the surrounding countryside. Konishi's latest cruelties infuriated the starving captives, who were swiftly losing the strength briefly regained from their days of gorging. "The Japanese are not complying with the agreement they made with us," Patty recorded in her diary on January 18. "They have not allowed anything to come into the gate. They're meaner than all get out."[52]

Amid frequent explosions around Los Baños throughout the last week of January, the captives could only speculate how soon U.S. forces might arrive. *Which would come first, the American troops or death by starvation?* "There have been lots of heavy explosions around here, whether it's demolition or not we don't know," Patty wrote on January 25. "There's supposed to be strong fighting in Quezon City. Others say the boys are only in Cabiao, which is 30 miles from the main city of Manila. I always said MacArthur would take Manila by his birthday, which is the 27th."[53]

Yet January 27 passed without an announcement of MacArthur's capture of Manila. Instead, the day brought the killing of another internee at the hands of the guards. "This morning we were awakened at 6:30 by a bullet shot," Patty wrote. "Right away, we thought someone had been shot, either going out or coming in....His name was George Louis from California and he worked for Pan American. He was caught coming back with two gunny sacks of food....Of course, this lowered morale of the camp a great deal."[54]

Louis had suffered only a minor shoulder wound when shot by a guard while trying to slip through the fence. Dr. Nance attempted to treat him as he lay on the ground, but Japanese guards kept him away. After nearly two hours passed, Louis was carried by the Japanese into a guardhouse. Lieutenant Konishi handed his pistol to one of the guards, and Louis was executed with a shot to the head. The Executive Committee sent a letter of protest to the commandant, but Iwanaka was unmoved.[55]

The guard shootings dramatically underscored the captives' peril, but dietary deficiency was the real killer in camp. The resultant beriberi cases were unlike anything seen by Dr. Nance even in his years of practicing wartime medicine in China. Almost all internees were suffering to varying degrees by the wet or dry kind of the disease. The dry sufferers seemed to be shriveling up as they wasted away; the wet sufferers—like Patty and Selma Croft—experienced painful swelling in their extremities. The wet beriberi was more lethal as it could bring on pulmonary edema and congestive heart failure. By late January, Dr. Nance knew that without improvements in the captives' diet, he would be recording deaths on a daily basis.[56]

"Roosevelt's birthday and nothing has happened yet," Patty began her diary entry on January 30. "Gosh, I give up!!" But she didn't. In that same entry she wrote of a rumor that Lt. Gen. George Grunert was leading an army toward Los Baños. "I sure hope it's true because there's only enough rice until the 15th." Grunert had left the Philippines just before the Japanese attack started and was still in the States at the time, so Patty's hope was forlorn. But she and her fellow captives desperately needed this or any kind of hope, even if just a rumor.[57]

As January turned into February, the captives could hear the Japanese guards drinking and carousing until the early morning hours. The internees hoped this presaged another sudden departure by their captors, and the Executive Committee made plans for this eventuality. Yet despite the raucous parties every night, the Japanese remained. "They probably realized they didn't have much of a future," Patty later reflected, "so why not live it up and get drunk every night."[58]

On February 3, Japanese guards went into the barracks offering to trade cigarettes and sugar for rings and watches. The desperate captives were being fleeced of their last few valuables. Patty speculated in her diary that the captives were being starved partly to encourage their trading personal items of value for food.[59]

By early February artillery shelling south of Manila was a distant rumble to the north of Los Baños. News of the First Cavalry's liberation of Santo Tomás the first week of February would not reach most of the Los Baños captives for more than a week later. But looking to the north, they could readily see big events were underway. "Manila is on fire," Patty wrote in her diary the evening of February 3. "At least that's how it looks from here."[60]

The captives at Los Baños had to wonder: Would the fires of Manila liberate them—or consume them?

# CHAPTER 8

✿ ✿ ✿

# America by Air, Land and Water

THE MANILA THAT PATTY CROFT viewed to the north was indeed on fire. Retreating with most of the Japanese army to the mountains of eastern Luzon, General Yamashita had declared Manila an open city, just as General MacArthur had three years earlier. Yet some 30,000 Japanese troops remained in the heart of the city and resolved to fight to the last man. Led by Rear Admiral Sanji Iwabuchi, these mostly diehard sailors and marines wreaked havoc on the Pearl of the Orient in an orgy of burning, rape and murder. Warsaw, Poland, was the only Allied city to suffer more destruction during the war than Manila.

Just four days after the First Cavalry's flying column shoved into Santo Tomás on February 3, MacArthur triumphantly entered Manila's city limits. Two days before his entry, the general released a communiqué. "Our forces are rapidly clearing the enemy from Manila," the message proclaimed. "Their [the Japanese defenders'] complete destruction is imminent." Newspapers and magazines in the States quickly ballyhooed the recapture of the Philippine capital city. In fact, MacArthur and the media's announcement of this near *fait accompli* proved premature. Bitter fighting in the city would continue for another month.[1]

The day the general arrived in Manila, he made an emotional visit to newly liberated Santo Tomás Internment Camp and Old Bilibid Prison, just north of the Pasig River. Bilibid housed thousands of the U.S. troops captured nearly three years earlier with the Japanese invasion of Luzon. "I looked down the lines of men bearded and soiled," MacArthur later wrote of this reunion with his lost command. "Here was all that was left of my men of Bataan and Corregidor."[2]

Shaken from his visit with the survivors at Santo Tomás and Old Bilibid Prison, the general sought action closer to the front lines. He found it just outside the ancient Walled City where Japanese holdouts were making a stand. Behind the high, thick walls, enemy troops were proving difficult to dislodge. To the dismay of his staff, MacArthur glared at distant Japanese defenders behind the walls as sniper rounds snapped around him. The old warrior needed this proximity to the fighting to distract him from the melancholy aspects of the war around him, including the wanton murder of Filipino civilians in the city.[3]

As fighting around the Walled City continued, MacArthur joined a patrol of the 37th Infantry Division as it crept up to the Manila Hotel, where he had abandoned his penthouse and almost all of his personal belongings three years earlier. As the general watched U.S. troops rid the historic hotel of remaining Japanese defenders, flames suddenly engulfed the penthouse. "I watched, with indescribable feelings, the destruction of my fine military library, my souvenirs, my personal belongings of a lifetime," he wrote. Like most of his fellow American *Manileño*s with whom he had lived before the war, MacArthur would lose most of his family's belongings and personal reminders of that tranquil life in Manila in the 1930s.[4]

Driving hard from south of Manila to link up with MacArthur's liberators streaming from the north, troops from General Swing's Eleventh Airborne Division saw the same flames devouring Manila that Patty Croft could see from the internment camp at Los Baños. A week after Santo Tomás was liberated, troops from the Eleventh reached the southern boundary of Nichols Field and faced stiff opposition by the Japanese. To provide unity of command in the recapture of Manila, on February 10 the Eleventh was transferred from Eichelberger's Eighth Army to Lt. Gen. Oscar Griswold's XIV Corps, a part of Krueger's Sixth Army.

As the paratroopers fought for control of Nichols Field and nearby Ft. McKinley, MacArthur landed at the airfield in a small spotter plane. With bullets still flying around the contested air base, MacArthur met with General Swing and Lt. Col. Doug Quandt, the Eleventh Airborne's operations officer (G-3). "Joe, I want you to liberate Los Baños as soon as you can," MacArthur told the Eleventh's commander. "And if you're going to do this, Joe, do it right." It was not unusual for MacArthur to appear at the front lines, but it was unusual for him to personally give an order to an officer several links below him in the chain of command.[5]

After the meeting with MacArthur, Quandt immediately returned to division headquarters in Parañaque, just south of Manila, to begin planning the Los Baños rescue with the division's G-2, Henry Muller. Muller, of course, had already accumulated substantial intelligence on the internment camp courtesy of Major Vanderpool and his Filipino guerillas. Quandt emphasized MacArthur's "do it right" comment to Muller, and both agreed this would require diverting a substantial force of Eleventh Airborne troops from the fighting in Manila.[6]

By February 12 the Eleventh had secured Nichols Field and a day later the airborne troopers linked with elements of XIV Corps's three divisions, including First Cavalry's Santo Tomás liberators. Enemy troops had been expelled from much of Manila, but isolated pockets of resistance would remain until early March. By then, a burned-out and gutted Manila would have little resemblance to its former status as a tropical paradise in the western Pacific. Worse still, around 100,000 *Manileños* would be dead.[7]

By mid-February, Swing's division was moving south and east of Manila to seize towns on the western shore of Laguna de Bay, whose southern shores harbored the town of Los Baños. On February 17, Swing received the formal written directive from his new commander to "prepare to carry out the Los Baños special mission on order by Commanding General, XIV Corps." General Griswold set February 23 as the target date for rescue of the 2,100 internees at Los Baños Internment Camp. The stage was almost set for what would arguably be the most daring, complicated and successful airborne operation of World War II.[8]

HAVING WATCHED THE DISTANT FIRES of Manila and heard the faint explosions the first few days of February, the internees at Los Baños were dismayed by a lull in the violence on February 6. The leaping flames and thundering guns had at least meant U.S. troops were getting closer, the captives thought. The sudden quiet on the northern horizon was disconcerting and depressing. It could mean a delay in their liberation.[9]

Even a brief stay in the troops' arrival would mean death by starvation for some of the captives. "Today is our last day for rice and then we run out," Patty Croft recorded in her diary the evening of February 7. "The food situation seems to be the worst. Only enough food until the 19th.

After that, I guess we go hungry." Since the captives were already starving from inadequate rations, her wording of going "hungry" after February 19 actually meant going without *any* food. Unless a new source was found, in less than two weeks not even a scrap would be available for the prisoners.[10]

The afternoon of February 9, the captives noted two U.S. planes flying low over their camp. The planes made several passes as if trying to get a better view of the camp's layout. Patty noted this curious flyover in her diary that evening: "Two planes flew over here really low. They were so low that we could see the star on the wing and also the pilot. They seemed to be looking the camp over because they flew over too many times."[11]

The two planes were likely requested by Eleventh Airborne's G-2, Lieutenant Colonel Muller. Swing and Quandt's meeting at Nichols Field with MacArthur on the liberation of Los Baños was probably not until February 10, the day after the two planes surveilled the Los Baños camp. But the resourceful Muller was not about to be caught flat-footed. Since his meeting with the Filipino grower in late December, he had devoted some of his limited time to thinking about a rescue operation. General Swing might not have approved early on, but as events unfolded, he—and the internees—was fortunate to have a G-2 with Muller's initiative.

Although the captives sensed their situation was about to change, they suffered even more as conditions deteriorated. The camp was blacked out at night, and a visit to the latrine could be a frightening ordeal. Not even a sliver of light guided the way down the dirt-covered hallway in the barracks. Some of the desperate internees captured fireflies in bottles to mark the pitch-black pathway.[12]

The ever-sadistic Lieutenant Konishi found a new way to torment the captives by restricting salt in the camp rations. Salt beds were plentiful in the Philippines, and the captives had never imagined a shortage in camp. Coupled with the intense hunger pangs from slow starvation, the suffering from salt-deficiency added to the camp's miseries. Only by refusing work details were the captives able to pressure Konishi to restore a minimal amount of salt to their rations.[13]

Chilling to the internees, the Japanese were digging a large ditch in camp. A machine gun was positioned on a slope overlooking this long trench. The captives were well aware of the Japanese history of never freeing prisoners. *Was Konishi planning a mass execution of the internees as American forces neared?* "When the Japanese started digging that big ditch, they told us they were going to put a building there," Patty remembered. "I think they planned to execute us." The starving, tormented captives could only wonder.[14]

"Two Philippine Island scouts came into camp last night and had a conference with the committee and wanted to know the conditions of the camp," Patty noted in her February 13 diary entry. "They were told the camp was badly in need of food and that one man died yesterday because of starvation." The two daring Filipinos were likely part of Vanderpool's guerilla coalition gathering information about the camp in preparation for the rescue.

The Japanese collected all the shovels in camp earlier that day, just as they had before suddenly leaving in early January. Excitement ran high among the internees.[15]

The next day, Patty made her first diary entry acknowledging the liberation of Santo Tomás more than a week after the camp's dramatic rescue and where she had languished for nearly three years. "Rumor is that St. Tomas [sic] has been freed and that the American Red Cross is feeding the camp," she recorded. "They would have to free it first now that I left the place. Gosh, that makes me mad." Obviously, the news was bittersweet for her—happy that her former fellow prisoners were finally free but frustrated that she was not among them. Patty had been against the December transfer to Los Baños, but her mother had prevailed.[16]

By the middle of February, activity in camp had slowed to a bare minimum. Most of the internees were too weak to work, and the increasingly nervous Japanese guards greatly restricted their movements around camp. When camp leaders requested they be allowed to negotiate with locals for rice or coconuts, Konishi disingenuously told them the local Filipinos had all fled to the hills and not to expect more food. "Of course, that makes us all depressed," Patty understated in her February 15 diary entry. "We're getting weaker and weaker and thinner and thinner."[17]

The captives could hear the sound of distant battle growing louder each day. Flames on the horizon were now seen in several different directions. A Japanese supply truck came into camp covered in blood—an indication the Japanese were under attack by local guerillas, the internees speculated. And almost daily now, American planes swooped low over the camp.

As tension built, the camp's dwindling rice rations stopped completely on February 19. Konishi announced that future camp rations would be limited to *palay*, unhusked rice. The captives' daily ration would consist of 500 grams, which after husking would provide a couple of hundred calories at most. Consuming raw *palay* caused bleeding in the digestive tract, so each internee would have to laboriously husk their ration and cook the meager proceeds.[18]

"We had tables in the dining area where we were husking the *palay*," Patty recalled. "But our sight was not that great, and our fingernails were not that great. Somebody came up with the idea of using two boards to grind the *palay* between. And then you had to pick out the kernels of rice individually. I still think about that now every time I cook rice."

Husking *palay* became a full-time obsession and all-hands effort by the starving internees. They knew they were only buying time with their husking and could not survive much longer. "We hope to have some extra rice or else we would have to stay up all night in order to get some rice for breakfast," Patty wrote in her diary on February 20. "We worked all day trying to get enough to eat. Our eyes are ready to fall out. Everyone is so depressed."[19]

Yet, momentous events were at hand. The night of February 18, captives Ben Edwards, Freddy Zervoulakos and Prentice "Pete" Miles "went over the wall," Patty noted in her diary. "They were supposed to have gone to join the force." There were no walls at Los Baños Internment Camp, so she meant the three men had escaped under or over the fences. The "force" that they were to join was a reference to the local guerrillas now working with the U.S. military on Luzon.[20]

"I knew Ben Edwards better than the other two," Patty recalled. "I remember he was with Pan Am before the war. I knew him just well enough to say 'hi' when we met in camp. We didn't really know for sure what they were up to, but we might not have survived without them."

THREE DAYS BEFORE THE TRIO made their escape, 20-year-old Freddy Zervoulakos had helped Executive Committee member George Gray sneak out of camp for a night meeting with local guerilla leader Tavo Inglés. Affiliated with the Hunters ROTC guerillas, Inglés told Gray of the camp's impending rescue by American troops and Filipino guerillas. The guerillas had just learned of this from their U.S. liaison, Major Vanderpool. The Eleventh Airborne planned to liberate Los Baños on February 19, Inglés said. Unknown to the guerilla leader, rescue planners had changed the date to February 23 to ensure availability of enough C-47 transport planes.[21]

Gray's news of the rescue both excited and frightened internee leaders. The captives immediately began planning to send an American internee to speak directly with U.S. military planners. Veteran of numerous nighttime forays outside camp, the half-Filipino Zervoulakos was selected to guide Edwards and Miles under the fences the evening of February 18. Just an hour after their escape, the three rendezvoused with a group of Filipino guerillas led by Romeo Espino, *nom de guerre* Colonel Price.[22]

The escapees were startled to see an American soldier with these guerillas. Sgt. John Fulton was wearing what looked to the Americans like a German army helmet. Fulton was the first American soldier seen by the internees in more than three years and before the U.S. Army replaced the shallow World War I helmet with the newer head cover. The Eleventh Airborne radio operator was working behind enemy lines to keep the guerillas in communication with division headquarters in Parañaque. "Hiya, Mac!" was all Fulton said to the surprised escapees as the guerillas quickly hustled the three away. The party needed to reach the shores of Laguna de Bay by daylight, where they would travel first by *banca*, the native outrigger dugout, and then overland to Parañaque to confer with the rescue planners at Eleventh Airborne headquarters.[23]

Around noon the next day, the escapees and their guerilla escort landed their *bancas* at Barrio San Roque, where they met guerilla leader Abdinago Ortiz. Colonel Ortiz's guerillas would guide them the rest of the way to Parañaque, ten more miles by *banca* and ten miles on foot. After Ortiz described the hazards of this journey, the escapees decided to send Pete Miles first. If he were captured or killed by the Japanese, then another of the runaways would attempt the journey. After Miles's first full meal in months, he sailed for Parañaque later in the afternoon.[24]

Eleventh Airborne's temporary headquarters in Parañaque was in a stylish old Spanish villa with a formal garden and swimming pool. Here Muller and Quandt had been collaborating on a plan to rescue the captives since General MacArthur had personally assigned this task to General Swing. The morning of February 20, the two planners brought in Maj. Hank Burgess, commander of the First Battalion of the Eleventh's 511th Parachute Infantry Regiment (PIR). Burgess's troopers had been pulled from the fighting at Fort McKinley for the rescue mission.

Muller and Quandt had earlier determined that the rescue of the 2,100 internees depended first and foremost on the element of surprise—*a big, lethal surprise.* Any forewarning of the raid on the camp would likely mean death for many or all of the captives. The First Cavalry's liberation of Santo Tomás had worked well enough, but the raid on Los Baños was different. At Santo Tomás, the flying column had essentially moved the front lines of U.S. forces to the internment camp. The captives remained in camp guarded by the cavalrymen as more U.S. forces swept into the heart of Manila. The Los Baños internees, however, were some ten miles behind firm enemy lines and within twelve miles of an estimated 8,000 to 10,000 Japanese troops of Maj. Gen. Masatoshi Fujishige's Eighth Infantry Division. After the camp's guards were eliminated, the captives would need to be evacuated—*and fast*.[25]

The operation as planned by Muller and Quandt would be unavoidably complex with forces converging on the camp by land, air and water. The land force would be an understrength reconnaissance platoon from the Eleventh acting as pathfinders and supported by Filipino guerillas. This covert force would make the initial assault on the camp guards. Simultaneously, a company from Major Burgess's battalion would parachute in and join the attack. Coordinating with the land and air assaults, the remainder of Burgess's battalion was to motor across Laguna de Bay in fifty-four amtracs, amphibious armored vehicles, and then across the two miles from lakeshore to camp. After the camp was secured, the troops would coordinate the evacuation of the 2,100 captives in the amtracs, which were to return to American lines across the bay.

Creating a diversion as the rescue began, the Eleventh's 188th Glider Infantry Regiment would mount a coordinated, ground attack on the small town of Calamba, off Highway 1 about five miles northwest of Los Baños. This diversionary attack was intended to deter Fujishige's Eighth Infantry Division from sending troops to Los Baños if the rescue bogged down. Most of Fujishige's troops had been positioned astride Highway 1 about twelve miles southwest of Los Baños to prevent U.S. troops from moving down the highway into southern Luzon. The U.S. diversionary force also planned to break through near Calamba and move eastward with troop trucks to link with and evacuate Burgess's battalion of paratroopers.[26]

Violating a cardinal rule of this type of military operation—simplicity—the rescue mission had numerous moving parts. Any number of things could go wrong. This would be an unpracticed Hail Mary pass by units of what would be called the Los Baños Force.

Concerned with the complexity of the raid, the planners knew they needed a more detailed picture of the camp and the daily routines of the guards and captives. Drawn from aerial photos, their maps of the sprawling camp lacked specificity. How many guards were in the camp? What was their fighting capability? Where were the guards' strong points? What was the physical condition of the internees? How many sickly captives would need to be carried to the amtracs? In short, they needed an insider's view of Los Baños. H-hour was less than seventy-two hours away.

As if providence intervened, that very afternoon the planners got their insider when a bedraggled Pete Miles was led to the Eleventh's headquarters by the division's recon platoon leader, Lt. George Skau. The perceptive Skau had joined Miles behind enemy lines after learning that he was en route to Parañaque. Understanding the trove of useful information Miles could provide, the recon veteran personally escorted the escapee to division headquarters, where Muller, Quandt and Burgess were puzzling over the details of the rescue operation.

Miles had not slept since leaving Zervoulakos and Edwards at Barrio San Roque early the previous day, but he was eager to give the planners key details of the camp—information that only an insider could provide. The mission planners could hardly believe their good luck. Not only had Miles been a captive at Los Baños, but he also had an eye for precision and detail like the mining engineer he had been before the war. Miles even produced a crumpled map of the camp that he had drawn earlier with details and distances on gates and guard posts. He described the poor condition of the internees and the deaths each day from starvation.[27]

After pumping every detail of the camp's layout from Miles, Muller suggested they discuss the daily routine of the guards and captives. Miles explained the daily roll calls, when the captives were awakened by the camp's gongs, and almost as an afterthought mentioned the guards' morning routine of outdoor calisthenics.

Muller seized on the offhand remark about the guards' exercise routine. *"Every morning?"* he asked excitedly. *"What time?"*[28]

"They start exercising at quarter to seven," Miles replied, giving details about the 30-minute daily routine performed in an open area away from the captives' barracks. The escapee described the "saber-dancing ritual" most of the camp's eighty guards performed while stripped to their G-string-like *fundoshi* undergarments—and with their rifles stacked inside a nearby building.[29]

It didn't take a military genius to grasp the significance of the Japanese morning calisthenics. Muller and Quandt quickly agreed to change H-hour on February 23 from 8 a.m. to 7 a.m.—right in the middle of the unarmed guards' daily workout in an open field. Both must have thought: *This is too good to be true!*[30]

Using Miles's insider information, the G-2 and G-3 finalized plans for the mission and began the assembly phase. Lt. John Ringler's B Company, 1st Battalion, 511th PIR, was selected for the jump. The paratroopers were pulled out of the fighting east of Nichols Field on February 21. Down to eighty men after the fierce combat around the airfield, Company B would be reinforced for the jump with a light-machine gun platoon from 1st Battalion's Headquarters Company.[31]

On February 20, fifty-four Water Buffalo amtracs of the 672nd Amphibian Tractor Battalion pulled away from the fields of the Manila Polo Club where they had bivouacked for two weeks. Resembling a Sherman tank without the turret, the noisy transports began a circuitous three-day journey southward to the community of Mamatid, nestled against the southwest shores of Laguna de Bay and about seven miles northwest of Los Baños Internment Camp. Within range of enemy artillery, the amtracs assembled along the lakeshore as darkness descended the evening of February 22. Absent B Company, Major Burgess's 1st Battalion troopers slept on the sandy beach alongside the amtracs. Embedded with the paratroopers was an exhausted Pete Miles, who insisted on joining the rescue effort.[32]

The afternoon of February 22, nine C-47s airplanes of the 65th Troop Carrier Squadron lined up beside a runway at Nichols Field. The men of Lieutenant Ringler's B Company would spend a restless night under the wings of the planes that would transport them over Los Baños at daybreak. "We realized we might be dropping into a hornet's nest, which could result in considerable casualties," Ringler later said. But despite the danger, he noted, the paratroopers' morale was high. "This was truly an ideal airborne mission, and this is what we were trained for."[33]

As the paratroopers settled in under the C-47s that evening, members of Lieutenant Skau's recon scouts and more than one hundred Filipino guerillas met in a one-room schoolhouse in the village of Nanghaya, about ten miles east of Los Baños. After a briefing by Skau, they split into six teams around 10 p.m. and began an all-night march to the camp. Four of the teams were to creep into position around the guard posts and initiate the assault at 7 a.m. in coordination with the parachute drop. Immediately preceding the attack, the other two teams were to detonate phosphorous grenades to mark the landings for the paratroopers to the east of camp and the amtracs to the north. Accompanying the recon force that evening were Freddy Zervoulakos and Ben Edwards. Like Pete Miles, they were selflessly returning to Los Baños to help liberate their fellow captives.

Zervoulakos fell in with one of the teams that included Sergeant Fulton, the Eleventh Airborne radioman that the escaped captives had briefly seen two nights earlier with the guerilla group. On February 20, Fulton had sent a crucial radio message to Eleventh Airborne headquarters from guerilla leader Colonel Price. The message read: "URGENT: ...Have received reliable information that Japs have Los Baños scheduled for massacre." Since sending this message, Fulton had been working frantically with the guerillas to save the captives.[34]

THE INTERNEES AT LOS BAÑOS knew the end of their captivity was near; they just weren't sure how. Liberation, death by starvation, execution—each was a possibility. Since February 19 they had received only *palay* for rations. Those physically able spent their hours trying to separate the precious kernels of rice from the husks, hoping to collect enough to live another day. "You could hear the hungry little children crying in the night," Patty recalled. "I could hardly walk. Beriberi was in my feet. My mother and I both had swollen legs. My younger brother was so pitiful."

Patty's diary entry the evening of February 22 gives no hint the captives suspected American troops were only hours from entering the camp. "Washington's birthday," the entry begins—like a number of earlier references to American holidays. "This afternoon, there was a wonderful bomb just over the hill. There were 10 P-38s dropping bombs on some troop concentrations. This, of course, lifted our morale." So profound was the desperation of the captives that U.S. bombs falling nearby raised their spirits more than frightened them.[35]

With the starving internees sleeping as best they could in the hours just before dawn, the various units of the Los Baños Force began to converge on the camp. The lumbering Water Buffaloes were the first of the main rescue force to get underway. The fifty-four amtracs rolled across the beach at Mamatid and into the dark waters of Laguna de Bay at 5:15 a.m. The two companies of paratroopers filled only about half the amtracs, which noisily crossed the lake waters in a column of threes at 5-miles-per-hour. They embarked with plenty of time to ensure the 7 a.m. H-hour landing on the south shore of the lake. Using only hand-held compasses to guide them through the darkness, the amtrac operators steered a 7-mile southeasterly arc toward the beach north of the internment camp.[36]

As the last of the amtracs chugged away from the shoreline at Mamatid, a raging General Swing rushed to the edge of the lake waters shouting profanely. He had intended to be riding in the lead amtrac, but his jeep driver had become hopelessly lost in the predawn darkness, nearly driving over the edge of a deep gorge. The general soon took to the sky in a single-engine spotter plane to observe the action from above Los Baños. Although most of Swing's division was still fighting in Manila, he was all too aware of MacArthur's personal interest in this rescue mission. Swing was determined not to disappoint a five-star general.[37]

Loaded with the paratroopers of B Company and the light-machine gun platoon, the nine C-47s roared away from Nichols Field at 6:40 a.m. as scheduled. After orbiting the airfield one time, the formation of "three Vs of Vs" leveled off to 1,000 feet heading southward. The 20-minute flight to Los Baños provided the troopers just enough time to go through their pre-jump checks. The planes dropped to 800 feet as they neared the drop zone, a strip about 500-yards wide by 1,000-yards long. This would put paratroopers on the ground about 800 yards northeast of the internment camp.[38]

As jumpmaster for the drop, Lieutenant Ringler stood in the doorway of the lead C-47 as the formation neared the drop zone, which he had selected from a map only the day before. He had cautioned his paratroopers to avoid the railroad tracks just outside the landing area and the nearby power line. "If you hit it, you're fried," he warned the paratroopers of the transmission line. Standing by the glowing red light next to the jump door, Ringler gave the command to "Stand up and hook up." He searched the ground ahead for the smoke marking the drop zone.[39]

Having left the Nanghaya schoolhouse briefing shortly after 10 p.m., Ben Edwards had joined a recon team led by Sgt. Martin Squires, one of the few troopers in the Eleventh who wore glasses. The glasses gave him a studious look leading one recon scout to give him the nickname "Martin the Thinker." Seeing that Edwards was armed only with two hand grenades, Squires had reluctantly given the civilian his .45 automatic. After hiking all night, Squires's team moved into position on the camp's northwest section by the old YMCA building. A few minutes before 7 a.m., a dog suddenly attacked one of the guerillas in Squires's group. Reacting reflexively, the Filipino shot the animal. The blast shattered the early morning silence of the camp. Inexplicably, the guards seemed undisturbed by the shot.[40]

As the blast echoed across the Los Baños campus, Lieutenant Skau and his team were still a quarter mile from the camp. Their Filipino guide had briefly become confused in the dark, and the group had fallen behind schedule. Skau's force, including some of the best guerilla fighters of Hunters ROTC, had the all-important task of destroying the building that held the exercising guards' stacked rifles. It was imperative that the team be in position by 7 a.m. Still some distance from the camp as they heard the drone of the approaching C-47s, they began a desperate sprint to the main gate.[41]

JUST BEFORE H-HOUR, 7 a.m. on February 23, the sound of the morning roll-call gongs reverberated through camp. The weak, sleepy captives swung out of their bunks for their morning assembly. Patty and her mother shuffled out of their cubicle and exited their barracks heading to roll call. Hearing the drone of the C-47s just northeast of camp, Patty looked skyward. She was immediately transfixed by the sight of parachutes blossoming in the light of early dawn. "We all at first thought it was food being dropped for us," Patty recalled. "But then we could see the soldiers hanging from the parachutes. We all went wild!"[42]

They also were jolted by a continuous stream of gunfire erupting across camp. "That's when my mother said we'd better go back to the barracks and get under our bed," Patty said. "We took off. I didn't know who was doing all the shooting, but I sure didn't want to get shot."

Breathing heavily as they collapsed near the front gate, Lieutenant Skau's team had barely made it before the first parachute opened—the predetermined signal for the recon scouts and guerillas to begin the assault. Seeing that first parachute pop, Skau tapped the head of the scout next to him signaling the trooper to fire a bazooka that demolished the stone pillbox guarding the front entrance. Bursting into camp, Skau's team raced against the Japanese troops toward the building that held the stacked rifles.[43]

Watching the C-47s northeast of camp, Ben Edwards and Sergeant Squires's recon team had nervously awaited the first parachute's opening. Seeing the first chute blossom, Edwards pulled the pin on one of his grenades and lobbed it over the fence at a guardhouse. Scaling the outer fence and crawling under the inner one, he fired his newly acquired .45-caliber pistol at two guards running from their post. To his amazement, one of the guards dropped. Explosions and gunfire erupted all around him. A bullet hit the ground just in front of him causing small, painful wounds to his shins. He suddenly thought how the well-worn khaki shorts from his internment years were not the proper dress for battle.[44]

Skau's team beat the scrambling Japanese troops to their stored weapons. The lieutenant tossed a white-phosphorous grenade inside the building housing the rifles, and it erupted in flames. Unarmed and nearly naked, scores of guards ran in all directions trying to escape the ferocious American and Filipino assault teams. The guards were cut down like cattle to slaughter, many falling under the lethal bolo knives of the guerillas. Only a handful from the Japanese garrison escaped into the nearby woods. Among those who got away, the internees would learn to their dismay, was the hated Lieutenant Konishi.[45]

After running the half mile from drop zone to camp, the airborne troopers of B Company charged through the front gate about 7:20. The jump had gone well, only one ankle injury to a paratrooper who had landed on the rail track that Lieutenant Ringler had warned about. But the locked-and-loaded troopers saw little action after rushing into camp. The recon platoon and guerillas had violently and efficiently annihilated the Japanese garrison in the minutes after H-hour began. The primary task of the paratroopers would now be boarding the sickly, frightened captives onto the amtracs. They fanned out to bring the internees out of the barracks where most of them had taken refuge when the shooting started.[46]

In Patty's barracks, Filipino guerillas with limited English-speaking skills entered before the paratroopers. "In the excitement when the guerillas came in," she said, "we all thought they told us to get our hands up. They had actually asked if there were any Japs in our barracks."

After the guerillas left and while still sheltering under her bed, Patty heard heavy footsteps outside her cubicle. "I heard this *clomp, clomp, clomp*," she said. "We had a dirt floor in the hallway dividing the barracks. Of course this soldier had his rifle and other equipment on him, so he was hitting the dirt pretty hard. I got out from under the bed and stepped out of the cubicle into that hallway."

She suddenly froze, staring at what she considered the best-looking American GI she had ever seen. "Are...you...a marine?" she asked haltingly, her eyes widening by the second.

"Hell, no! I'm a paratrooper," he retorted.

Looking oddly disappointed, Patty complained to the GI, "All my days at Los Baños, I've dreamed of being rescued by a Marine. And you're not a Marine!"

Despite her momentary disillusionment, Patty of course celebrated with her fellow internees. America had finally arrived—in the form of giant paratroopers with bloused fatigue pants stuffed into combat boots. These seemingly huge, heavily muscled GIs were the most beautiful sight the puny, scruffy captives could imagine. The healthy, handsome young Americans had come to liberate them. After three years of demoralizing isolation and latent concern that their fate had been overshadowed by the war effort—*America had not forgotten them!*

Not realizing the imperative of a quick evacuation, the more than 2,100 captives quite understandably only wanted to celebrate, frustrating the paratroopers who struggled to get the revelers' attention. The internees couldn't grasp the fact that they were still in grave danger when all they could see around them were well-armed American troops. They were joyously oblivious to being well behind enemy lines and uncomprehending of the threat posed by a division of Japanese troops within twelve miles of camp. They could also be fired on by the handful of guards who had escaped the slaughter and several enemy detachments around Los Baños.[47]

The additional troops from 1st Battalion soon arrived in the amtracs. The beach landing had gone as planned, and the paratroopers had readied for a fight as they lumbered over the two miles to camp. With Major Burgess aboard, the first amtrac smashed through the camp's barbed-wire fences around 7:30. But instead of hearing the expected gun battle upon their arrival, they mostly heard cheering internees. With the camp rapidly filling with the huge Water Buffaloes, the rest of the amtracs began lining up outside the front gate.

Burgess deployed A and C Companies in blocking positions around the camp to protect against a counterattack. With the Japanese Eighth Infantry Division within a few hours of Los Baños, General Fujishige could easily send a large force to spoil the party. But the celebrating civilians just didn't understand their peril and showed no urgency to climb aboard the amtracs. They attempted joyous small talk with their anxious rescuers and begged food and cigarettes. Many were determined to pack their accumulation of worn personal belongings despite the sudden irrelevance of this mostly junk.[48]

One of the amtracs parked just outside Patty's barracks, and that was as far as she and her mother ventured into the raucous camp. "The troops said we would be leaving in the tanks and could take one bag with us," she said. "I grabbed my accordion. It was the only thing I still had that was worth anything." She also packed a few personal items, including her no-longer secret diary. Sitting in the armored confines of the amtrac, she never saw the scores of Japanese bodies scattered around camp, many horribly mutilated from the Filipinos' bolo knives.

Scrambling aboard the amtrac with her daughter, Selma Croft took only one bag. She worried about her young son, Bill, who was nowhere in sight. She could only hope for the best. She and Patty were surprised to see other internees trying to carry all of their virtually worthless possessions with them—empty cans, broken toys, ragged garments. Some of these possessions were remnants of the once-affluent lives of these civilians before the war. "I even saw my friend Eileen's dad trying to carry his *filthy mattress* with him!" Patty said, still amazed by this recollection.

With so many of the civilians wanting to continue the celebration and others laboriously packing all of their possessions, the rescuers became frustrated. The need to get the internees into the amtracs had become urgent. In desperation, Lieutenant Ringler suggested to Major Burgess that the troops set fire to the barracks to get the internees moving. Burgess concurred, and the paratroopers began igniting the dry *sawali* structures. With that, the holdouts abandoned most of their useless effects and started boarding. They began to leave behind a dark chapter of their lives.[49]

Loaded with 1,500 of the liberated captives, the caravan of amtracs began the two-mile return to the beach about 9:30. The remaining 600 or so refugees in camp would have to walk to the beach and await the amtracs' return later in the day. Men, women and children rode in the first convoy of armored vehicles with around 150 of the weakest on stretchers. Taking a well-earned rest in one of those stretchers was returned escapee Pete Miles. Having provided vital information about the camp to the rescue planners in Parañaque several days earlier, he had gallantly returned for his fellow internees in one of the amtracs. After three days with almost no sleep, he collapsed from exhaustion once the camp was secured.[50]

As the long column noisily clamored the two miles to the beach, scattered gunfire from Japanese troops in the surrounding woods occasionally pinged the armored sides of the amtracs. As oblivious to the gunfire as those inside the armored vehicles, Filipinos came out of their houses to cheer the passing parade. Patty and her mother hunkered down with two dozen mostly Catholic nuns in their vehicle. Most of the civilian passengers were surprised that the Water Buffaloes barely slowed as they lumbered from land to water and began to churn northward across the lake.[51]

"After we got in the water, I went up on top with the GIs," Patty recalled. "I wanted to get into their rations. I wanted *some food. Oh, those candy bars!* They were wonderful." The soldiers were happy to pass out field rations, candy bars, and American cigarettes to the newly liberated captives. Despite the festive mood, a soldier on each side of the amtrac stood ready with a .50-caliber machine gun to discourage distant Japanese troops taking potshots.

"While I was eating, the Japs started shooting down on us from the side of a mountain," Patty said. "One of the paratroopers pushed me down onto the motor of the amtrac and burned my leg." It was a minor injury easily ignored in the joy of the moment. Suppressing fire from the .50-calibers soon quieted the Japanese guns on the distant hillsides.[52]

"That was scary for a while," Patty said, "and the amtrac went so slow across the lake. It seemed like hours to me to get to the beach at Mamatid. I don't remember much on that ride except thinking I was finally free and could eat as much as I wanted. That was enough! I only briefly thought about where they might be taking us." She was for certain they were being taken out of the hands of their Japanese captors—that, too, was enough.

Soon after the amtracs left with the first group, the remaining 600 internees assembled with most of the paratroopers to begin the two-mile march to the beach. Some of the troops formed a rear guard to protect the internees, but the scattered gunfire from the distant Japanese was largely ineffective. Filipino guerillas carried baggage for many of the weak, tired evacuees. By 11:00, most of the remaining internees and troops were assembled at the beach awaiting the amtracs' return.[53]

After the former captives were safely out of camp, the original plan had been for most of the 1st Battalion paratroopers to advance westward through the town of Los Baños and to link up with the diversionary force on Highway 1. This force, consisting mostly of the Eleventh's 188th Glider Infantry Regiment, was to provide troop trucks for the paratroopers' return to American lines. Major Burgess, however, was unable to make radio contact with the diversionary force and didn't know how far the regiment had been able to advance down Highway 1. Moreover, he was concerned that troops from Fujishige's nearby infantry division might be moving northward, which could block his planned linkup with the diversionary force.

When General Swing, circling above in the spotter plane, contacted Burgess by shortwave radio around midmorning, the commander on the ground told Swing that he wanted to cancel the planned linkup and instead evacuate his paratroopers in the returning amtracs with the remaining civilians. Swing, on the other hand, saw no reason for a change in plans. He suggested 1st Battalion make the linkup with the Eleventh's glider infantry regiment and help hold the new ground taken by the diversionary force. "Could you do this without heavy casualties?" Swing asked hoping for an affirmative response.[54]

Burgess hesitated. He knew his troops were completely exhausted from their earlier fighting in Manila and the still-underway rescue mission. Plus, 1st Battalion's advance to the linkup on Highway 1 could turn into a disaster if Fujishige's troops intervened. And the weary paratroopers had already given out most of their rations to the hungry internees. Turning the shortwave radio off, Burgess never responded to his commanding officer. He told the radioman to stow the radio as it would no longer be needed. Radio communication was notoriously bad in this part of Luzon, the major considered, and General Swing would just have to understand. Burgess and the rest of his battalion would remain on the beach and ride back on the amtracs with the rest of the civilians that afternoon.[55]

Lt. Col. Henry Muller had spent a frantic morning at headquarters in Parañaque trying to communicate with the rescue units. The division G-2 wouldn't learn of the mission's progress until the first group of liberated civilians arrived at Mamatid around midday. Muller had been especially concerned about Fujishige sending some of his infantry to Los Baños and wrecking the rescue. By 5 p.m. Muller had received word that the last of the civilians and paratroopers had landed safely at Mamatid.[56]

By any measure, the historic rescue was a spectacular success. Of the 2,146 rescued, around 1,600 were Americans, a little more than 300 were British, and the rest represented seven other Allied nations. Miraculously, none of the civilians had been killed in the daring raid, although one, Margaret "Betty" Silen, had taken a bullet to her hip. Three other civilians were slightly wounded by a single bullet that passed through the arm of one, the abdominal wall of another, and into the hand of a third. Two of the Filipino guerillas had died in the initial assault on the camp, and two more were wounded along with two of the Eleventh's recon scouts.[57]

Muller, who had planned the rescue effort since his meeting with the Filipino grower in late December, could turn in that evening with a feeling of relief and pride. "Everything that could have gone wrong didn't go wrong," he later noted of the complex mission. "Everything that had to go right did go right. Murphy's miserable law was suspended for twenty-four hours."[58]

Patty and her mother arrived at Mamatid with the first group of evacuees in the amtracs around noon. "I didn't see any town," she remembered. "There was just an open area by the edge of the lake. There we got on troop trucks to take us to New Bilibid Prison." The trucks didn't arrive for several hours, so the weakened civilians waited on the beach in the tropical sun. Many became badly sunburned, their skin fragile from malnutrition. Still, the former captives maintained a celebratory mood while begging for any remaining rations from the GIs around them.[59]

Midafternoon, they boarded the troop trucks for the twenty-mile drive northward to New Bilibid Prison in Muntinlupa. The Japanese had held U.S. civilian and military prisoners at the facility, which had only recently been liberated by American troops and cleaned in preparation for the Los Baños evacuees. Upon arrival, the former captives were greeted by the glorious sight of a huge American flag billowing over New Bilibid's administration building.

Climbing from the trucks, the civilians formed lines to receive a chocolate bar, a pack of cigarettes, and dated Red Cross mail from friends and family in the States. After claiming floor space in their dormitory-like cells, the weary but jubilant civilians formed a long queue that evening for a scrumptious meal of corned beef and vegetable stew. Dinner was served out of sparkling-clean garbage cans, and ravenous refugees wept openly as they savored the plain fare. Many returned for seconds and thirds. The heavy eating was too much for long-empty stomachs, and many became violently ill soon afterward.[60]

After an evening of overeating and socializing with internee friends, Patty returned to her quarters with her mother, where they would sleep in true freedom for the first time in nearly thirty-eight months. Even after the momentous events of the day, she took the time for her final diary entry after years in captivity. "Today was one of the most wonderful days in history—the day we were freed," she wrote. "At 7:00 o'clock, the roll call gong went off and we started out for roll call when a plane [sic] flew over and dropped about 200 parachutists. We of course knew the time had come. We all went hysterical."[61]

It had been a day of days for the young woman, who had gorged on a variety of foods that afternoon and evening, and blissfully retched over a toilet in her new quarters. Barely twenty years old at the time of her rescue, memories from that day would fill her with joy and awe all the years of her long life. "God, those parachutes falling were a wonderful sight," she said seventy-eight years later. "I'll never forget it. Whenever I'm a little down or depressed, I just think about that sight."

# CHAPTER 9

※ ※ ※

# Farewell to the Islands

MANY OF THE RESCUED INTERNEES began their first full day of freedom with a chapel service and communion. With New Bilibid Prison serving as both a refugee camp and a military hospital, recovering U.S. soldiers attended the Sunday morning services with the freed civilians. Not in attendance were any of the weary heroes of the Eleventh Airborne. The paratroopers returned early that morning to the front lines of battle in nearby Manila. The tired GIs had barely gotten to meet the freed captives, many of whose lives were likely saved by the troopers.

Still busy with the fighting, General MacArthur sent an appropriate message to the newly liberated civilians. "Nothing could be more satisfying to a soldier's heart than this rescue," he wrote. "I am deeply grateful. God was certainly with us today."[1]

Extolling Swing and the Eleventh Airborne's execution of the rescue mission as "magnificent," MacArthur was elated that none of the civilians had been killed. Yet stateside news about this brilliantly executed rescue was eclipsed by a concurrent wartime event. As Patty Croft motored across Laguna de Bay with the first group of evacuees the morning of February 23, five marines and a navy corpsman hoisted an American flag atop Mt. Suribachi on the island of Iwo Jima far to the northeast of the Philippines.

A photo of this iconic scene won a Pulitzer Prize for Associated Press wartime photographer Joe Rosenthal, and the U.S. celebrated this step toward seizing this strategic island less than 800 miles from Tokyo. Bitter fighting on Iwo Jima continued for several weeks afterward, however, with U.S. newspapers and magazines giving much of their coverage of the Pacific theater to this bloody struggle. The Eleventh Airborne's remarkable rescue of the civilians faded from the news.

Exploring her new surroundings on her first full day at the repurposed New Bilibid Prison, Patty was impressed with the hospitality of what had been a dreary wartime prison camp not long before the arrival of the rescued civilians. "Bilibid was quite large and spread out, just one-story high," she remembered, "but it was actually pretty clean. The army had done a good job getting it ready for us." She would be sleeping in a bunk bed above her mother, and their large, unlocked cell would be shared with a number of other civilians.

"We really didn't have any more privacy at Bilibid than we had at Los Baños," Patty said. "But we weren't used to privacy, so it didn't really matter. The first few days we mostly sat around in our quarters and talked." They also ate three good meals a day for the first time in years. Their food was prepared by the army, and the civilians dined in the luxury of the facility's large mess hall. Within a month, most of the former captives gained back much of the weight they had lost.

A few days after settling into their new billet, Patty and Selma were reunited with younger brother, Bill, who was quartered in a different area of the sprawling facility. "He was really thin, but he appeared to be doing alright," Patty remembered. "But he had been in that barracks at Los Baños with those seamen and rough-type people. To me, he never seemed quite the same after those years." Patty and Selma learned that family friend Hilton Carson had suffered a slight head wound during the rescue when grazed by a bullet or piece of shrapnel, but he was recovering and resting at New Bilibid with the others.

Despite the relative safety of their new residence, many of the liberated civilians became frightened by Japanese shelling in the area as fighting around Manila continued. Some of the women were terrorized by a weak Japanese attack on New Bilibid. After all they had endured, the thought of falling back into Japanese hands was too much for some of the stressed former captives. Several screamed hysterically before U.S. troops quickly repelled the Japanese assault.[2]

Feeding the thousands of refugees at New Bilibid posed a supply problem for the military, who struggled to truck in the daily food requirements with Japanese artillery menacing the roadways. Supply officers devised a novel solution, and once again the civilians stared up in wonder as multi-colored parachutes drifted from the sky. But this time crates of food were being dropped instead of paratroopers. The various colors of the para-chutes signified the types of food being supplied. These drops restarted the rumor mill among the still-nervous civilians with some speculating that a food shortage was leading to this desperate action by the army.[3]

The military caretakers showed great patience with the traumatized civilians, even catering to their obsession for tin cans. During captivity, tin cans were treasured possessions of the internees—all-purpose contain-ers for eating, drinking, cooking and cleaning. When soldiers saw former captives digging through garbage to salvage discarded cans, they tried to discourage this unnecessary habit. Giving up, the military began providing shiny, new cans to civilians who still felt they couldn't live without them.

Military doctors initially encouraged the internees to eat in small quan-tities, but most of course found this advice hard to follow. Many continued to suffer when their digestive systems rebelled against the suddenly over-whelming diet of full meals. Once the former captives became convinced that the bounty of food really would last, most began to relax and temper their eating habits.[4]

Within a few weeks of her new diet, Patty's beriberi cleared up, and she regained much of her weight. A large part of her eating consisted of foods mostly nonexistent over the previous three years. "I couldn't get enough sweets, cakes and pies," she said. "I was getting pretty thin before our rescue, but I wasn't as underweight as my mother. She was down to eighty pounds. She was really thin." Both Patty and Selma would return to their pre-war weight within a few months.

Besides malnutrition, examinations by the military doctors revealed that almost all the civilians had another condition in common—intestinal parasites commonly referred to as "worms." "Oh, my gosh, did I have worms," Patty recalled. "We all had worms. We were still taking pills to kill those worms after we returned to the States." Most of these parasites came from the captives eating unsanitary and often undercooked meals. Still, only 107 of the more than 2,100 rescued from Los Baños required hospitalization. This low percentage doubtless resulted from the effective self-administration established by the captives, including the heroic efforts of the overworked and undersupplied internee medical staff.[5]

As the rescued captives recovered from their long ordeal, tragically, the Filipinos who lived near the destroyed camp at Los Baños paid a horrendous price following the internees' liberation. Reports confirmed that the sadistic Lieutenant Konishi had been one of the few in the camp's garrison to escape the violent attack by the American and Filipino force. Gathering up the scattered Japanese troops in the vicinity of the camp, the ever-vindictive Konishi led an attack on the village of Los Baños. As punishment for the Filipino guerrillas aiding the paratroopers and locals cheering the rescued captives, the rampaging Japanese exacted a savage toll on the native civilians.[6]

On the Eleventh Airborne's return to the Los Baños area several weeks after the rescue, Maj. Hank Burgess, who had commanded the liberators of the camp, reported an overwhelming stench of death around the town. Upon investigation, Burgess reported that genocidal Japanese troops had "tied families beneath their homes with their arms behind their backs around the stilts, or posts, supporting the house....Men, women, and children were all tied, block after block, then the area was set afire." It was estimated that more than 1,500 natives of Los Baños paid for the camp's liberation with their lives, hundreds burned to death. The rescue had been a triumph for the Americans—but a catastrophe for the locals.[7]

In mid-March, Jean MacArthur visited the rescued civilians at New Bilibid. Many of them were old friends and acquaintances of Jean and the general from the halcyon years before the war came to Manila. In an earlier visit to the recovering civilians at Santo Tomás, she had been shocked at the sight of her starved fellow Americans in their ragged clothes. Embarrassed by her own stylish attire, she quickly discarded her hat and gloves. She was better prepared to greet the former internees at New Bilibid.[8]

"I remember sitting on my top bunk when Jean MacArthur came in," Patty said. "It was after we had settled in at New Bilibid. My mother of course knew her and had played bridge with her before the war. She came in to visit, and I sat on my bunk rocking my legs back and forth as she greeted my mother."

Patty had been surprised that MacArthur's wife had visited New Bilibid as the area was still technically in a war zone. She noted the esteemed visitor had several army guards with her and remembered Jean and her mother embracing as old friends would. "I didn't get a hug from her," Patty said, "but at least I could talk to her. She visited with my mother for some time as I sat on my bunk."

As her health returned, Patty felt an emotional tug from nearby Manila, the center of her childhood memories. Torn from her home by the Japanese before graduating high school, here she was more than three years later—a young woman filled with a chaotic jumble of difficult memories and unprocessed feelings. She longed to return, if only briefly, to the site of that orderly world in the final months of her senior year of high school.

Donning khaki skirts like those worn by army nurses, Patty and another New Bilibid resident, Betty Gardiner, hitched a ride in a jeep with a pair of friendly GIs. Approaching the heart of the former Pearl of the Orient, they quickly realized the city of their childhood no longer existed. They had seen the distant flames and heard the explosions, but they were not prepared for the endless blocks of burned-out buildings, the anguished Filipino faces, the smell of death. The scenic tropical streets of their childhood were now unrecognizable.

"We went to find Betty's house first, more in the center of Manila," she recalled. "We started down her street but someone warned us that the street was mined. So we got out of there in a hurry." They gave up trying to visit the apartment building in Pasay where Patty had lived, driving instead to the familiar confines of Santo Tomás Internment Camp. Most of the thousands of their former fellow captives were still convalescing there. They had warm reunions with a number of their friends including Patty's former roommate, Eileen Aaron.

But some of the internees they had known at Santo Tomás had died or been killed in the three months since Patty and her mother had left. One of the more notable deaths was that of Carroll Grinnell, the former General Electric executive who had been the leading figure among the civilians at Santo Tomás. Just before Christmas, Grinnell and several other camp notables had been arrested by the Japanese without explanation and taken away. Their bodies were found in late February north of Pasay near Harrison Park, where they had been executed. Patty had known Grinnell and his family since her early childhood in Santa Mesa. She would always remember him as a caring leader of the internees who did his best in an impossible situation.[9]

Hearing that fifteen of the newly liberated civilians at Santo Tomás had been killed when the Japanese shelled the camp on February 7, Patty was astounded to learn that one of those fatalities was a woman who had taken Selma's bed on the first floor of the Main Building. Probably out of spite, the Japanese had fired on the camp hours after General MacArthur's visit. The unfortunate woman had claimed Selma's bed shortly after Patty and her mother had left for Los Baños. If they had stayed at Santo Tomás, as Patty had argued, her mother might have died in the artillery attack. "My mother had always been kind of psychic," Patty said. "She had said she felt like something bad was going to happen if we stayed at Santo Tomás. She was sure right about that!"[10]

Driving back in the jeep to New Bilibid, they passed through an area still under fire from Japanese snipers. That was more than enough adventure for one day. "I don't think my mother even knew that I took that visit to Manila," Patty said. "She would have been pretty upset. But, you know, we were young and willing to take a chance."

With no shortage of handsome young soldiers around New Bilibid, Patty and her girlfriends' social lives improved as they convalesced. Many of these troops were from the First Cavalry Division, which was bivouacked at a nearby rest area. Bands occasionally performed in the mess hall at New Bilibid, and the female residents had their pick of dancing partners. "Those soldiers had not seen American girls in a long time," she said. "We might have been a little thin, but they thought we were something else. We girls never had it that good again in our whole lives."

Patty began seeing a First Cavalry captain from Arizona, and she arranged a date for her friend Betty with a 22-year-old lieutenant from Oklahoma named Paul J. Kelly, who served with the captain. "We all would dance when the bands played," Patty recalled, "but we mostly sat around and talked. We couldn't really go anywhere in a war zone. Betty sprained her ankle one day and wasn't around when Paul came to see her. Paul told me to quit pairing him up with Betty because he wanted to start seeing me."

Patty soon dropped her captain and began socializing with the handsome First Cavalry lieutenant. The two became good friends over the next few weeks, but Patty's thoughts were turning more to her impending repatriation in America. General MacArthur had ordered all American internees back to the States once they were given medical clearance by the military doctors. None of the civilians would be allowed to stay in the Philippines unless they could offer a compelling reason. By early April, Patty's brother Bill—ill and still thin—had already left for California. She and her mother began preparing for their own departure.[11]

In the early morning hours of April 10, Patty and Selma once again rode in a long convoy of troop trucks carrying them and hundreds of their fellow former internees to Manila harbor to board a navy transport ship bound for California. As the trucks made their way to the docks, the former captives waved back at cheering Filipinos along the route. But the departees were shocked by the devastation in the city. Many of the landmarks of Manila had been destroyed.

A Filipino band played "Farewell to You" as the civilians arrived at the bay to board the *USS Admiral E. W. Eberle*, a Benson-class troopship making its maiden active-duty voyage. Around 2,500 former captives, almost all Americans from the camps at Santo Tomás and Los Baños, struggled up the long gangplank for the three-week voyage to California. Shiny tin cans dangled from the bundles of many of the boarders, still nervous about their future after years of terror and uncertainty.

Escorted by two U.S. Navy destroyers, the *Eberle* pulled away rapidly from the Manila shoreline and into enemy-infested waters. The civilians took a long look at the former island paradise they had once made their home. For many of these doctors, nurses, teachers, engineers, missionaries, businessmen and children, it would be their final view of the devastated city, whose tropical beauty now existed only in their memory.[12]

Patty and Selma were assigned hammocks below decks where they shared space with other passengers in the crowded, sweltering ship's hold. "We were sleeping troop-style," Patty said. "There wasn't much room between the hammock below and the hammock above." Word soon passed around the ship that a Japanese submarine was stalking the *Eberle*. "We were sitting around the deck with life jackets on," Patty remembered. "We were afraid we were going to be torpedoed. After going through all we had, then to die at sea would have been awful."

A few days after departing Manila, the ship stopped briefly at the island of Leyte to pick up returning U.S. soldiers, and there the passengers learned that President Roosevelt had died the day before. "It was a big deal on the ship," Patty recalled. "But a lot of those coming back from the Philippines didn't like him because they believed he had left us stranded in Manila when the war started."

After leaving Leyte, the top-heavy ship was hit by a typhoon. The *Eberle* wallowed in the raging seas and nearly capsized several times. The long-suffering former internees endured the seasickness and terror. At least they were headed to the States. The Japanese submarine gave up its chase in the turbulent waters, a side benefit of the dangerous storm.[13]

One unfortunate passenger died at sea—a girl on the voyage home with her father. "That Reynolds girl was about fourteen and was sleeping not too far from me when she got really sick," Patty remembered. "Her dad had already lost his wife, and then his only child when she died. They buried her at sea. That was awful watching her body go down."

Near the end of April, the *Eberle* anchored briefly offshore Honolulu, where Selma had given birth to Patty decades earlier. Passengers were not allowed to leave the ship as many had no proof of U.S. citizenship. This security measure was a reminder that America was still at war. Most of the returnees' birth certificates, passports, and other vital records had been lost during their internment. Patty and Selma were among these undocumented passengers. U.S. officials came aboard and continued on to California, interviewing each of the former captives and beginning the process of restoring a record of their past and proving their identities.[14]

As the troopship neared the U.S. coast, excitement built among the passengers. Many were returning to an America that until only recently they had been unsure of seeing again. Having left behind their homes, careers, and in many cases, all their earthly possessions, the returnees were understandably anxious about their futures. But they were alive, and for the time being that would suffice.

The large transport slipped into the harbor at Los Angeles at 8 a.m. the morning of May 2. Welcoming strains of "California Hear I Come" greeted the disembarking passengers, many of whom dropped to their knees and kissed the ground. Patty and Selma didn't, but they shared the sentiment.[15]

The Red Cross oversaw the homecoming arrangements and declared the group's arrival the largest of the civilian repatriations from the Philippines. The 2,500 new arrivals were driven to the spacious Elks Temple at West Lake Park (later renamed MacArthur Park to honor the general) where they could unite with relatives and receive needed services and assistance by the Red Cross and other groups. The temple was a temporary refuge as the civilians confirmed their citizenship.[16]

The first repatriates to arrive at the temple that morning were Ernest and Gladys Wichman, and their two boys, Daniel, 3, and Douglas, 2. Obviously named for the captives' anticipated liberator, Douglas had been born at Santo Tomás Internment Camp, the only home he had ever known. The boys were taken to the children's reception center and given toys to play with, the first real play things little Douglas had ever held. Perplexed, he didn't know what to do with them.[17]

Patty and Selma had no relatives waiting at the Elks Temple. Like each of the repatriates, they received two hundred dollars from the Red Cross for new clothes, other personal items, and travel expenses. The Red Cross helped them with their plans to proceed to Oakland to join Bill, who had arrived a week or so before them. After completing required government paperwork, they departed the mass of former internees with whom they had shared what seemed like a lifetime of fear, sadness, starvation, boredom and anguish. "It may sound strange," Patty said, "but it wasn't that difficult to separate. Some of them we were happy to get away from. But I exchanged addresses and kept in contact with ones I was close to."

That evening Patty and Selma spent a restless night at a nearby hotel in downtown Los Angeles. They had grown used to sleeping in a large group and were bothered by the novelty of trying to rest alone in a crowded modern city. "Believe me, it was very hard to sleep with all the sirens going off and traffic noise," Patty recalled. "There were fire trucks and police cars making a lot of noise."

They left the next day on a train for Oakland where they would reunite with Bill at Selma's widowed father's house. Five days after their arrival, the surrender of German forces on May 8 set off VE-Day (Victory in Europe) celebrations across America. Patty didn't recall going out on the town to mark this red-letter day in World War II. "I think we were too tired," she said. The former internee briefly enjoyed celebrity status in her grandfather's neighborhood. "Everywhere I went people wanted to give me things to eat," she said. "When I went to the drug store in Oakland, they would give me free ice cream sodas."

As part of the former internees' repatriation process, a thorough medical examination was required. Patty's examination was scheduled at a hospital in San Francisco. "We didn't have a car," she recalled, "so I took a ferry across the bay and then a streetcar to Knob Hill. I checked in at the hospital and got in bed. The doctor came around and asked me what I was there for." She told him of having been asked to report to the hospital for an evaluation of her overall health and possible treatment. "He said, 'You don't need to stay here. You just have worms.' So he gave me medication and discharged me." She would continue to take pills and drink liquids for several more months as part of a de-worming regimen.

Patty began receiving letters regularly from Lt. Paul Kelly, still stationed with the First Cavalry in Manila. In June, Paul wrote that he was being transferred to Camp Atterbury in Indiana, where he would be discharged from the army. He wanted to visit her in Oakland while in transit. "He stayed at my grandfather's for about a week," Patty recalled, "and took me out on the town. We went to the best restaurants in San Francisco, to the Top of the Mark and the Fairmont." Their relationship became more serious.

In July, Patty took a train to Chicago to visit some of her mother's relatives. Paul invited her to stop along the way to meet his parents in Oklahoma City, where he was spending the remainder of his thirty-day leave before reporting to Camp Atterbury. Patty's reunion with Paul was covered by the local newspaper with the news account highlighting her years in captivity.

Continuing on to Chicago, Patty stopped off in Louisville, Kentucky, to visit high school friend Nancy Taylor, who had left Manila before the Japanese invasion. Once again the local media capitalized on Patty's internment story. Her interview by the *Courier-Journal* in Louisville was picked up by the Associated Press news service, and a subsequent front-page story by the *Cincinnati Enquirer* misidentified her as an "Army nurse captured on Bataan." These news accounts would be the first of many throughout her life about the extraordinary experience of her internment.[18]

Patty was still in Chicago on August 6 and August 9 when the atomic bombs were dropped on Japan. The Japanese surrender on August 14, V-J Day (Victory over Japan Day), set off a new round of celebrations in cities across America. The Japanese defeat had a special poignancy for Patty— as it did for most of the other civilian and military prisoners who had suffered at the hands of their Japanese captors. "I remember being in Chicago visiting some cousins I had never met when the Japanese surrendered," she said. "That was a big, big day for me. Got out in the street and celebrated."

Returning to Oakland after her Chicago trip, she enrolled in fall classes at nearby Armstrong College in Berkeley. With no record of her high school coursework and no diploma to show for it, Patty's college matriculation was unusual. She was allowed admission on a trial basis. If she was unable to keep up with her classmates, she would be expelled.

In September she began taking a bus to Armstrong each morning and sitting in a classroom surrounded mostly by 18- and 19-year-olds, whose experiences over the previous three years had been far different from those of a newly repatriated former prisoner of Japan. Walking around the Armstrong campus with no concern about hostile armed guards or her next meal, she was often struck by how much her life had changed from just months earlier. At times she felt she existed in a parallel universe. How could she now be a college freshman in such a comfortable, predictable world when just seven months earlier she was a wretched captive in a foreign land facing starvation or execution, desperately grinding *palay* to stay alive?

"It was a weird world for me," she admitted of that period. "Just weird. I had nothing in common with my classmates. I didn't have any friends among them." But her instructors seemed to understand her unusual background and took an interest. For an assignment in her freshman composition class, Patty wrote about her experiences growing up in Manila and her years of captivity. "Boy, was my teacher ever impressed!" she recalled. "She urged me to write a book about it."

She continued getting letters from someone who could relate to her experiences of the last few years—someone with whom she could identify. Lt. Paul Kelly had also spent years fighting to stay alive in New Guinea and the Philippines, and had been among the first American troops to embrace the emaciated captives of Santo Tomás and Los Baños. The bond between the two continued to grow. About to be discharged from the army, Paul visited Patty again that fall in Oakland. The war veteran provided a connecting bridge from her former world in the now-shattered Pearl of the Orient to her new world in an America that could scarcely understand whence she had come.

The America of her new home was a nation undergoing a convulsion. The millions of veterans streaming home from Europe and the Pacific were eager to begin or return to careers and family. The nation's conversion back to a peacetime economy would begin several decades of unprecedented growth and affluence. Patty found herself in a fast-paced society much in contrast with her years of confinement and the life she had known before the war. "To me, America was much more glamorous than the Philippines," she said. "All the stores and modern conveniences. It was a much faster lifestyle than I had known."

Christmas 1945 was a time of healing for Patty and her family in Oakland, just as it was for families across America. The war had been disruptive, if not tragic, for those who had lived through it. But that Christmas was a magical time for Patty Croft, barely 21-years-old, already with life experiences most could hardly imagine. Now she was engaged to be married to one of those young American heroes who had come for her and her fellow captives in their darkest hour.

Patty and Paul Kelly were married in Oklahoma City on February 24, 1946, one year and a day after Patty had been rescued from Los Baños

Internment Camp. Fittingly, Paul wore the dress uniform of an officer in the First Cavalry Division. The bride's hand in marriage was given by her older brother, Al, now a junior officer in the U.S. Navy.

Sadly, Selma was unable to attend her only daughter's wedding. She had returned to Manila the month before trying to regain money and property possessed before the war. Now officially divorced, the 52-year-old former captive was starting her life over practically destitute. She would be unable to recover any of her money or household furnishings.

Revisiting the burned-out barracks at Los Baños where she and Patty had been held the year before, Selma was slowly walking through the rubble of their cubicle when she felt something in the debris under her foot. Examining the fused mass she had stepped on, Selma recognized the set of silver spoons with the letter C on the back of each. The spoons were the parting gift to Patty from the elderly woman in their Santa Mesa neighborhood in the 1930s. Nearly destroyed in the barracks fire, the charred spoons would make a telling souvenir from their months at Los Baños— and a pleasant reminder of her family's happier years in pre-war Manila.

Selma found a kindred spirit when she visited former internee Hilton Carson, who had returned to his beach home in Manila after his rescue. Hilton could relate firsthand to Selma's uprooted existence. Their friendship soon grew into a romance, and they would marry in Manila.

In 1946, Selma attended the war crimes trial for Sadaaki Konishi in Manila. The sadistic officer had been captured on Luzon three weeks after the surrender of Japan. Her attendance at the trial, of course, was personal. Konishi had not only caused untold suffering and death in and around the internment camps, but also had threatened the lives of Selma and two of her children. Although the sadistic officer had eluded the guerillas and paratroopers at Los Baños, he would not escape justice before a military commission. He was tried at the former residence of the U.S. high commissioner of the Philippines and later hung at Sugamo Prison in Japan. Konishi was one of 920 Japanese soldiers and officials executed for war crimes.[19]

Selma and Carson eventually left the Philippines to live in Sarasota, Florida. By the time of their return to the States, the Philippines were no longer a commonwealth under the U.S. flag. On July 4, 1946, the United States kept its promise of independence, and the Philippine Republic was launched. American flags throughout the islands were lowered. Although some U.S. citizens stayed, Selma and Carson joined a contingent of Americans who returned to the States following the islands' forty-seven years of U.S. administration. The American era in the Philippines had ended.

Upon her move to Florida, Selma continued to safeguard the American flag she had provided for the emotional flag-raising ceremony at Los Baños in January 1945. It was the 48-state flag presented to her husband by Governor-General Leonard Wood in the early 1920s. It was the flag that in some respects symbolized the American experience in the Philippines.

Like millions of Americans after the war, newlywed Patty Croft Kelly set about building a marriage and before long raising a family. Living in the dry, windswept state of Oklahoma, her mind often wandered back to the lush, tropical islands of her youth. She eventually adjusted to her new life in a much different world—but the old memories never faded.

"I missed the Philippines for a long time after I got back to the States," she said. "It was home and where I had spent almost all my life. I remembered all the fun times we had with the social events at the Polo Club and other places like that. Oh...all the colored lights and the trees at the Polo Club. And not far away, the waves crashing on the beach. Lots of big dinner parties. It was a wonderful lifestyle, a slow easy life."

And she has never forgotten the sight of parachutes falling in the early light of a tropical dawn.

# EPILOGUE

ON A WINTER MORNING IN FEBRUARY 2018, Patty Kelly Stevens walked into the U.S. Army Airborne & Special Operations Museum on a special mission. Seventy-three years earlier to that very day, a U.S. Army airborne unit on another special mission had given her and more than 2,100 other civilian prisoners of Japan a gift—their freedom. Now, on the seventy-third anniversary of that February morning in 1945, Patty had a gift of her own to bequeath—a century-old symbol of freedom and liberty that had been a family treasure for most of its existence.

The Croft family's U.S. flag had followed the vicissitudes of America's presence in the Philippines for a quarter century before it started a new journey when Selma Croft Carson returned to the United States after the islands' independence. The flag began following the life changes of an American family. For two decades living in Florida, Selma continued to safeguard the large banner that she had risked her life to preserve in two internment camps. As time took its toll with Selma's death in 1968, the flag was passed down to her youngest son, Bill. The former American *Manileño* had experienced the trauma of internment as an adolescent in one war only to be called by his country a few years later to serve in another U.S. war, this one in Korea.

Two years after Bill's premature death in 1969, Patty Croft Kelly asked her widowed sister-in-law to send the flag to Oklahoma for the funeral of

Paul Kelly following the First Cavalry veteran's death in September 1971. "I remember that flag being flown out to Oklahoma City and hand carried by someone from Braniff Airlines," Patty said. "I don't think I had seen it since it was raised at Los Baños. My mother had kept it for nearly all those years."

The forty-eight-star banner had been presented by Governor-General Leonard Wood to Patty's father, raised over "Camp Freedom" at Los Baños, safeguarded by her mother and brother in Florida, and used to cover WWII veteran Paul Kelly's casket. Although she had been indifferent to the flag as a youth in Manila, the banner became a priceless family heirloom for the former internee, who became Patty Kelly Stevens with her remarriage in 1990.

By late 2017, Patty was 93 and once again widowed. Her son, Paul Kelly Jr., became concerned about what might happen to the family's treasured flag in the event of his mother's passing. His unease was heightened at the time by national anthem protests on television—especially disturbing to him after what his mother and grandmother had endured in the internment camps while preserving this national symbol of freedom. Paul and his sister, Carole Kelly Summers, might safeguard it for a while. But if passed down to Patty's grandchildren, would they understand this storied flag's significance to the family?

A friend of Paul's suggested finding a museum to preserve these colors. Considering the Eleventh Airborne Division's role in freeing the internees at Los Baños, Paul found what he considered the most appropriate permanent residence for the large banner. Late in 2017, he contacted officials at the U.S. Airborne & Special Operations Museum in Fayetteville, North Carolina. Learning the flag's proud history, museum director Jim Bartlinski was more than receptive to preserving it. "We have an obligation to care for that flag until the end of time," he said after Patty and family members traveled to Fayetteville to pass the heirloom to the museum.[1]

On February 23, 2018, Bartlinski and Patty spoke to a group gathered at the museum and told the long history of the old flag and the amazing rescue of the civilian internees at Los Baños. The presentation ceremony at the museum added a little extra to the day for Patty Kelly Stevens, but since 1945 she had always celebrated February 23. She still does. "If I want ice cream and cake, I have it," she said. "It's just a big day."

Patty Kelly Stevens stands at the display of her family's century-old U.S. flag with a paratrooper mannequin descending from above at the U.S. Airborne & Special Operations Museum in Fayetteville, N. Carolina. Patty and family members traveled to the museum to donate the banner on Feb. 23, 2018, the 73rd anniversary of her and 2,145 other captives' liberation by the 11th Airborne Division's 511th Parachute Infantry Regiment. *Photo courtesy of Carole Kelly Summers*

# NOTES

## CHAPTER 1: EASY LIVING IN PRE-WAR MANILA

1. "Fire Creates Panic at Manila Carnival," *San Francisco Chronicle*, Feb. 6, 1920, 8.

2. "Early Day Birdmen Meet After Long Separation," *Los Angeles Times*, Jan. 31, 1936, 30.

3. Ibid.

4. "New Air Mail Service Organized for Manila," *Hilo (Hawaii) Daily Tribune*, April 27, 1921, 6.

5. "Early Day Birdmen Meet," *Los Angeles Times*, 30.

6. "Chinese Maiden Is Adept Student in Aviation Class of Flyer From Texas," *Oklahoma City Times*, Aug. 10, 1922, 31; "Brings Record Tea Cargo," *Seattle Daily Times*, Sept. 19, 1922, 21.

7. "S.S. President Wilson," *Honolulu Advertiser*, February 14, 1926, 4.

8. Richard Ragodon, "What were the first car dealerships in the Philippines?" May 24, 2018, Top Gear Philippines website, https://www.topgear.com.ph/features/feature-articles/first-Philippine-dealerships-a52-20180524.

9. Doug Baker and Susan Hutchins, *American Journey,* vol. 2, 7th ed. (Oregon, Wisc.: Rainmaker Education, 2017) 187-9.

10. Ibid., 189-90.

11. Stanley P. Johnson, "Life Worth Living in Manila," *Mid-Pacific Magazine,* vol. 24, no. 1 (July 1922), 37-8.

12. Frances B. Cogan, *Captured: the Japanese Internment of American Civilians in the Philippines, 1941-1945* (Athens, Ga.: University of Georgia Press, 2000) 9-12.

13. Ibid.

14. Ibid., 14.

15. Ibid., 2.

16. Ibid., 12.

17. Manila Polo Club: The Early Years, Manila Nostalgia website, http://www.lougopal.com/manila/?p=1517.

18. The PanAm Clipper Arrives in Manila, Manila Nostalgia website, http://www.lougopal.com/manila/?p=1463..

19. Thomas M. Cleaver, *I Will Run Wild: The Pacific War from Pearl Harbor*

*to Midway* (New York: Osprey Publishing, 2020) 31-2.

20. Ibid., 32-3.

21. Cogan, *Captured*, 10.

22. Hiroshi Masuda, *MacArthur in Asia* (Ithaca, N.Y.: Cornell University Press, 2012) 6.

23. Ibid., 1-5; William Manchester, *American Caesar* (Boston, Mass.: Little Brown and Company, 1978) 162.

24. Manila Hotel: The Golden Years, Manila Nostalgia website, http://www.lougopal.com/manila/?p=3330.

## CHAPTER 2: WAR CLOUDS OVER THE PHILIPPINES

1. David M. Kennedy, *Freedom from Fear: The American People in Depression and War, 1929-1945* (New York: Oxford University Press, 2005) 397-402.

2. Manchester, *American Caesar*, 161.

3. Masuda, *MacArthur in Asia*, 5-6.

4. Manchester, *American Caesar*, 162.

5. John S. D. Eisenhower, *General Ike: a Personal Reminiscence* (New York: Free Press, 2003) 25-6.

6. Manchester, *American Caesar*, 173-4.

7. Ibid., 180-2.

8. Ibid.

9. Ibid., 182-3.

10. Ibid., 182-4.

11. Eisenhower, *General Ike*, 29-30.

12. Manchester, *American Caesar*, 166.

12. Manchester, *American Caesar*, 166.

13. The American School had been established by Americans, but Caucasian students from other nations also attended.

14. Grace W. Nash, *That We Might Live* (Scottsdale, Ariz.: SHANO Publishers, 1984) 11-6.

15. Cleaver, *I Will Run Wild*, 46-7.

16. Manchester, *American Caesar*, 184-5.

17. Ibid., 186.

18. Ibid., 186-90.

19. Cleaver, *I Will Run Wild*, 46-8.

20. Ibid., 11.

21. Manchester, *American Caesar*, 191-5.

22. A Day of Infamy, Manila Nostalgia website, http://www.lougopal.com/manila/?p=2573.

23. Cogan, *Captured*, 26-7.

24. "Sayre Wants Internees Paid," *Manila Daily Bulletin*, March 22, 1947, 1.

25. Nash, *That We Might Live*, 15.

26. A Day of Infamy, Manila Nostalgia website; Natalie Crouter, *Forbidden Diary* (New York: Burt Franklin & Company, 1980) 2.

27. Henry C. Clausen, *Pearl Harbor: Final Judgement* (New York: Crown Publishers, 1992) 67-70.

28. Ibid., 82.

29. Ibid., 136-8.

30. Kennedy, *Freedom from Fear,* 520-2.

31. Clausen, *Final Judgement,* 138.

32. Manchester, *American Caesar,* 205.

## CHAPTER 3: BLACK CHRISTMAS

1. Crouter, *Forbidden Diary*, 2-3.

2. Manchester, *American Caesar*, 210-2.

3. Ibid., 205-7.

4. Ibid., 206-12.

5. Ibid.

6. Ibid., 213.

7. Ibid., 213-5.

8. "Sayre Tells High Spirit of Filipinos," *The Long Beach (Calif.) Sun*, Dec. 13, 1941, 1.

9. "Two More Transports Damaged Off Legaspi," *The Los Angeles Times*, Dec. 15, 1941, 1.

10. Cogan, *Captured*, 43.

11. Manchester, *American Caesar*, 215-217.

12. Ibid.; Cogan, *Captured*, 43.

13. A. V. H. Hartendorp, *The Japanese Occupation of the Philippines,* Vol. 1 (Manila: Bookmark, 1967) 3-4.

14. R. P. Cronin Jr., "Defenders Withdraw 20 Miles in Lingayen Area North of Manila," *The San Francisco Examiner*, Dec. 27, 1941, 1.

15. Frank Hewlett, "Great Manila Fires Raze Historic Sites," *The Los Angeles Times*, Dec. 28, 1941, 2.

16. Manchester, *American Caesar*, 223-5.

17. Manchester, *American Caesar*, 218-20.

18. Hartendorp, *Japanese Occupation,* Vol. 1, 4.

19. Ibid., 5.

20. Cogan, *Captured*, 50.

21. Carol Talbot and Virginia Muir, *Escape at Dawn* (Wheaton, Ill.: Tyndale House Publishers, 1988) 16-7; Hartendorp, *Japanese Occupation,* Vol. 1, 306.

22. Hartendorp, *Japanese Occupation,* Vol. 1, 5-6.

23. Ibid., 6-7.

24. Jennifer Preyss, "Woman of War" (four-part series), *Victoria (Texas) Advocate*, Dec. 8, 2014, pg. A1, A3.

25. Frederick H. Stevens, *Santo Tomás Internment Camp* (U.S.A.: Stratford House, Inc., 1946) 78.

26. Hartendorp, *Japanese Occupation,* Vol. 1, 10.

# CHAPTER 4: "PROTECTIVE CUSTODY" AT SANTO TOMÁS

1. Hartendorp, *The Japanese Occupation,* Vol. 1, 8-12.

2. Cogan, *Captured,* 3; U.S. Prisoners of War and Civilian American Citizens Captured and Interned by Japan in World War II, Congressional Research Service Report for Congress, Naval History and Heritage Command website, https://www.history.navy.mil/research/library/online-reading-room/title-list-alphabetically/u/us-prisoners-war-civilian-american-citizens-captured.html#intern.

3. Stevens, *Santo Tomás Internment Camp,* 20-1, 23.

4. Hartendorp, *The Japanese Occupation,* Vol. 1, 1-14.

5. Ibid., 43-50.

6. Ibid., 50.

7. Stevens, *Santo Tomás Internment Camp,* 23-4.

8. Hartendorp, *The Japanese Occupation,* Vol. 1, 18.

9. "Commercial Feeding Begins Tuesday or Wednesday," *Internews*, Jan. 24, 1942, 1.

10. Stevens, *Santo Tomás Internment Camp,* 187-8.

11. Hartendorp, *The Japanese Occupation,* Vol. 1, 20.

12. Ibid., 4, 21.

13. Hartendorp, *The Japanese Occupation,* Vol. 1, 88.

14. Ibid., 88-93.

15. "Internee Escapes Result in Swift Cancellation of Special Privileges," *Internews*, Feb. 14, 1942, 1.

16. Hartendorp, *The Japanese Occupation,* Vol. 1, 93-94.

17. "American School Seniors Hold Mock Graduation," *Internews*, March 21, 1942, 2.

18. Hartendorp, *The Japanese Occupation,* Vol. 1, 34-5.

19. Stevens, *Santo Tomás Internment Camp,* 178.

20. Hartendorp, *The Japanese Occupation,* Vol. 1, 84, 101.

21. Manchester, *American Caesar,* 270-1.

22. Masuda, *MacArthur in Asia,* 70.

23. Manchester, *American Caesar,* 253-6.

24. Ibid., 257-63, 270.

25. Ibid., 270-1.

26. Ibid., 271.

27. Cleaver, *I Will Run Wild,* 189-91.

28. Ibid., 195-7.

29. Hartendorp, *The Japanese Occupation,* Vol. 1, 28-31.

30. Stevens, *Santo Tomás Internment Camp,* 32-3.

31. Ibid., 33.

32. Stevens, *Santo Tomás Internment Camp,* 110-17; Hartendorp, *The Japanese Occupation,* Vol. 1, 28.

33. Hartendorp, *The Japanese Occupation,* Vol. 1, 174.

34. Stevens, *Santo Tomás Internment Camp,* 115-6.

## CHAPTER 5: A MISERABLE ROUTINE

1. Hartendorp, *The Japanese Occupation,* Vol. I, 39-40; Stevens, *Santo Tomás Internment Camp*, 398.

2. Stevens, *Santo Tomás Internment Camp*, 31.

3. Ibid., 233-7.

4. Hartendorp, *The Japanese Occupation,* Vol. I, 54-5.

5. Stevens, *Santo Tomás Internment Camp*, 256.

6. Ibid., 324-7.

7. Ibid., 344-5.

8. Ibid., 369; email correspondence between authors and Martin Meadows, Jan. 2, 2024.

9. Bruce Henderson, *Rescue at Los Baños* (Harper-Collins Publishers: New York, 2015) 265.

10. Stevens, *Santo Tomás Internment Camp*, 40; "Repatriation Seen for 130 in Japan," *San Bernardino County Sun*, Sept. 25, 1942, 12; "Woman Freed by Japs Brings News of Captives," *Los Angeles Times*, Sept. 16, 1942, 8.

11. "Woman Freed by Japs," *Los Angeles Times*, 8.

12. Hartendorp, *The Japanese Occupation,* Vol. I, 48-9.

13. Ibid; Stevens, *Santo Tomás Internment Camp*, 403.

14. Stevens, *Santo Tomás Internment Camp*, 404.

15. Ibid., 353-4; Hartendorp, *The Japanese Occupation,* Vol. 1, 332-3.

16. Hartendorp, *The Japanese Occupation,* Vol. 1, 328-34.

17. Ibid., 334.

18. Patty Croft diary entries (Jan. 1, 1943-Feb. 23, 1945) at Santo Tomás and Los Baños internment camps, Luzon, P.I.

19. Croft diary entries, Jan. 7-8, 1943.

20. Manchester, *American Caesar*, 296.

21. Ibid., 297-8.

22. Ibid., 299.

23. Ibid., 303.

24. Ibid., 313.

25. Kennedy, *Freedom from Fear*, 562.

26. Manchester, *American Caesar*, 330-2.

27. Ibid., 336-7; Kennedy, *Freedom from Fear,* 563-4.

28. Manchester, *American Caesar*, 337.

29. Stevens, *Santo Tomás Internment Camp*, 227-230.

30. Hartendorp, *The Japanese Occupation,* Vol. 1, 366.

31. Hartendorp, *The Japanese Occupation,* Vol. 1, 367-9.

32. Ibid., 373.

33. Croft diary entries, Jan. 10 and Feb. 3, 1943.

34. Stevens, *Santo Tomás Internment Camp*, 409, 487-97; Croft diary entry, Feb. 20, 1943.

35. Croft diary entries, February through April, 1943.

36. Ibid., May 5, 1943.

37. Hartendorp, *The Japanese Occupation,* Vol.1, 522.

38. Ibid., 523-4.

39. Ibid., 523-6.

40. Ibid., 530-1; Croft diary entry, May 14, 1943.

41. Hartendorp, *The Japanese Occupation,* Vol.1, 531.

42. Stevens, *Santo Tomás Internment Camp,* 418.

43. Ibid., 414.

44. A. V. H. Hartendorp, *The Japanese Occupation of the Philippines,* Vol. II (Manila: Bookmark, 1967) 1-5; Stevens, *Santo Tomás Internment Camp,* 420.

45. Hartendorp, *The Japanese Occupation,* Vol. II, 10.

46. Ibid., 8.

47. Stevens, *Santo Tomás Internment Camp,* 418.

48. Stevens, *Santo Tomás Internment Camp,* 424; Croft diary entry, Nov. 19, 1943.

49. Hartendorp, *The Japanese Occupation,* Vol. II, 43.

50. Ibid; Stevens, *Santo Tomás Internment Camp,* 51, 426.

51. Stevens, *Santo Tomás Internment Camp,* 427.

## CHAPTER 6: THE STARVING TIME

1. Patty Croft diary entries, January 1944 and Feb. 1, 1944; Hartendorp, *The Japanese Occupation,* Vol. II, 148.

2. Stevens, *Santo Tomás Internment Camp,* 369; Hartendorp, *The Japanese Occupation,* Vol. II, 148-9.

3. Hartendorp, *The Japanese Occupation,* Vol. II, 132.

4. Ibid., 157; Stevens, *Santo Tomás Internment Camp,* 142.

5. Stevens, *Santo Tomás Internment Camp,* 428, 431-2.

6. Ibid., 147-8.

7. Ibid., 125.

8. Hartendorp, *The Japanese Occupation,* Vol. II, 165, 170.

9. Ibid., 181-2.

10. Ibid., 191.

11. Stevens, *Santo Tomás Internment Camp,* 428, 434.

12. Hartendorp, *The Japanese Occupation,* Vol. II, 198-9.

13. Stevens, *Santo Tomás Internment Camp,* 435-6.

14. Croft diary entry, April 3, 1944.

15. Ibid., April 4, 1944.

16. Ibid., April 6, 1944.

17. Henderson, *Rescue at Los Baños,* 34, 134.

18. Croft diary entry, April 27, 1944; Stevens, *Santo Tomás Internment Camp,* 369.

19. Croft diary entry, April 27, 1944.

20. Ibid.

21. Stevens, *Santo Tomás Internment Camp,* 64.

22. Croft diary entry, April 27, 1944.

23. Henderson, *Rescue at Los Baños*, 111.

24. Jennifer Preyss, "A Woman of War" (four-part series), *Victoria (Texas) Advocate*, Dec. 8, 2014, 3-4.

25. Croft diary entry, June 7, 1944.

26. Stevens, *Santo Tomás Internment Camp,* 443.

27. Hartendorp, *The Japanese Occupation,* Vol. II, 301.

28. Ibid., 308.

29. Ibid., 308-9; Stevens, *Santo Tomás Internment Camp,* 150.

30. Stevens, *Santo Tomás Internment Camp,* 150-1.

31. Croft diary entry, Sept. 21, 1944.

32. Ibid.

33. William F. Halsey, *Admiral Halsey's Story* (New York: McGraw Hill Book Co., 1947) 191.

34. Manchester, *American Caesar*, 346-51.

35. *Reports of General MacArthur: The Campaigns of MacArthur in the Pacific,* Vol. 1 (Dept. of the Army: Washington, D.C., 1966) 165.

36. Manchester, *American Caesar*, 363-5.

37. Ibid., 368.

38. Ibid.

39. Ibid., 369.

40. Ibid., 370.

41. Ibid., 371-2; *Reports of General MacArthur*, 173.

42. *Reports of General MacArthur*, 178, 181-2, 190.

43. Ibid., 198-9; Manchester, *American Caesar*, 385.

44. Joseph Connor, "Shore Party: the Truth Behind the Famous MacArthur Photo," https://www.historynet.com/shore-party-macarthur-photo/.

45. Croft diary entry, Oct. 1, 1944.

46. Nash, *That We Might Live*, 146.

47. Stevens, *Santo Tomás Internment Camp,* 462.

48. Ibid.

49. Ibid., 462-3; Croft diary entry, Nov. 5, 1944.

50. Croft diary entry, Nov. 25, 1944.

51. Stevens, *Santo Tomás Internment Camp,* 161.

52. Ibid.

53. Ibid., 126-7.

54. Croft diary entries, Dec. 1-2, 1944.

55. Nash, *That We Might Live*, 148-51.

56. Croft diary entry, Dec. 3, 1944.

## CHAPTER 7: DESPERATION AT LOS BAÑOS

1. Henderson, *Rescue at Los Baños*, 38-40; Anthony Arthur, *Deliverance at Los Baños* (New York: St. Martins Press, 1985) 49.

2. Talbot and Muir, *Escape at Dawn*, 192D (illustration).

3. Croft diary entry, Dec. 5, 1944.

4. Nash, *That We Might Live*, 151-2.

5. Henderson, *Rescue at Los Baños,* 116-120.

6. Arthur, *Deliverance at Los Baños*, 61.

7. Henderson, *Rescue at Los Baños,* 80-1.

8. Ibid., 84.

9. Ibid., 108-12.

10. Ibid., 112.

11. Ibid., 109.

12. Croft diary entry, Jan. 1, 1945.

13. Croft diary entries, Jan. 2-3, 1945.

14. Nash, *That We Might Live*, 188.

15. Croft diary entry, Jan. 6, 1945.

16. Arthur, *Deliverance at Los Baños*, 123-4.

17. Henderson, *Rescue at Los Baños,* 124.

18. Croft diary entry, Jan. 7, 1945.

19. Henderson, *Rescue at Los Baños,* 125.

20. Croft diary entry, Jan. 8, 1945.

21. Arthur, *Deliverance at Los Baños*, 129.

22. Croft diary entry, Jan. 10, 1945.

23. Croft diary entry, Jan. 12, 1945.

24. Henderson, *Rescue at Los Baños,* 126; Talbot and Muir, *Escape at Dawn*, 120.

25. Manchester, *American Caesar*, 382-3, 390-3.

26. Ibid., 403-5.

27. Ibid., 405.

28. Ibid., 406-7.

29. Ibid.

30. "General Douglas MacArthur Lands in Philippines at Lingayen Gulf on Luzon, January 9, 1945," Smithsonian website, https://www.si.edu/object/nmah_1303377.

31. Manchester, *American Caesar*, 406-9.

32. Ibid., 410-11.

33. Arthur, *Deliverance at Los Baños*, 178-9.

34. Ibid., 179; Maxwell Bailey, "Raid at Los Baños," *Military Review,* vol. 63, May 1983, 52.

35. Arthur, *Deliverance at Los Baños*, 179.

36. Ibid.

37. Ibid., 179-80; Talbot and Muir, *Escape at Dawn,* 120.

38. Bailey, "Raid at Los Baños," 54.

39. Stevens, *Santo Tomás Internment Camp*, 366-8.

40. Talbot and Muir, *Escape at Dawn,* 165; Bailey, "Raid at Los Baños," 52-3.

41. Henderson, *Rescue at Los Baños,* 171.

42. Ibid., 51, 105-7.

43. Ibid., 143-5.

44. Bailey, "Raid at Los Baños," 54; Henderson, *Rescue at Los Baños,* front matter.

45. Talbot and Muir, *Escape at Dawn,* 121.

46. Nash, *That We Might Live,* 196-7.

47. Henderson, *Rescue at Los Baños,* 10-11, 114.

48. Croft diary entry, Jan. 14, 1945.

49. Talbot and Muir, *Escape at Dawn,* 124-6.

50. Ibid., 127; Nash, *That We Might Live,* 201-6.

51. Croft diary entry, Jan. 16, 1945.

52. Croft diary entry, Jan. 18, 1945.

53. Croft diary entry, Jan. 25, 1945.

54. Croft diary entry, Jan. 27, 1945.

55. Talbot and Muir, *Escape at Dawn,* 128-9; Arthur, *Deliverance at Los Baños,* 145-6.

56. Henderson, *Rescue at Los Baños,* 103-4.

57. Croft diary entry, Jan. 30, 1945.

58. Croft diary entries, Jan. 31 and Feb. 3, 1945.

59. Croft diary entry, Feb. 3, 1945.

60. Ibid.

## CHAPTER 8: AMERICA BY AIR, LAND AND WATER

1. Manchester, *American Caesar,* 413-4.

2. Ibid.

3. Ibid., 415.

4. Ibid.

5. Henderson, *Rescue at Los Baños,* 173.

6. Ibid.

7. Bailey, "Raid at Los Baños," 52.

8. Ibid., 52, 60.

9. Croft diary entry, Feb. 6, 1945.

10. Croft diary entry, Feb. 7, 1945.

11. Croft diary entry, Feb. 9, 1945.

12. Talbot and Muir, *Escape at Dawn,* 172-3.

13. Nash, *That We Might Live,* 208.

14. Henderson, *Rescue at Los Baños,* 202.

15. Croft diary entry, Feb. 13, 1945.

16. Croft diary entry, Feb. 14, 1945.

17. Croft diary entry, Feb. 15, 1945.

18. Croft diary entries, Feb. 18-20, 1945.

19. Croft diary entry, Feb. 20, 1945.

20. Croft diary entry, Feb. 19, 1945.

21. Arthur, *Deliverance at Los Baños,* 188-91, 209.

22. Ibid., 186-94.

23. Ibid., 194-5.

24. Ibid., 195-6.

25. Ibid., 211-12; Henderson, *Rescue at Los Baños*, 190.

26. Bailey, "Raid at Los Baños," 57-9; Henderson, *Rescue at Los Baños*, 192-3.

27. Arthur, *Deliverance at Los Baños*, 213; Henderson, *Rescue at Los Baños*, 193.

28. Henderson, *Rescue at Los Baños*, 195.

29. Ibid.

30. Ibid.

31. 511th Parachute Infantry Regiment website, The Raid at Los Baños: 75 Years Later, https://511pir.com/blog/luzon/225-the-raid-at-los-banos-75-years-later.

32. Henderson, *Rescue at Los Baños*, 226-9.

33. 511th Parachute Infantry Regiment website, The Raid at Los Baños.

34. Bailey, "Raid at Los Baños," 57; Henderson, *Rescue at Los Baños*, 214-7.

35. Croft diary entry, Feb. 22, 1945.

36. Bailey, "Raid at Los Baños," 61.

37. Henderson, *Rescue at Los Baños*, 230-1, 261.

38. Bailey, "Raid at Los Baños," 60-1.

39. 511th Parachute Infantry Regiment website, The Raid at Los Baños.

40. Henderson, *Rescue at Los Baños*, 97, 240-2.

41. Ibid., 243.

42. Croft diary entry Feb. 23, 1945.

43. Henderson, *Rescue at Los Baños*, 243-4.

44. Ibid., 242-3.

45. Ibid., 243-4.

46. Ibid., 254.

47. 511th Parachute Infantry Regiment website, The Raid at Los Baños.

48. Henderson, *Rescue at Los Baños*, 254-259.

49. Arthur, *Deliverance at Los Baños*, 249-252.

50. Ibid., 252; Henderson, *Rescue at Los Baños*, 257-9.

51. Arthur, *Deliverance at Los Baños*, 252.

52. Henderson, *Rescue at Los Baños*, 258-9.

53. Ibid., 260-1; Arthur, *Deliverance at Los Baños*, 252-3.

54. Henderson, *Rescue at Los Baños*, 262-3.

55. Ibid., 263-4.

56. Ibid., 267.

57. Ibid., 268; "2,146 More Prisoners Rescued From Japanese," *The (San Mateo, Calif.) Times*, Feb. 24, 1945, 2; 511th Parachute Infantry Regiment website, The Raid at Los Baños; Interview with liberated female internee Georgette Kramer from the Los Baños Japanese Internment Camp, website entitled Critical Past, https://www.criticalpast.com/video/65675040436_Prisoners-from-Los-Banos_Bilipid-prison_internment-camps_Manila-City-jail.

58. Henderson, *Rescue at Los Baños*, 268-9.

59. Nash, *That We Might Live,* 221.

60. Ibid., 221-2; 511th Parachute Infantry Regiment website, The Raid at Los Baños.

61. Croft diary entry, Feb. 23, 1945.

## CHAPTER 9: FAREWELL TO THE ISLANDS

1. Talbot and Muir, *Escape at Dawn,* 268-9.

2. Ibid., 274-5.

3. Ibid., 273.

4. Ibid., 276.

5. Ibid; Cogan, *Captured,* 307.

6. Cogan, *Captured,* 308.

7. Ibid., 308-9.

8. Manchester, *American Caesar,* 425.

9. Stevens, *Santo Tomás Internment Camp,* 473, 483.

10. Hartendorp, *The Japanese Occupation,* Vol. II, 544; former Santo Tomás internee Martin Meadows unequivocally states a Japanese shelling of Santo Tomás occurred on Feb. 7, 1945 after MacArthur's visit, but sources vary.

11. Cogan, *Captured,* 309-10.

12. Talbot and Muir, *Escape at Dawn,* 301.

13. Nash, *That We Might Live,* 226.

14. Talbot and Muir, *Escape at Dawn,* 303.

15. "2959 Freed From Japs Arrive Here," *Los Angeles Times,* May 3, 1945, 1-2.

16. "2,800 Liberated From Philippines Land at L.A.," *The San Francisco Examiner,* May 3, 1945, 18.

17. "Wichmans Become First Repatriates From Prison Camps to Arrive in L.A.," *Evening Vanguard* (Venice, Calif.), May 4, 1945, 1.

18. "Double Reunion Brings Happiness To Home in City," *The Daily Oklahoman,* July 26, 1945, 10; (item) *The Courier-Journal* (Louisville, Ky.), July 22, 1945, 16; "Bataan Nurse Has Idea for Ending Meat Lack," *The Cincinnati Enquirer,* July 26, 1945, 1.

19. Henderson, *Rescue at Los Baños,* 276-7, 303.

## EPILOGUE

1. "WWII prisoner donates U.S. flag to Airborne & Special Operations Museum," *The Fayetteville Observer,* Feb. 23, 2018, https://www.fayobserver.com/story/news/military/2018/02/23/wwii-prisoner-donates-us-flag-to-airborne-amp-special-operations-museum/14136712007/.

# BIBLIOGRAPHY

## PERSONAL DIARY

Nichols Hills, Oklahoma. Internment diary of Patty Gene Croft (1943-1945).

## GOVERNMENT DOCUMENT

Dept. of the Army. *Reports of General MacArthur: The Campaigns of MacArthur in the Pacific,* Vol.1. Washington, D.C.: 1966.

## JOURNAL

Maxwell Bailey. "Raid at Los Baños." *Military Review* vol. 63 (May 1983): 51-66.

## NEWSPAPERS

*Cincinnati Enquirer*, 1945.
*Courier-Journal* (Louisville, Ky.), 1945.
*Daily Oklahoman*, 1945.
*Evening Vanguard* (Venice, Calif.), 1945.
*Hilo* (Hawaii*) Daily Tribune*, 1921.
*Honolulu Advertiser*, 1926.
*Internews*, 1942.
*Long Beach* (Calif.) *Sun*, 1941.
*Los Angeles Times*, 1936, 1941, 1942, 1945
*Manila Daily Bulletin*, 1947.
*Oklahoma City Times*, 1922.
*San Bernardino County Sun*, 1942.
*San Francisco Chronicle*, 1920.
*San Francisco Examiner*, 1941, 1945.
*Seattle Daily Times*, 1922.
*Times, The* (San Mateo, Calif.)*,* 1945.
*Victoria* (Texas) *Advocate*, 2014.

## MAGAZINE

Johnson, Stanley P. "Life Worth Living in Manila," *The Mid-Pacific Magazine,* July 1922, 37-42.

## BOOKS

Arthur, Anthony. *Deliverance at Los Baños.* New York: St. Martins Press, 1985.

Baker, Doug and Susan Hutchins. *American Journey,* vol. 2, 7th ed. Oregon, Wisc.: Rainmaker Education, 2017.

Clausen, Henry C. *Pearl Harbor: Final Judgement.* New York: Crown Publishers, 1992.

Cleaver, Thomas M. *I Will Run Wild: The Pacific War from Pearl Harbor to Midway.* New York: Osprey Publishing, 2020.

Cogan, Frances B. *Captured: the Japanese Internment of American Civilians in the Philippines, 1941-1945.* Athens, Ga.: University of Georgia Press, 2000.

Crouter, Natalie. *Forbidden Diary.* New York: Burt Franklin & Company, 1980.

Eisenhower, John S. D. *General Ike: a Personal Reminiscence.* New York: Free Press, 2003.

Halsey, William F. *Admiral Halsey's Story.* New York: McGraw Hill Book Co., 1947.

Hartendorp, A. V. H. *The Japanese Occupation of the Philippines,* Vol. 1 & Vol. 2. Manila: Bookmark, 1967.

Henderson, Bruce. *Rescue at Los Baños.* New York: Harper-Collins Publishers, 2015.

Kennedy, David M. *Freedom from Fear: The American People in Depression and War, 1929-1945.* New York: Oxford University Press, 2005.

Manchester, William. *American Caesar.* Boston, Mass.: Little Brown and Company, 1978.

Masuda, Hiroshi. *MacArthur in Asia.* Ithaca, N.Y.: Cornell University Press, 2012.

Nash, Grace W. *That We Might Live.* Scottsdale, Ariz.: SHANO Publishers, 1984.

Stevens, Frederick H. *Santo Tomás Internment Camp.* U.S.A.: Stratford House, Inc., 1946.

Talbot, Carol and Virginia Muir. *Escape at Dawn.* Wheaton, Ill.: Tyndale House Publishers, 1988.

## PERSONAL CORRESPONDENCE

Email correspondence between authors and former Santo Tomás internee Martin Meadows, Dec. 15, 2023.

## ONLINE SOURCES

A Day of Infamy, Manila Nostalgia website. http://www.lougopal.com

Connor, Joseph. "Shore Party: the Truth Behind the Famous MacArthur Photo," HistoryNet website. https://www.historynet.com.

"General Douglas MacArthur Lands in Philippines at Lingayen Gulf on Luzon, January 9, 1945," Smithsonian Institution website. https://www.si.edu.

Interview with liberated female internee Georgette Kramer from the Los Banos Japanese Internment Camp, Critical Past website. https://www.criticalpast. com.

Manila Hotel: The Golden Years, Manila Nostalgia website. http://www. lougopal.

Manila Polo Club: The Early Years, Manila Nostalgia website. http://www.lougo-pal.com/manila/?p=1517.

Richard Ragodon. "What were the first car dealerships in the Philippines?" Top Gear Philippines website. https://www.topgear.com.

*The Fayetteville Observer*, Feb. 23, 2018. https://www.fayobserver.com.

The PanAm Clipper Arrives in Manila, Manila Nostalgia website. http://www. lougopal.

"The Raid at Los Baños: 75 Years Later," 511th Parachute Infantry Regiment website. https://511pir.com.

U.S. Prisoners of War and Civilian American Citizens Captured and Interned by Japan in World War II, Congressional Research Service Report for Congress, Naval History and Heritage Command website. https://www.history.navy.mil.

# INDEX

Made in the USA
Coppell, TX
01 August 2025

52536906R00128